T0140547

Lecture Notes in Computer Science　14673

Founding Editors

Gerhard Goos
Juris Hartmanis

The series Lecture Notes in Computer Science (LNCS), including its subseries Lecture Notes in Artificial Intelligence (LNAI) and Lecture Notes in Bioinformatics (LNBI), has established itself as a medium for the publication of new developments in computer science and information technology research, teaching, and education.

LNCS enjoys close cooperation with the computer science R & D community, the series counts many renowned academics among its volume editors and paper authors, and collaborates with prestigious societies. Its mission is to serve this international community by providing an invaluable service, mainly focused on the publication of conference and workshop proceedings and postproceedings. LNCS commenced publication in 1973.

Maryam Lotfian · Luigi Libero Lucio Starace
Editors

Web and Wireless Geographical Information Systems

21st International Symposium, W2GIS 2024
Yverdon-les-Bains, Switzerland, June 17–18, 2024
Proceedings

 Springer

Editors
Maryam Lotfian 🆔
University of Applied Sciences and Arts
Western Switzerland, School of Business
and Engineering (HEIG-VD)
Yverdon-les-Bains, Switzerland

Luigi Libero Lucio Starace 🆔
University of Naples Federico II
Naples, Italy

ISSN 0302-9743   ISSN 1611-3349 (electronic)
Lecture Notes in Computer Science
ISBN 978-3-031-60795-0   ISBN 978-3-031-60796-7 (eBook)
https://doi.org/10.1007/978-3-031-60796-7

This Springer imprint is published by the registered company Springer Nature Switzerland AG
The registered company address is: Gewerbestrasse 11, 6330 Cham, Switzerland

Paper in this product is recyclable.

Preface

This volume contains the papers selected for presentation at the 21st International Symposium on Web and Wireless Geographical Information Systems (W2GIS 2024), hosted by the University of Applied Sciences and Arts Western Switzerland, School of Business and Engineering Vaud (HEIG-VD) in Yverdon-les-Bains, Switzerland, on June 17–18, 2024. W2GIS 2024 aimed to provide a platform for discussing advancements in theoretical, technical, and practical aspects within web and wireless-based approaches for disseminating, using, and processing geo-referenced data. W2GIS is a unique forum to address new research challenges in developing location-based solutions and GIS, representing a recognized and regular event within the research community. This year's conference highlighted the emerging fields of citizen science and volunteered geographic information. To explore these topics from different perspectives, we invited two keynote speakers: Christopher Beddow, a geospatial data engineer at Meta, and Anna Berti Suman, a research fellow at Luiss School of Law, Rome. Christopher Beddow focused on crowdsourcing as the critical part of the infrastructure data in the age of AI, while Anna Berti Suman addressed citizen science and environmental justice.

The 2024 edition of W2GIS received 20 submissions from 66 authors coming from more than 30 different institutions from 11 different countries. Each paper received at least two rigorous, single-blind reviews and, based on these reviews, 15 papers were selected for presentation at the symposium and inclusion in the conference proceedings, with a 75% acceptance rate. In addition to the regular *Research Track*, which invited scientific contributions in the form of full or short papers, W2GIS 2024 also included a dedicated *Industry Session*, intended for works with a larger focus on industrial impact and at least one author with an industrial affiliation. Furthermore, W2GIS 2024 also featured a *Doctoral Symposium* where doctoral students had the chance to submit an overview of their research as a short paper, present their activities and receive feedback from well-known researchers in the field.

Among the 15 selected contributions, 10 belong to the Research Track (7 full papers and 3 short papers), 2 to the Industry Session (1 full, 1 short paper), and 3 to the Doctoral Symposium. The W2GIS 2024 proceedings had the privilege to accept an invited paper authored by Anna Berti Suman, entitled *Civil society mobilising geospatial data to demonstrate environmental incompliance*.

The accepted papers demonstrate remarkable quality, and are at the forefront of research and development in Web and Wireless Geographical Information Systems, addressing pressing challenges and exploring novel solutions. From advanced techniques for data aggregation and analysis to the integration of generative artificial intelligence and machine learning into geospatial applications, the contributions showcased in these proceedings demonstrate the breadth and depth of Web and Wireless GIS research.

We sincerely thank all the authors for their valuable contributions to the 2024 edition of W2GIS. We would also like to thank the Program Committee members for their meticulous reviews and insightful feedback, which helped ensure the quality of the accepted papers, and the Steering Committee members, for their ongoing guidance and support. Special thanks are also due to the members of the local organizing committee, particularly Jens Ingensand and Florent Joerin, for their tireless efforts in planning and coordinating the conference.

June 2024

Maryam Lotfian
Luigi Libero Lucio Starace

Organization

Program Committee Chairs

Maryam Lotfian	HEIG-VD, Switzerland
Luigi Libero Lucio Starace	University of Naples Federico II, Italy

Steering Committee

Michela Bertolotto	University College Dublin, Ireland
Christophe Claramunt	Naval Academy Research Institute, France
Sergio di Martino	University of Naples Federico II, Italy
Jérôme Gensel	University of Grenoble, France
Farid Karimipour	Institute of Science and Technology Austria, Austria
Miguel R. Luaces	University of A Coruña, Spain
Sabine Storandt	University of Konstanz, Germany
Kazutoshi Sumiya	Kwansei Gakuin University, Japan
Martin Tomko	University of Melbourne, Australia
Ki-Joune Li	Pusan University, South Korea
Mir Abolfazl Mostafavi	University of Laval, Canada

Local Organizing Committee

Nicolas Blanc	HEIG-VD, Switzerland
Bertil Chapuis	HEIG-VD, Switzerland
Maxime Collombin	HEIG-VD, Switzerland
Alain Dubois	Hepia, Switzerland
Olivier Ertz	HEIG-VD, Switzerland
Jens Ingensand	HEIG-VD, Switzerland
Florent Joerin	HEIG-VD, Switzerland
Maryam Lotfian	HEIG-VD, Switzerland
Jean-Christophe Loubier	HES-SO VS, Switzerland
Jakob Rager	HES-SO VS, Switzerland
Daniel Rappo	HEIG-VD, Switzerland

Program Committee

Hoda Allahbakhshi	University of Zurich, Switzerland
Christine Bassem	Wellesley College, USA
Camille Bernard	Université Grenoble Alpes, France
Alain Bouju	La Rochelle University, France
Maria Antonia Brovelli	Politecnico di Milano, Italy
Elena Camossi	NATO CMRE, Italy
Bertil Chapuis	HEIG-VD, Switzerland
Zhixiang Fang	Wuhan University, China
Rob Feick	Waterloo University, Canada
Gregory Giuliani	University of Geneva, Switzerland
Eric Guilbert	Laval University, Canada
Jens Ingensand	HEIG-VD, Switzerland
Stephane Joost	EPFL, Switzerland
Thierry Le Pors	ISEN, Brest University, France
Songnian Li	Toronto Metropolitan University, Canada
Jean-Cristophe Loubier	HES-SO Valais-Wallis, Switzerland
Feng Lu	Chinese Academy of Sciences, China
Miguel Mata	UPIITA-IPN, Mexico
Kamaldeep Singh Oberoi	CESI-LINEACT, Toulouse, France
Daniele Oxoli	Politecnico di Milano, Italy
Kostas Patroumpas	Athena Research Center, Greece
Peng Peng	Chinese Academy of Sciences, China
Andres Perez-Uribe	HEIG-VD, Switzerland
Franca Rocco di Torrepadula	University of Naples Federico II, Italy
Luigi Libero Lucio Starace	University of Naples Federico II, Italy
Nico Van de Weghe	Ghent University, Belgium
Shoko Wakamiya	Nara Inst. of Science and Technology, Japan
Yuanyuan Wang	Yamaguchi University, Japan
Yousuke Watanabe	Nagoya University, Japan
Francisco Javier Zarazaga-Soria	University of Zaragoza, Spain

Additional Reviewers

Sergio Martin-Segura	University of Zaragoza, Spain
Taketoshi Ushiama	Kwansei Gakuin University, Japan

Contents

Keynote

Civil Society Mobilising Geospatial Data to Demonstrate Environmental Incompliance

Anna Berti Suman[1](✉) ⬚ and Gabriel Rojas Verdugo[2] ⬚

[1] Libera Università Internazionale degli Studi Sociali 'Guido Carli' (Luiss), Via Parenzo 11, 00197 Rome, Italy
abertisuman@luiss.it
[2] Universität zu Köln, Albertus Magnus Platz, 50923 Köln, Germany

Abstract. User-generated geospatial data have opened up new opportunities for a wide range of applications. In particular, civic monitoring initiatives based on volunteered geographic information (VGI) have allowed ordinary people to mobilise Earth Observation technologies for environmental monitoring to detect non-compliance with environmental laws and regulations. Through review of illustrative cases, this article will show how such data have played a key role in triggering investigations by public prosecutors and are grounding claims in front of the judiciary by affected citizens. The article will also discuss cases where civil society used geospatial data to demonstrate non-compliance with environmental rules, ban extractive operations and demand reparation for environmental damage.

Keywords: Civic Environmental Monitoring · Citizen-Gathered Data · Volunteered Geographic Information · Law Enforcement

1 Civic Environmental Monitoring and Volunteered Geographic Information (VGI)

Civic environmental monitoring is the use by ordinary people of monitoring devices (e.g., sensors) or their senses (e.g., smell; hearing) to detect environmental issues [1]. This concept borders other typologies of civic engagement with environmental matters, such as citizen sensing, citizen science, and mobile crowd-sensing [2, 3]. At times, civic environmental monitoring initiatives rely on volunteered geographic information (VGI), and the intersection of these two practices will be the focus of our analysis.

Civic monitoring initiatives offer an example of decentralized and non-hierarchical environmental surveillance systems, driven by care of civil society for specific matters of concern [4]. The recognition of the complementary value of civic monitoring practices is growing. Such initiatives can indeed support both short-term and long-term official monitoring, increasing its accuracy and granularity [5]. Civic monitoring and adjacent practices can be a powerful source of evidence for law enforcement, especially when they shed light on official informational gaps associated with the shortages of public agencies' resources to detect environmental wrongdoings. The practice can also contribute to

M. Lotfian and L. L. L. Starace (Eds.): W2GIS 2024, LNCS 14673, pp. 3–19, 2024.
https://doi.org/10.1007/978-3-031-60796-7_1

the provision of public services, strengthening official environmental monitoring and compliance assurance by offering valuable data from the ground [1].

The specific use of VGI as part of data collected through civic environmental monitoring offers dual benefits. It provides a valuable contrast to remote sensing, enhancing accuracy, while also generating ground-level data that would otherwise be unavailable. This approach has wide-ranging impacts, including the creation of up-to-date and decentralized databases where citizens can feed information, the supplementation of inadequate public authority databases, and even the provision of evidence in legal proceedings. The development of efficient input systems for VGI data has accelerated data submission, and the availability of such data through public databases broadens its audience beyond its original scope [6].

The struggles of governments and agencies to monitor efficiently all the existing environmental issues is not new and persist as an important concern. As for 2000, in the United States (U.S.) just the 19% of water bodies were monitored and complied with the Clean Water Act [7]. In this sense, citizen-gathered data could fill such data gaps and provide data over spatial and temporal scales that would otherwise not be possible [7].

Between June 2020 and August 2023, the first author of this article led as principal investigator the 'Sensing for Justice' research project (SensJus) [8] at the Digital Economy Unit of the European Commission's Joint Research Centre [9]. Building on the learnings from this project, the article will discuss how civil society actors mobilize Earth Observation technology and capabilities to produce citizen-gathered data that can help detecting non-compliance with environmental laws and regulations (Fig. 1).

Fig. 1. A graphic representation of the Sensing for Justice project's aims. Source: contracted illustrator Aelisir Illustration.

Our article, focusing on the intersection between civic monitoring and VGI, transfers this discussion to the field of environmental law enforcement. We also offer an overview of existing legislative frameworks and scholarship discourses that help legitimize the contribution of civic evidence to law enforcement.

Subsequently, we review cases studied for the SensJus project where geo-referenced civic data offered evidence for triggering investigations by public prosecutors (i.e., the case of oil-extraction associated environmental issues in the Southern Italian region of Basilicata, Italy) and are grounding civic claims for local environmental mismanagement (i.e., the case of air pollution and fires associated with waste management and other industrial activities in the Valle Galeria area, Lazio region, Italy). We also discuss cases from the U.S. where civil society used geospatial data to demonstrate non-compliance with environmental rules through litigation (i.e., the court saga revolving around coal ash pollution in North Carolina) and from Latin America, Ecuador, where participatory mapping served the identification of unmapped gas flaring sites and triggered a ban on gas flaring in the region.

We conclude outlining key lessons learned from this brief case review and sketch promising avenues for evolutions in the field. We also offer a few key elements for a future research agenda that should be aimed at further exploring and leveraging the contribution of VGI-supported civic monitoring for environmental law enforcement.

2 Environmental Law Enforcement

Environmental enforcement encompasses the set of actions that institutions – such as governmental environmental agencies – take to ensure the compliance with and implementation of environmental laws, and the measures aimed to correct or halt situations or activities that endanger the environment or public health.

The 'environmental rule of law' describes the situation in which environmental laws are widely understood, respected, and enforced and embraces also the societal and planetary benefits of environmental compliance. It essentially offers a framework for addressing the gap between environmental laws on the books and in practice [10]. Environmental law enforcement could be achieved through many different strategies, pursuing compliance through environmental litigation or through policy and legislative interventions.

Our proposition is that citizen-gathered evidence based on VGI can support the environmental rule of law. For example, a civic monitoring initiative can offer evidence to demonstrate that certain environmental standards are not being respected. One could identify different scenarios, where civic evidence is confronted with supra-national standards when the standards for environmental quality are missing at the national level, insufficient or not respected [4], or when there is compliance according to the local and international standards, but people still resort to civic monitoring due mistrust or by perceiving that the issue has not been addressed [4].

The 2023 United Nations Environmental Programme (UNEP) report, discussing the global status of the environmental rule of law, affirms that civic engagement with monitoring the environment can offer precious data on local conditions, filling gaps in official data and reducing dependence on data generated by governmental actors or companies [6, 10]. Already in 2019, the first UNEP Global Report on the Environmental Rule of Law [11] noted that data collected through civic monitoring initiatives can enhance environmental rule of law by supporting decision-making processes and assisting in the identification of violations through monitoring various environmental indicators.

The 2023 UNEP report cites several successful cases where civic evidence proved to be valuable for law enforcement, in different countries around the world. UNEP recognizes the advancements that scientific studies and policy interventions have offered for greater use of civic monitoring in official interventions. For example, the work by the SensJus project [8] is recognized as providing research capacity on the ability of civic monitoring to inform environmental law enforcement [10].

At a policy level, the 2020 European Commission Report on Best Practices in Citizen Science for Environmental Monitoring is mentioned, with specific recommendations to enhance the use of citizen-generated data for environmental monitoring [12]. On the U.S.-side, in 2016, the Crowdsourcing and Citizen Science Act was adopted, encouraging the use of civic environmental data by federal agencies.

UNEP [10, 11], however, also argues that, despite authorities increasingly recognize the importance and role of civic contributions, there may be legal barriers to its use in official enforcement. For example, barriers may be related to the need of using only data that have undergone a formal peer-review processes or the law itself may exclude the possibility of reliance on civic evidence for administrative decisions and judicial processes.

UNEP also points to the fact that further research is still needed to assess the actual and potential contribution of civic monitoring to law enforcement [10]. This article, showcasing selected examples, aims at contributing to address this request. In the next section, we develop arguments aimed at legitimising this contribution under international legal frameworks and relevant scholarly discourses.

3   Legitimizing Civic Monitoring

3.1   The International Framework

Despite some challenges, civic environmental monitoring has garnered recognition and finds its legitimization in international policy and legislative frameworks. Agenda 21's Chapter 40 from the 1992 Rio Declaration[1] affirmed everyone's right to use and also *provide* information. The European Commission's 2020 Report on Best Practices in Citizen Science for Environmental Monitoring in its Recommendation 5.1 outlined considerations for citizen-contributed data [12].

Furthermore, during the 7th Meeting of the Parties of the Aarhus Convention in 2021[2], there was acknowledgment that broader citizen science provides a new source of environmental information. It was suggested that citizens could have a right to produce environmental information, which, if meeting appropriate standards, should be accepted by authorities to fill data gaps and support monitoring efforts. In the following sub-sections, we discuss two selected international instruments that can be regarded as particularly

---

[1] United Nations Conference on Environment and Development, Rio de Janeiro, 1992.

[2] United Nation Economic Committee for Europe, 7th Session of the Meeting of the Parties to the Aarhus Convention, Geneva. 2021.

suitable to legitimize civic contributions in the forms of submitting environmental data for law enforcement.

3.1.1 The Aarhus Convention

The Aarhus Convention[3] (hereinafter referred to as "the Convention") implemented by the United Nations Economic Commission for Europe (UNECE), which came into effect in 2001, is crucial for legitimizing civic environmental monitoring efforts [13]. It grants citizens and environmental organizations procedural environmental rights, aiming to enhance access to environmental information (Article 4–5), facilitate public participation in decision-making (Article 6–8), and enable challenges to public decisions in courts through environmental justice mechanisms (Article 9). The Convention employs clear and inclusive language to promote these rights, emphasizing the importance of public access to information, participation in decision-making processes, and access to justice in environmental matters.

Key provisions include ensuring public access to information, support from authorities in seeking information and promoting dissemination, and measures to enhance broader access to information, public participation, and environmental justice. The Convention mandates that, if information is unavailable, the authority should redirect the request to the presumed holder of the information (Article 4, par. 5) and refuse it only if it is not in the possession of any public authority. However, it lacks detailed provisions for cases where information is insufficient or not held by any public authority, which would be the cases where civic data could play an essential role.

The Convention currently recognizes only traditional data flows from governmental actors to citizens, meaning that accessible environmental information is limited to what authorities possess, often sourced from private actors' reports, such as those mandated by the Pollutant Release and Transfer Register established by the Kyiv Protocol of 2009 [13]. Research conducted by Berti Suman [4] in the framework of the SensJus project explores how civic environmental monitoring can be legitimized under the Aarhus Convention by addressing questions related to the utilization of civic evidence based on existing and new rights, as well as the legal and governance adaptations needed to ensure greater reliance on such monitoring and evidence.

The Aarhus Convention 7th Meeting of the Parties, acknowledged the significance of civic contributions, particularly citizen science, as a legitimate source of environmental information. The UNECE called for a consultation on electronic information tools within the Convention, with inputs from the European Citizen Science Association (ECSA) to broaden the inclusion of citizen science and civic environmental monitoring in supporting official environmental monitoring and broader environmental governance. This amendment was discussed and adopted during the 2021 7th Meeting of the Parties. However, the effectiveness of contributing civic data is limited without a duty for competent authorities to consider the data submitted and respond [4, 13, 15].

---

[3] Convention on Access to Information, Public Participation in Decision-Making and Access to Justice in Environmental Matters, Aarhus. 1998.

Despite the right to contribute information has not been officially recognized to date, the research of Berti Suman [13] argues that *implicitly* the right could be regarded as already foreseen in the letter of the convention, in particular by Article 5(1)(a) of the Aarhus Convention stating that authorities have the duty to "possess and update environmental information which is relevant to their functions". This duty could be interpreted as compelling authorities to accept civic-gathered information where they do not hold the relevant information on a given environmental matter.

3.2 The Escazú Agreement

The Regional Agreement on Access to Information, Public Participation and Justice in Environmental Matters in Latin America and the Caribbean[4] (here referred to as 'the Escazú Agreement'), provided by the Environmental Commission for Latin America and the Caribbean (ECLAC), which entered into force in 2021, guarantees access to environmental information[5], public participation, and environmental justice[6], emphasizing principles like good faith and precautionary measures[7]. It promotes a wide environmental information provision to the public, favours regulations granting broader access to environmental rights, and encourages favourable interpretations to civil society[8]. Similar to and inspired by the Aarhus Convention, it advocates for environmental information disclosure, provides procedures for cases where information is lacking, and emphasizes using effective means for information delivery during emergencies. It encourages the generation of comprehensive environmental information databases by public authorities, incorporating up-to-date data from various sources, including private entities. Additionally, it openly acknowledges the possibility of altering the burden of proof regarding access to environmental justice; and foresees strategies to eliminate barriers to participation and envisages specific provisions for human rights defenders engaged in addressing environmental matters (Article 9).

Its Article 7(4) explicitly states that due consideration should be given to the observations of the public, so they can contribute to the process. Article 7(8) argues that each Party shall ensure that, once a decision has been made, the public is informed in a timely manner thereof and of the grounds and reasons underlying the decision, including how the observations of the public have been taken into consideration.

While the Escazú Agreement addresses correcting asymmetries, neither it nor the Aarhus Convention offers solutions for situations where information is absent. It raises the question of whether the existing legal framework could be interpreted to recognize the generation of information through alternative means when conventional sources are unavailable.

---

[4] Regional Agreement on Access to Information, Public Participation and Justice in Environmental Matters in Latin America and the Caribbean, Escazú. 2018.

[5] Ibid., art 2 (c).

[6] Regional Agreement on Access to Information, Op. cit.., art 1.

[7] Regional Agreement on Access to Information, Op. cit.., art 3, (d) (e) (f).

[8] Regional Agreement on Access to Information, Op. cit.., art 4 (8).

3.3 Recognition of the Right to Contribute Information

Different ways on how to frame the right to frame information have been proposed. Authors [14] have outlined certain conditions to be met to ground a new right such as: 1. The matter is not duly monitored or addressed by the competent authorities creating a matter of concern for civil society 2. Access to information obligations is not (properly) complied with by the authorities; 3. And/or in any instance in which the civic data produced is of quality and robustness that can reasonably complement to official data. For point 3, the authors note that civic data does not need to equal government data in terms of data quality because even less precise data can still provide useful complementary information.

Further research by Berti Suman [4] explores a right to contribute environmental information, particularly when official data is lacking or insufficient, emphasizing the term 'contribute' to recognize the meaningful engagement of citizens in monitoring activities and sharing data with authorities to inform environmental law enforcement. Moreover, Whittaker [15] building on Berti Suman [13] examines the pros of guaranteeing a general right to submit environmental information and offers a hypothetical regime to implement the proposed right.

The absence of provisions in international agreements for situations with no available environmental information makes institutions more inclined to simply denying civic access to information. To address this gap, exploring new ways to bring forth civic information or present evidence is crucial.

Analysing the precautionary principle alongside due diligence obligations offers insights. The precautionary principle, a customary rule of general international law, mandates preventive measures when there is a risk of serious environmental harm, even without clear scientific evidence. It justifies taking cost-effective measures to prevent irreversible environmental damage [16], thereby potentially validating new mechanisms to gather information for use in legal or administrative proceedings.

As part of environmental international law is soft (i.e., non-binding) law, urging compliance with its obligations presents challenges. However, framing the precautionary principle as a due diligence obligation of result can hold states accountable for not achieving expected outcomes in averting environmental risks. This approach emphasizes the importance of implementing measures to prevent harm and grants discretion to the norm addressee in choosing appropriate actions.

Kayikci [17] suggests that, in order to prevent significant environmental damage, the norm addressee should consider all cost-effective measures. The authors of this article believe that these measures could include the exploration of new methods of producing or *co-producing* environmental information and could lead to new regulations supporting these new information streams.

While the Aarhus Convention and the Escazú Agreement offer mechanisms to broaden access to information and promote disclosure by public authorities, they do not explicitly endorse or incentivize the development of new information-generation methods. At the Inter-American level, instead, public participation in environmental decision-making is recognized in Article 23 of the American Convention on Human Rights which provides for the right of every citizen "to take part in the conduct of public affairs and to receive and *impart* information". In the U.S., the Clean Water Act and the Endangered Species Act both provide for the reliance on community monitoring for realizing their respective aims of monitoring and reporting. The Crowdsourcing and Citizen Science Act also provides for the use of civic environmental data by federal agencies.

As exposed in Berti Suman [4], however, a legal recognition – on one side – may respond to this gap but – on the other side – could hamper innovation and exclude civic environmental monitoring initiatives which do not meet the established legal conditions. Such an argument highlights how civic environmental monitoring is already influencing the way authorities handle environmental matters, leading to adaptations in governance models and challenging traditional responsibilities [14]. Even without formal integration into governance or legal frameworks, civic monitoring and its data can inform decision-making and law enforcement.

4 Citizen-Generated Data and VGI: Reliability and Standards

4.1 Citizen-Generated Data

Jasanoff's [18] concept of "coproduction of science and society" illustrates the intertwined development of scientific knowledge and social order. Civic monitoring exemplifies this intertwinement by blending scientific knowledge production with civic epistemologies, as institutionalized practices for collective decision-making [4]. It offers civil society actors a constructive way to contribute to both knowledge creation and institutional decisions [4].

The process of co-production of knowledge has to pass through processes of data validation. Such validation will depend on the standards against which is it confronted. In general, data collected through civic environmental monitoring may have to adhere to certification mechanisms such as those set by the International Standardization Organization (ISO) or sector-specific regulations to be considered valid for particular cases [19].

There may also be the possibility of standards set by groups of peers, for example within the ECSA [19]. Furthermore, different databases have their standards for data inclusion [4], for example, the 'Hackair' platform enables citizens to generate and publish geo-located information relevant to human exposure to outdoor air pollution. Additionally, the 'AirBase' public air quality database system of the European Environmental Agency collects information on monitoring air quality. To what extent these databases allow for the input of citizen-generated data?

The adoption of electronic data transmission systems for environmental data sharing, along with growing data availability through platforms, spurred the development and harmonization of electronic data standards. This led to the creation of the Infrastructure for Spatial Information in the European Community (INSPIRE) Directive[9] in 2007, establishing an EU-wide spatial data infrastructure and technical standards to promote data interoperability and sharing. Recognizing the potential of citizen-gathered data, the European Commission through the Communication EC (2017)312 on "Actions to

---

[9] Directive 2007/2/EC of the European Parliament and of the Council of 14 March 2007 establishing an Infrastructure for Spatial Information in the European Community (INSPIRE).

Streamline Environmental Reporting"[10] launched Action 8 to promote citizen science for complementing environmental reporting (p. 11). Despite civic data not being widely used for official monitoring due to potential disparities with more sophisticated monitoring systems, the cases that we discuss further in this article demonstrate that civic monitoring can still prompt official reporting and actions.

4.2 Data Quality

Data quality has been one of the main constraints for the further development and use of VGI spatial data. Concerns about quality arise from various aspects, from data collection to data analysis [20]. Challenges include data gathered with errors and bias due to a lack of strict data management in general VGI initiatives, management and analysis of high amounts of heterogeneous data and the interpretation of data derived from poorly described sources with almost no metadata [21].

The counterpoint to VGI-generated data is what is called the authoritative geographic data sets, which are considered accurate and reliable [20]. This term describes the data produced by professional mapping institutions [20] following strict protocols, guidelines, and best practices. Important differences between authoritative and VGI data lie in the dynamic nature of VGI, including data and contributor heterogeneity, potential biases, and lack of specifications on data collection protocols [24].

Despite these challenges, VGI can sometimes be completer and more accurate than authoritative datasets [23] and despite the concerns regarding reliability and accuracy, VGI provided by non-professionals or experts has had a growing reliance and acceptance due to its ability to persist in time and react efficiently, providing highly accurate, complete, in time and practical and usable scale [22]. The quality of VGI is crucial for its integration with authoritative data [24]. Therefore, it is important to establish reliable protocols for civic monitoring activities [21].

Recommendations to address data quality issues in VGI highlight the importance of protocols in meeting minimum data quality requirements. Clear instructions and a dedicated focus on data collection processes, self-assessment stages, data submission, and community feedback are proposed [24]. For instance, Mooney et al. [24], suggest a generic and flexible protocol for collecting VGI vector data, aiming to standardise data collection processes while encouraging participation. The protocol consists of five main stages: Initialization, Data Collection, Self-Assessment/Quality Control, Data Submission, and Feedback to the Community. Yet, it is encouraged not to design overly complex protocols and to find a balance between data quality and participation [24].

To enhance the reliability of VGI data, local regulations should also be taken into account when determining the level of stringency required for a protocol. However, due to the scope of this paper, a detailed analysis of different local legal frameworks is not possible. Therefore, this article limited its focus to the main international standards used by VGI providers, which can offer insight into law enforcement scenarios due to their global recognition.

---

[10] European Commission COM (2017)312 on 'Actions to Streamline Environmental Reporting'.

4.3 Quality Assessment of VGI

The International Organization for Standardization (ISO) 19157[11] indicates a set of standards for evaluating the quality of spatial data, which are followed by professional communities according to their protocols. However, these guidelines and standards have not been developed with the *nature* of VGI in mind [23]. The research of Fonte et al. [23] emphasizes the application of ISO 19157 standards for spatial data quality to VGI and propose additional measures tailored to VGI's unique characteristics.

To address these challenges, the ISO 19157 quality elements can be applied to VGI, including positional accuracy, thematic accuracy, completeness, temporal quality, logical consistency, and usability [23]. Additionally, specific indicators for VGI are needed, such as the inclusion of data-based indicators, demographic and socio-economic indicators, and contributor indicators, as proposed by Antoniou and Skopeliti [26]. It is important to note that these indicators aim to assess data reliability rather than accuracy, considering factors like agreement with other data sources, contributor history, recognition, and behaviour.

Other contributions such as the one proposed by Cho [22] involve a different method of assessing the quality of data and controlling contributions where contributors make additions, correct inaccuracies, and edit invalid data to improve the quality of the geospatial database. There are, however, no experts to ensure quality control, but rather the same contributors "through iterative corrections" [22].

As shown, civic monitoring offers opportunities but also poses challenges, such as ensuring reliable data collection, addressing biases, and acknowledging the influence of personal perspectives on data collection. Overcoming these challenges is key for ensuring that the practice can be regarded as a reliable source of information. This goal requires considering not only statistical corrections and protocols but also the social dimension of civic monitoring.

Certain barriers to the acceptance of citizen-gathered evidence have been identified in the literature [7] such as professional scepticism; uncertainty about rapidly changing technology; restrictions on the use of citizen science data by agencies; and legal barriers to the gathering of data by citizens. Another take regarding the barriers that civic monitoring might face according to Berti Suman [4] are, first, to ensure that the kind of monitoring is not prohibited as such or does not harm legally protected interests and, second, that applicable requirements are met so the initiative can offer a valid monitoring for the specific purposes to which it is aimed.

5 Case Studies

5.1 Case Studies

Several cases studies discussed in the literature cited throughout this article demonstrate that civic evidence, especially in the field of VGI, can complement official evidence to foster environmental law enforcement. These findings provide precious and cutting-edge material for interested actors, such as academics researching civic monitoring, non-governmental organizations and individuals relying on civic monitoring, environmental

---

[11] International Organization for Standardization (ISO), 2013. ISO 19157: 2013 Geographic Information – Data quality.

lawyers and, lastly, for governments and competent authorities but also corporations that are facing social and judicial conflicts around environmental matters. Below, we briefly discuss cases in which VGI-based civic data was useful for law enforcement. Our cases have been identified as relevant through purposive sampling by the research performed for the SensJus project discussed earlier and should not be considered as representative of the multiform reality of civic monitoring initiatives.

5.2 Oil Contamination Mapping in Basilicata

An interesting case of civic monitoring using VGI for environmental law enforcement is situated in Basilicata, South of Italy, in which the local inhabitants are monitoring environmental and public health problems associated with oil extraction. A thorough discussion of the case is offered by Berti Suman [27] and Berti Suman [4]. What is distinctive of this case is that the local inhabitants, acting under the 'Analyze Basilicata' initiative are operating as local alerts to spot environmental problems. When they identify an issue by first-hand experience (e.g., an oil spill), they search for official data on the problem including accessing national, European and global geo-spatial information. If official information is missing, inaccurate or inaccessible to civil society, the citizens run their own monitoring on the ground. They also situate the data collected on maps which become a form of communicating local issues on public web pages. In case they identify a discrepancy between official data and their measurements, they first share the results with other social actors and the media. Then, they often resort to the data collected to file a formal notification to the competent environmental agency or to the public prosecutor office. They essentially act as an 'early warning' system for compliance assurance. They also proactively engage with public institutions, asking for information release based on the Aarhus Convention and the Italian legislation on access to information, i.e., the 2016 Freedom of Information Act. For example, they demonstrate ability to strategically use the Pollutant Release and Transfer Register established by the Kyiv Protocol under the Aarhus Convention (Fig. 2).

5.3 Demonstrating Coal Ash Pollution in North Carolina

The saga on coal ash pollution in North Carolina – widely discussed in Berti Suman and Burnette [29] – demonstrate the contribution of civic environmental monitoring in driving environmental law compliance through litigation. Local community organizations and environmental groups joined efforts to detect pollution from coal ash impoundments through ongoing water quality monitoring and the collection of scientific data, leading to legal action against the responsible company, Duke Energy. The Asheville Powerplant case demonstrates the effectiveness of citizen-collected evidence in prompting legal enforcement actions for Clean Water Act violations. Sampling results from streams and groundwater, along with data from public records, provided critical evidence that led to guilty pleas and fines against Duke Energy, triggering important regulatory responses such as the Coal Ash Management Act in 2014 and enforcement actions. At the Allen Powerplant, riverkeepers and environmental organizations monitored coal ash basins to identify pollution and advocate for regulatory intervention. Overall, these cases demonstrate the importance of civic environmental monitoring in mobilizing communities,

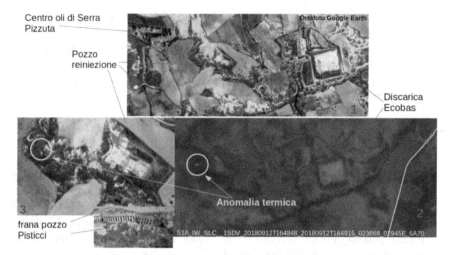

Fig. 2. Civic monitoring of gas flaring in Basilicata by the grassroots collective CovaContro. Source: CovaContro article, https://covacontro.org/le-torce-petrolifere-lucane-viste-dallo-spazio-un-problema-volutamente-sottostimato-da-terra/, last accessed 2024/04/05.

informing regulatory decisions, and holding polluters accountable. Through decentralized yet coordinated efforts, citizen scientists and environmental organizations played a crucial role in addressing coal ash pollution and demanding justice for affected communities. Technology, such as online mapping, facilitated the visualization of affected areas. In addition to traditional methods of data collection, the utilization of VGI and spatial data mapping played a significant role. Through VGI, community members and environmental organizations were able to collect and share geospatial data, enhancing the visualization and understanding of pollution impacts. Online mapping platforms provided a means to disseminate scientific findings to a broader audience, facilitating public engagement and awareness. By leveraging VGI and spatial data mapping, civic actors were able to pinpoint pollution hotspots, identify overlooked seepage sites, and advocate for regulatory action. This integration of VGI not only empowered communities to monitor environmental conditions but also facilitated collective action and informed decision-making processes at both the local and governmental levels.

5.4 Tackling Gas Flaring in Ecuador

Another relevant case comes from Latin America, the so-called 'Mecheros case' in the Amazon Rainforest, Ecuador, Facchinelli et al. The case revolves around a ruling, issued on 26 January 2021, by the Court of Nueva Loja, which banned gas flaring in the Ecuadorian Amazon. The data submitted by the litigants relied in part of civic monitoring. Facchinelli et al. [28] refer specifically to independent spatial information gathered through participatory mapping with indigenous and farmer communities. The mobilisation of local civil society was a response to the lack of independent information about oil activities and in particular on gas flaring. This gap has led to the monitoring of gas flaring through satellite imagery by civic actors, which achieved remarkable results in terms of data quality and accuracy, argue Facchinelli et al. [28]. The case is also notable for the approach adopted, that is, a "community-based participatory action research approach to develop a participatory GIS process, aiming both to provide reliable data and to support social campaigns for environmental and climate justice" [28]. Interestingly, to ensure long-term sustainability of the mapping project, only open access data and open-source applications and software have been employed. VGI data from the participatory mapping played a key role for conducting ground truth validation of existing official datasets. The initiative identified 295 previously unmapped gas flaring sites, demonstrating that gas flaring activities were considerably more than the official data provided by the Ecuadorian Ministry of Environment and National Oceanic and Atmospheric Administration Nightfire annual datasets [28]. The case shows that VGI-based civic evidence can have tangible effects in court, provide reliable data from the ground filling official gaps, empower local actors affected by oil extraction, and support social campaigns for environmental and climate justice.

5.5 Documenting Waste-Disposal Associated Air Pollution Around Rome

The Valle Galeria area, located in the outskirt of the city of Rome, the capital of Italy, has long been affected by various environmental problems, due to the concentration in it of multiple highly impactful activities. Among the other sources of environmental impacts we find the Malagrotta landfill, the largest in Europe, now shut down since 2013 for legal issues associated with its operations, and which – over the last years – have been affected by recurring fires causing the release of pollutants in the surrounding air, water and soil. The Regional Environmental Protection Authority (ARPA Lazio) regularly carries out monitoring in the area, and controls in the Valle Galeria area. Some of these monitoring activities have been performed also in support of the judicial authority, the Italian Public Prosecutor. Frequently, olfactory and acoustic ailments have been reported by the local inhabitants and such impacts associated with the plants present in the area have under official controls. Sampling of atmospheric emissions and of water quality of the local river, Rio Galeria, was also carried out by competent local institutions. All these activities are aimed to verify compliance with existing environmental regulations. Local citizens, particularly concerned for their health and the preservation of the local environment, are also exploring judicial avenues. In particular, they are launching class actions and requests to access relevant documents and data held by the public administration, pursuant to the Italian Freedom of Information Act (FOIA) and the Aarhus Convention. Local citizens in 2019 founded a committee to defend the territory, named Valle Galeria Libera, and are currently building strategic cooperations with local associations such as the independent ecological organization A Sud [30]. Since 2021, the organization supports civic monitoring activities in the context of the RomaUp program, a program, for participatory mapping of urban environmental issues [31]. The results of VGI-based civic monitoring performed in the area denounced how the significant presence of industrial plants generates a direct impact on air quality, causing distress for the local inhabitants [32]. It is still to be seen how this evidence will be used in ongoing and forthcoming judicial proceedings.

6 Conclusion

6.1 Concluding Remarks

The exploration of civic monitoring, particularly through the lens of Volunteered Geographic Information (VGI), presents a promising avenue for enhancing environmental law enforcement. The cases discussed in this article highlight the potential of citizen-generated data to complement official evidence, mobilize communities, inform regulatory decisions, and hold polluters accountable. However, several challenges and opportunities emerge from this discussion.

Firstly, the legitimacy of civic monitoring within the framework of international agreements such as the Aarhus Convention and the Escazú Agreement is crucial. While these agreements recognize the importance of public participation and access to information, there is still a need for further clarification regarding the acceptance of citizen-generated data by competent authorities. Addressing legal barriers and promoting the integration of civic data into decision-making processes are essential steps toward realizing the full potential of civic monitoring.

Secondly, ensuring the reliability and standardization of citizen-generated data is paramount. While civic monitoring offers valuable insights into environmental conditions, addressing issues such as data quality, biases, and validation processes is necessary to enhance its credibility. Establishing certification mechanisms, adhering to international standards, and promoting collaboration between stakeholders can contribute to the robustness and official uptake of citizen-gathered data.

The protocols and guidelines performed by citizen scientists especially in the field of conservation and ecology are well-developed and accepted by contributors. This could be an important starting point for promoting trust in civic data and increasing institutional recognition of such data sources.

The data provided by volunteers can be valuable for research, policy and practice, as well as for citizens themselves to address local environmental issues and has the potential to enhance their participation in environmental decision-making and advocacy, promoting a collaborative environmental governance.

Overall, civic monitoring blends scientific knowledge with civic epistemologies and institutionalized practices for collective decision-making. Embracing this collaborative approach can foster innovation, improve governance models, and empower communities to address environmental challenges effectively.

6.2 Future Research Agenda

Looking ahead, future research should focus on further legitimizing civic monitoring within legal and policy frameworks, enhancing data reliability and standardization, and exploring innovative approaches to address emerging environmental issues. In addition, empirical studies on actual (successful and failed) cases of civic monitoring aimed at promoting environmental law enforcement should be conducted, in order to offer first hand data to peer communities, scientists and decision-makers.

By leveraging the potential of citizen-generated data and VGI, stakeholders can advance environmental law enforcement, promote environmental justice, and safeguard the well-being of communities and ecosystems, as well as strengthen institutional responses to environmental law breaches.

Special attention on the increase of VGI may also increment the heterogeneity of contributions and hence solving quality issues for assessing VGI usability may become harder in the future. Finding ways to address this while these practices are continuously evolving it is a complex task but highly needed.

In the field of civic environmental monitoring, good quality data is achieved through standardised protocols, particularly in the field of conservation and ecology, which are accepted by participants. Further dialogues between these two bodies of practice could enhance overall the reliability and accuracy of volunteered data.

Several methods for ensuring data quality have been proposed, from standardization, to protocols, iterative editing, and creation of codes of practices by volunteers 10 [24]. It would be interesting to explore a more detailed approach on which methods could perform better depending on the environmental issue that the initiative tries to cover.

Acknowledgments. Part of the research discussed in this article by author Anna Berti Suman was supported by the Marie Skłodowska-Curie grant n. 891513, awarded under European Union's Horizon 2020.

Disclosure of Interests. The authors have no competing interests to declare that are relevant to the content of this article.

References

1. Berti Suman, A.: Civic monitoring for environmental enforcement. Exploring the potential and use of evidence gathered by lay people, European Commission, JRC132206 (2023). https://publications.jrc.ec.europa.eu/repository/handle/JRC132206
2. Berti Suman, A., van Geenhuizen, M.: Not just noise monitoring: rethinking citizen sensing for risk-related problem-solving. J. Environ. Planning Manage. **63**(3), 546–567 (2020). https://doi.org/10.1080/09640568.2019.1598852
3. Haklay, M., et al.: Contours of citizen science: a vignette study. R. Soc. Open Sci. **8**(8), 202108 (2021). https://doi.org/10.1098/rsos.202108
4. Berti Suman, A.: Civic Monitoring for Environmental Law Enforcement. Edward Elgar (in print, forthcoming in 2024)
5. Pocock, M.J.O., Chapman, D.S., Sheppard, L.J., Roy, H.E.: Choosing and Using Citizen Science: a guide to when and how to use citizen science to monitor biodiversity and the environment. Centre for Ecology & Hydrology (2014)
6. Moodley, K., Wyeth, G., Oo, J., Fouse, S.: Citizen Science Programs at Environmental Agencies: Best Practices Environmental Law Institute. Best Practices (2020). https://www.eli.org/research-report/citizen-science-programs-environmental-agencies-best-practices
7. Wyeth, G., Paddock, L., Parker, A., Glicksman, R., Williams, J.: The impact of citizen environmental science in the United States. Environ. Law Report. **49**(3) (2019). https://core.ac.uk/reader/232646900
8. Sensing for Justice. https://sensingforjustice.webnode.it. Retrieved 6 April 2024. The project was developed thanks to the support of the Marie Skłodowska-Curie grant n. 891513, under H2020-EU, and to the concluded research grant of the Dutch Research Council NWO, the Rubicon fellowship n. 66202117

9. Civic monitoring for environmental enforcement. European Commission Joint Research Centre. https://joint-research-centre.ec.europa.eu/scientific-activities-z/innovations-public-governance/civic-monitoring-environmental-enforcement_en. Retrieved 6 April 2024
10. United Nations Environment Programme. Environmental Rule of Law: Tracking Progress and Charting Future Directions. United Nations Environment Programme (2023). https://doi.org/10.59117/20.500.11822/43943
11. United Nations Environment Programme. Environmental Rule of Law: First Global Report (2019). https://wedocs.unep.org/20.500.11822/27279
12. European Commission. Best Practices in Citizen Science for Environmental Monitoring. Brussels (2020). https://data.consilium.europa.eu/doc/document/ST-9973-2020-INIT/en/pdf
13. Berti Suman, A.: Citizen sensing from a legal standpoint: legitimizing the practice under the Aarhus framework. J. Eur. Environ. Plann. Law, 18(1–2), 8–38 (2021). https://doi.org/10.1163/18760104-18010003
14. Berti Suman, A., Balestrini, M., Haklay, M., Schade, S.: When concerned people produce environmental information: a need to re-think existing legal frameworks and governance models? Citizen Sci. Theory Pract. 8(1), 10 (2023). https://doi.org/10.5334/cstp.496
15. Whittaker, S.: Exploring a right to submit environmental information under international environmental law. J. Environ. Law 35(3), 401–418 (2023). https://doi.org/10.1093/jel/eqad025
16. Cooney, R.: The Precautionary Principle in Biodiversity Conservation and Natural Resource Management: An Issues Paper for Policy-Makers, Researchers and Practitioners. Elsevier (2004). https://doi.org/10.1016/B978-0-12-811989-1.00003-8
17. Kayikci, M.S.: The Burden of Proof within the Scope of the Precautionary Principle: International and European Perspectives (SSRN Scholarly Paper), Rochester, NY, 6 July 2012. https://doi.org/10.2139/ssrn.2101613
18. Jasanoff, S. (ed.): States of Knowledge. The Co-Production of Science and the Social Order. Routledge (2004)
19. Berti Suman, A.: Between freedom and regulation: investigating community standards for enhancing scientific robustness of Citizen Science. In: Reins, L. (ed.) Regulating New Technologies in Uncertain Time, pp. 31–46. T.M.C. Asser Press (2019). https://doi.org/10.1007/978-94-6265-279-8_3
20. Rak, A., Coleman, D., Sue, N.: Legal liability concerns surrounding volunteered geographic information applicable to Canada. In: Spatially Enabling Government, Industry and Citizens Research and Development Perspectives (Abbas Rajabifard & David Coleman, pp. 125–141). GSDI Association Press (2013)
21. See, L., Estima, J., Pődör, A., Arsanjani, J.J., Bayas, J-C.L., Vatseva, R.: Sources of VGI for mapping. In: Foody, G., et al. (eds.) Mapping and the Citizen Sensor, pp. 13–35. Ubiquity Press, London (2017). https://doi.org/10.5334/bbf.b
22. Cho, G.: Some legal concerns with the use of crowd-sourced Geospatial Information. IOP Conf. Ser. Earth Environ. Sci. 20(1), 012040 (2014). https://doi.org/10.1088/1755-1315/20/1/012040
23. Fonte, C.C., et al.: Assessing VGI data quality. In: Foody, G., et al. (eds.) Mapping and the Citizen Sensor, pp. 137–163. Ubiquity Press, London (2017). https://doi.org/10.5334/bbf.g
24. Minghini, M., et al.: The relevance of protocols for VGI collection. In: Foody, G., et al. (eds.) Mapping and the Citizen Sensor, pp. 223–247. Ubiquity Press, London (2017). https://doi.org/10.5334/bbf.j
25. Mooney, P., Minghini, M., Laakso, M., Antoniou, V., Olteanu-Raimond, A.-M., Skopeliti, A.: Towards a protocol for the collection of VGI vector data. Int. J. Geogr. Inf. 5(11), 217 (2016). https://doi.org/10.3390/ijgi5110217

26. Antoniou, V., Skopeliti, A.: Measures and indicators of VGI quality: an overview. In: ISPRS Annals of the Photogrammetry, Remote Sensing and Spatial Information Sciences. Presented at the ISPRS Geospatial Week 2015, ISPRS Annals, La Grande Motte, France, pp. 345–351 (2015)
27. Berti Suman, A.: Striving for good environmental information: civic sentinels of oil pollution in the South of the North. Law Environ. Dev. J. (LEAD J.) 17(2), [i]-179 (2022). https://doi.org/10.25501/SOAS.00037890
28. Facchinelli, F., et al.: Extreme citizens science for climate justice: linking pixel to people for mapping gas flaring in Amazon rainforest. Environ. Res. Lett. 17(2), 024003 (2022). https://doi.org/10.1088/1748-9326/ac40af
29. Berti Suman, A., Burnette, A.: Exploring the role of civic monitoring of coal ash pollution: (Re)gaining agency by crowdsourcing environmental information. Law Ethics Human Rights 17, 227–256 (2024). https://doi.org/10.1515/lehr-2023-2009
30. A Sud Homepage. https://asud.net/. Accessed 6 April 2024
31. A Sud RomaUp Project. https://asud.net/progetto/romaup-2/. Accessed 6 April 2024
32. A Sud 'Valle Galeria, terra ai margini della città'. https://asud.net/ultima/valle-galeria-terra-ai-margini-della-citta/. Accessed 6 Apr 2024

Spatiotemporal Data Analysis

A Novel Framework for Spatiotemporal POI Analysis

Negin Zarbakhsh$^{(\boxtimes)}$ ⓘD and Gavin McArdle ⓘD

UCD School of Computer Science University College Dublin, Belfield Dublin 4,
Ireland
negin.zarbakhsh@ucdconnect.ie, gavin.mcardle@ucd.ie

Abstract. Urban landscapes are rapidly evolving, integrating diverse
Points of Interest (POIs) to accommodate city dwellers' needs, highlighting the necessity for efficient analytical frameworks. This study presents a
preprocessing framework using KNIME, known for its user-friendly interface and robust data management, for efficient POI preprocessing. We
integrated the Advan mobility dataset with the Census dataset, allowing
us to consider both the POI features of the location and the characteristics of the people using these POIs. We also introduce two novel
POI features that link visitors to POIs: median dwell time at POIs and
visitor travel distance from home to POI, to deepen our understanding
of POI dynamics. We used the framework to conduct spatiotemporal
analyses across 31 POI categories, identifying significant temporal variations linked to daily human behaviour within these categories. For our
spatial analysis case study, due to healthcare disparities across various
geographic divisions in the US, we selected the outpatient care services
category of POIs for deeper analysis. The study underscores a significant correlation between our two novel features and variances in both
geographic (land area) and demographic (population density) aspects
across nine US divisions. This research makes a substantial contribution to urban studies, providing a solid framework for POI analysis and
introducing other influential features along with visitors' check-in data
for examining POIs in cities.

Keywords: Dwell time · Movement analysis · Points of Interest ·
Spatiotemporal data mining · Travel distance

1 Introduction

To study human behaviour in cities, it is essential to analyze the places that people visit daily. These places, also known as Points of Interest (POIs), could be
categorized by their functionalities such as religious organizations, restaurants
and other eating places, offices of dentists and physicians, gasoline stations and
so on. In the physical world, these POIs serve as hubs for daily activities and are
characterized by their precise latitude and longitude coordinates, which are fundamental components of mapping platforms like Google Maps and Open Street

© The Author(s), under exclusive license to Springer Nature Switzerland AG 2024
M. Lotfian and L. L. L. Starace (Eds.): W2GIS 2024, LNCS 14673, pp. 23–40, 2024.
https://doi.org/10.1007/978-3-031-60796-7_2

Map (OSM), Location-based Social Networks (LBSN) like Foursquare and Yelp, and tourism-related platforms such as Booking.com, Airbnb, and TripAdvisor. The evolution of these platforms coincides with the recent advancements in big data management which are further enhanced by cutting-edge developments in artificial intelligence (AI) and machine learning (ML) algorithms. This opens up new possibilities for utilizing the data they collect to make more informed decisions for our cities. Analyzing factors such as the sentiments towards these places, the overall quality of experiences as reflected in their ratings, the timing, and duration of visits, the length of commutes, and subsequent destinations chosen and so forth help urban planners to unlock valuable insights [21]. It has been a long-standing question in the literature to provide a precise definition of these places. In 1987, John Agnew [1] introduced three fundamental dimensions of places: location, locale, and sense of place. The location of a place is a significant aspect, as every place possesses specific geographical coordinates on the Earth's surface that can be pinpointed on a map. In addition to that, Agnew emphasizes that each place has distinctive physical characteristics that set it apart from others. Having defined the place by its location and occupied it with physical form, the third element is a sense of place that connects people to places based on the feeling and experience they have in that place. Over the years researchers have tried to add more aspects to place definition such as Seamon [24] who equated place with mobility using the phrase 'place-ballet', explaining how daily routines in a place affect the sense of place to include all aspects that could make *a place a place*.

To analyze POIs in cities effectively, we need to collect comprehensive data that provides new perspectives on various aspects of these POIs. This includes not only information about the characteristics of the place itself but also the experiences and feelings of the people who visit it. Current literature has only examined the relationship between people and POIs from the perspective of check-in attributes data [10,21,23], the demographic profile of visitors by census data [18] and visual characteristics by street-level imagery's [22,29,31], but we believe there is more to explore. Our research delves deeper and includes new features such as the median dwell time of visitors in different categories of POIs, the average distance people commute from home to visit different categories of POIs, the popularity of different categories at different times of day, and differences between weekdays and weekends. Therefore, our studies include the analysis of visitors demographic background by features such as their origin (Not Hispanic or Latin, Hispanic or Latin), age (18–24, 25–34, 35–54, ages 55), race (American Indian and Alaska, Native Asian alone, Native Hawaiian and Other, Pacific Islander Some other race alone, Two or more race). It also includes the economic situation of the visitors in terms of their income (Less than $49,999, $50,000 To $99,999,$100,000 Or More), their social aspect including educational attainment (less than High School Diploma, HS Diploma or GED, Some College and/or Associate's Degree, Bachelor's Degree, Master's, Doctorate, and Prof Degree). All of these features are estimated based on the census block group the visitors travel from to a POI and census data for the population living in these blocks. The main contribution of this study is to include the sense of place by defining the behaviour and engagement of visitors by including the median distance, bucket of dwell time at a POI, and distance from home along with the total check-in data that includes features such as raw visit numbers along with the days and hours which are popular for that specific POI. We included these features from the Advan company dataset. We also provide our analysis based on the North American Industry Classification System (NAICS)[1], a standardized classification system utilized for the categorization and classification of industries across the United States.

Our research introduces a novel framework for preprocessing human visitation data, which encompasses a detailed analysis of how individuals interact with various categories of POIs. This includes metrics such as visit frequency, median dwell time, commuting distance, and peak visitation times and days. Additionally, our method integrates this data with census-related datasets, enabling the creation of intricate socio-economic and demographic profiles. To achieve this, we have employed a graphical workflow system that models complex preprocessing steps through a network of interconnected nodes. Specifically, we utilize KNIME, an open-source platform introduced by Berthold et al. in 2007 [3]. KNIME stands out for its extensibility, strongly typed data system, and comprehensive workflow documentation features [9]. It provides a robust, user-friendly environment that facilitates the integration of various analytical tools and techniques, effectively tackling prevalent data processing challenges. In our study, KNIME's intuitive graphical interface and superior data integration capabilities have been instrumental in enhancing the preprocessing of POI datasets. This method facilitates a deeper understanding of both place characteristics and human interactions at POIs, representing a notable progression in POI data analysis. It enriches the geospatial domain by simplifying and enhancing the user-friendliness of POI data analysis, thereby broadening its accessibility and applicability in the field. Our study also adds an extension to previous research [7] focusing on the mobility aspect using KNIME. Having this framework ready, this study demonstrates its utility by addressing the following research questions (RQ):

- **RQ1 (Temporal Aspect)**: How do visitors' engagement patterns with different categories of POIs vary across weekdays and weekends, as well as at different times of the day?
- **RQ2 (Spatial Aspect)**: How do geographic and demographic factors influence outpatient care centres accessibility in the US, as reflected in median dwell time at care facilities and the distance patients travel to a POI from their home?

RQ1 focuses on the temporal aspect of this study, and in RQ2, we chose "Outpatient Care Centers" categories of POI as a case study for the spatial differences analysis of this study due to current health disparities issues such as rural-urban differences in the US [14,34]. We also account for population density and land use as demographic and geographic factors, given their demonstrated influence on outpatient care centres in previous studies [6,20].

---

[1] https://www.census.gov/programs-surveys/economic-census/year/2022/guidance/understanding-naics.html.

2 Literature Review

POI datasets, integrating both geographical (e.g. POI address, precise coordinates, POI building footprint polygons, etc.) and non-geographical (e.g. operational details such as working hours, and their website, categories describing their functionality, etc.) are crucial in urban studies. These POIs typically adhere to a hierarchical structure classification, starting with a broad category that represents a general type of POIs, for example, "food service," into finer levels of specificity like "Italian fast-food restaurant," which offers a more detailed and specific description of the type. This hierarchical structure enhances the accuracy and relevance of navigation and location-based services [29].

Apart from these categories, POIs serve as a focal point for daily human activities; therefore, data on human mobility may help understand POIs. The study of human mobility has undergone a significant transformation with the advent of smartphones [16]. Traditionally, this field has depended on data sources like national censuses, which provide macro-level insights into population characteristics and form a foundational understanding of demographic and socioeconomic aspects. Additionally, localized surveys have been instrumental, offering micro-level information such as the purpose of each trip and the chosen mode of transportation, thus facilitating a deeper understanding of mobility dynamics [2]. While these datasets are invaluable for studying human mobility, their collection process can be resource-intensive, prone to statistical inaccuracies, and challenging to apply in dynamic contexts [22,28]. In recent years, smartphones have transformed our world, reshaping our lifestyles, societal norms, and behavioural patterns. In 2022, mobile technologies had already contributed $5.2 trillion which is equivalent to 5% of the global Gross Domestic Product (GDP). This figure is projected to approach nearly $6 trillion by 2030, highlighting the widespread impact of mobile technology in improving productivity and efficiency on a global scale[2]. With over 8.44 billion cellular subscriptions globally, the ubiquity of these devices has opened up new avenues for understanding human movement patterns around POIs. These smart devices are equipped with Personal Global Positioning System (GPS) trackers, enabling continuous monitoring of individuals' movements throughout the day. These developments have led to companies collecting information on people's movements in these places to better understand how these places are being used [4,5,11,12,28–31].

This study aims to seize the opportunities presented by the wealth of information available on human mobility patterns around the POIs and the utilization of both geographical and non-geographical attributes of POIs to construct a preprocessing framework to provide a comprehensive view of POI visit patterns not only by check-in data but also by features such as median dwell time and distance from home, the popularity of the day and hours of the week, socio-economic and demographic estimation of visitors.

---

[2] https://www.gsma.com/mobileeconomy.

Studies on a Regional Functionality (Coarse-grained Scale). Research in assessing the physical characteristics and human activities within geographical areas has significantly advanced, focusing initially on coarse-grained land use categorizations like agricultural, residential, commercial, and industrial sectors, and land cover types (materials cover the surface of the earth such as water, soils, rock, roads, and so on). Liu *et al.*'s [19] comprehensive survey of 102 scholarly articles on urban function analysis revealed that 35% of studies relied exclusively on POI datasets, with 49.02% using multi-source data sets. This indicates a growing trend towards integrating diverse data streams for a more holistic understanding of urban dynamics. Through this integration, researchers can leverage the collective strength of several sources to enhance the understanding of the region's functionality by providing semantic information and improving spatial and temporal resolution. Human mobility data sets have recently emerged as a viable source for investigating land use functioning in much finer temporal, spatial, and social dimensions [8]. The integration of various data sources, including satellite imagery, POI data, human mobility patterns, and spatial graphs, has proven effective in enhancing our comprehension of regional functionalities, as evidenced by the RegionEncoder model described in [13]. This model served as a powerful tool in addressing significant urban challenges, including house price prediction and the assessment of regional popularity. Underscoring the potential of multi-modality for land use classification has been further proven in previous research [17,25,33].

The foundational approach to regional functionality is key to comprehending the broader societal and environmental roles of specific areas. This perspective, as outlined by [27], provides a macro-level view of urban landscapes. However, the evolving landscape of geographic analysis and urban planning demands a more nuanced, fine-grained examination. Recognizing the significant impact of individual POIs within these regions, researchers have shifted focus to understanding how these specific locations contribute to urban life. As Milias et al. (2021) [22] highlighted, these POIs are not just mere locations on a map; they are dynamic hubs of activity, each with its unique function and influence. By analyzing the distinct roles and interactions of these POIs, we gain a deeper understanding of the micro-level dynamics that shape the urban experience.

Studies on a POI's Functionality (Fine-grained Scale). On a finer scale, the exploration of POIs' presence and persistence in cities has become crucial for urban planning and governance to make informed decisions about the selection of business sites, POI recommendations for tourism, and appraisals of real estate [22]. Extensive research [10,22] has developed models to categorize POIs with the help of ML models. Some [10] propose that minimal metadata, such as textual names and neighbourhood-based attributes extracted primarily from sources such as OSM, suffices. Conversely, there exists a body of research [21,22] that advocates for an array of features that extends beyond the fundamental, encompassing a broader spectrum of features to predict POI functionality. McKenzie's study [21] on the temporal aspects of human behaviour about POIs highlighted the stability and regional variability of temporal signatures, influencing POI categorization and the reliability of check-in behaviours. Other researchers [23]focused on linking POIs to their surroundings, exploring the frequency of visits, interactions with the POIs, and the surrounding environment's impact on their longevity. There is another line of research that relates visitors to POIs which includes using demographic data sourced from census records or geo-tagged/geocoded social media profile posts data [18]. Other researchers [22, 29, 31] focus on visual characteristics, such as street-level images. Other research extends to improving the quality of POI tags in location-based services, with innovative solutions like the triadaptive collaborative learning framework (to automatically fill in missing tags and correct incorrect ones) [32], the Geographic-Enhanced and Dependency-Guided Sequence Tagging model (which extracts POI mentions and identifies their associated accessibility labels from unstructured text) [26], and character-based LSTM models for semantic tag completion [15].

Despite existing advances, a comprehensive understanding of the various characteristics of visitors and locations within POI analysis, particularly among diverse categories, is still lacking. Additionally, there is a demand for reliable tools that provide uniform preprocessing results for POI data. Our study aims to fill these gaps by presenting an innovative set of features used for analysing POI data. We introduce this sophisticated framework utilizing KNIME, which serves to refine the analysis and extend the practical use of POI information.

3 Data Preperation Framework

Our study focuses on segmenting features into two key dimensions: People-related and Place-related attributes. Therefore, we use a variety of datasets, including census Bureau data[3] and the Advan mobility dataset[4] (originally owned by Safegraph). For the people-related aspect, we examined demographics like visitors' origins, ages, and races, alongside economic factors such as income levels and social elements like educational attainment. Addressing privacy and data anonymization constraints, which limited access to detailed visitor information in the Advan dataset, we estimated visitor features using aggregated census data based on home census block groups (CBG) information. To infer visitor demographics at POI, we used Advan's visitation pattern dataset[5], which provides information on visitor home origins and visit counts. By applying census data percentages to raw visit counts, we estimated visitor profiles for each POI, providing insight into demographic compositions based on their home CBG data. Our final data includes the features below:

- **Raw Visit Counts:** This metric indicates the number of distinct visitors from the Advan panel to a specific POI.

---

[3] https://data.census.gov/.
[4] https://advanresearch.com/.
[5] https://docs.safegraph.com/docs/monthly-patterns.

- **Normalized Visits by Region NAICS Visits:** This represents the ratio of raw visit counts to the total number of visits within the same state or province and within the same NAICS code during the same time frame.
- **Distance from Home:** This is measured as the median commute distance in meters for visitors to a POI.
- **Bucketed Dwell Times:** This feature categorizes the duration of visits into predefined time buckets, such as "<5 min", "5–20 minutes", "21–60 minutes", "61–240 minutes", and ">240 min". Each category includes the count of visits falling within that time range.
- **Popularity by Hour:** This measures the volume of visits to the POI during each hour of the day, and specifies the most popular one.
- **Popularity by Day:** It calculates the total number of visits for each day of the week, from Monday to Sunday, and highlights the most popular day.

Understanding the temporal characteristics of human activities at different POIs is vital for analysing them, as highlighted in McKenzie et al., 2015 [21]). For instance, the peak times for restaurants during lunch and dinner hours or the typical shopping hours at clothing stores are crucial factors in identifying these locations. These comprehensive feature sets enhance our understanding of visitor demographics and engagement patterns, offering a fuller view of human activities and sentiments at various places, thereby addressing both RQ1 and RQ2 effectively. In the following, we explain the KNIME workflow.

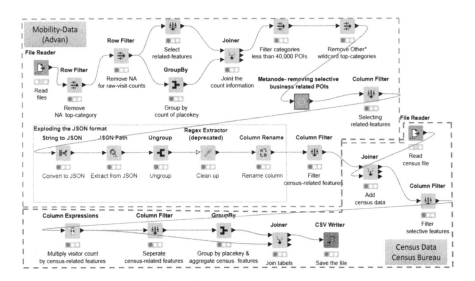

Fig. 1. KNIME workflow for cleaning Advan data and its integration with census data.

3.1 KNIME Workflow for Data Preparation

Managing extensive city-related datasets poses major big data challenges, with data preprocessing being the most time-intensive yet vital stage in model development. To improve reproducibility, we introduce a KNIME workflow, chosen for its efficiency and robust data handling capabilities, illustrated in Fig. 1, designed to integrate Census data with Advan mobility data.

Our KNIME workflow begins with the 'File Reader' node, handling CSV files from Advan mobility datasets encompassing 12,570,900 POI records. We then apply 'Row Filter' and 'Column Filter' nodes to remove rows with missing values (top category and raw counts of visitors) and select essential features for modelling. A key step involves grouping POIs by their top categories using unique Placekey identifiers, ensuring a representative sample for each category. We further refine our data by excluding categories marked as "other" or irrelevant to our study, using a 'Row Filter' node with wildcard text matching. This includes "accounting, tax preparation, bookkeeping, and payroll services," "Agencies, brokerages, and other insurance-related activities," "offices of real estate agents and brokers," "lessors and real estate," and building-related businesses such as building material and suppliers, dealers and building finishing and equipment contractors. This filtration focuses on business-related categories and results in 3,004,101 POI records.

Next, we eliminate POIs with missing visitor home CBG data and integrate census data, requiring the 'String to JSON' node to transform and manipulate data formats effectively. The dataset contains POI data, including complex structures like dictionaries and lists. For example, the "visitor_home_cbgs" field shows the number of visitors from specific CBG IDs. We streamlined these data using techniques such as converting string representations to a structured JSON format, facilitating the integration of census data to enrich our analysis. This transformation process, crucial for our study, involved extracting key information from the JSON format and refining data representations for better clarity and analysis. Key steps included employing data manipulation nodes for efficient handling and merging of visitor counts with demographic data from the census, thereby enhancing our understanding of visitor profiles. By summarizing these enriched POIs by their unique Placekeys (their unique identifiers), we achieved a detailed overview of visitor demographics at these locations.

4   Results

In Sect. 3, we explained the preprocessing steps required to obtain a clean dataset representing visitation patterns over one month, from December 1, 2022, to January 1, 2023. The dataset contains a vast amount of visit counts, totalling 624,422,510, associated with 3,033,869 distinct POIs. The POIs are classified into 31 unique NAICS top categories, further subdivided into 87 subcategories, and distributed across 55 regions within the US This includes a set of 22,766 cities in the US, as shown in Fig. 2. As seen in the city density plot, this includes the US states and the US territories. Over 35% of POIs are situated in the four regions of California, Texas, Florida, New York, and Pennsylvania, in that order. The top five cities with the highest number of POIs are Houston, Los Angeles,

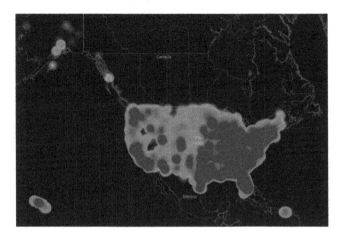

Fig. 2. City POI Density Map. Cities with a higher concentration of POI are highlighted in red colour. (Color figure online)

Chicago, Brooklyn, and New York. With the use of the KNIME framework, we have obtained a highly refined and well-structured data set that includes essential features. These features are crucial in addressing research questions associated with temporal and spatial analyses in Sect. 1.

4.1   Temporal Analysis

Our KNIME framework, as detailed in Sect. 3.1, effectively filtered business-related POI categories, enabling a detailed comparison of people's behaviours across these categories. We further refined the framework by integrating JSON nodes, which were instrumental in identifying peak visit times and days. This allowed us to quantify the flow of visitors to specific POI categories at different times, providing a richer understanding of temporal visitation trends to address RQ1. For RQ1, we compared visitor engagement with various POI categories on weekdays versus weekends. Initially, we assessed the data distribution, and the Shapiro-Wilk test results revealed a non-normal distribution for both Weekday and Weekend data (p-values < 0.05). Consequently, we employed the non-parametric Wilcoxon signed-rank test for comparison. This test revealed a significant difference in engagement between weekdays and weekends (p-value = 0.0007), highlighting distinct patterns for different POI categories. Additionally, we calculated the median differences for each category to understand the direction and magnitude of these variations and below are the comparison results of different POI categories:

– Higher Weekday Engagement: Categories like "Elementary and Secondary Schools", "Outpatient Care Centers", "Child Day Care Services", "Automobile Dealers", and "Depository Credit Intermediation" show significantly higher engagement during weekdays compared to weekends.

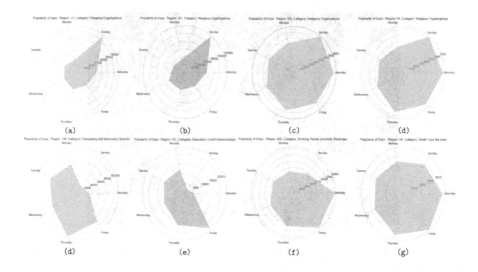

Fig. 3. Radar plots for popularity of a particular category within different regions across days of the week. Each radar plot corresponds to a unique POI category and represents a specific region. The values on the radar plot represent the popularity of the specified category within the given region for each day of the week.

- Higher Weekend Engagement: Categories such as "Traveler Accommodation", "Drinking Places (Alcoholic Beverages)", and "Religious Organizations" tend to have higher engagement during weekends.
- Minimal Differences: Some categories like "Death Care Services", "Grocery Stores", "General Merchandise Stores" and "Clothing Stores show only minor differences in engagement between weekdays and weekends.

To explain this further, we use the radar plot to visualize and compare the popularity of different days of the week across different POI categories and regions. Each spoke on the radar plot corresponds to a different day of the week and the values on each spoke represent the magnitude or level of popularity for that day within the category or region. The farther the value is from the centre of the plot, the higher the popularity for that day, and vice versa as shown in Fig. 3. Shifting focus from weekdays to time-of-day popularity, we aggregated total visits for all POIs, categorized by function. We divided the day into distinct periods: morning, noon, evening, and night, and normalized visit counts across categories to enable comparison between categories as shown in Fig. 4. Additionally, we utilize our two key features, median dwell time and travel distance, to enhance our understanding and comparison of these aspects across all 31 POI categories as shown in Fig. 5.

4.2 Spatial Analysis

Our KNIME framework (Sect. 3.1) facilitates the integration of POI datasets with census data, adding detailed US geographical divisions down to the state

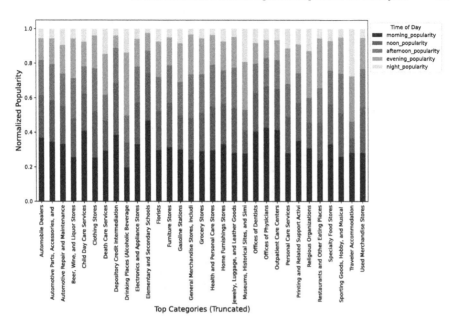

Fig. 4. stacked bar plots for the popularity of a particular category within the different times of the day.

level. This enables the analysis of these datasets across various geographical scales, enriching the geographic granularity of the study. In addressing RQ2, we adopt the standard US subdivisions into geographic divisions (New England, Middle Atlantic, West North Central, South Atlantic, East South Central, West South Central, Mountain and Pacific[6]). We select outpatient care centres as a case study to study the visitor's behaviour spatially. Then, we aggregate our POI values into their geographic divisions by using the Census Bureau 500k shape file and summing the amount of land, 2020 total population, and averaging the distance from home and median dwell time of all the POI coordinates into their bigger geographical divisions. Table 1 shows these values, where we calculated the population density in these regions (Total Population ÷ Land Area). Regions such as New England and the Middle Atlantic have higher median dwell times, while West South Central has the lowest. The Pacific division shows the highest average distance travelled from home and East South Central and South Atlantic also have higher distances. To investigate how geographic and demographic factors influence outpatient care centres' POIs, we chose land area, population density, and the two key metrics (median dwell time and distance from home) in understanding healthcare service dynamics across different US geographic divisions. For this purpose, we calculated the correlation and show it in Fig. 6.

---

[6] https://www.cdc.gov/nchs/.

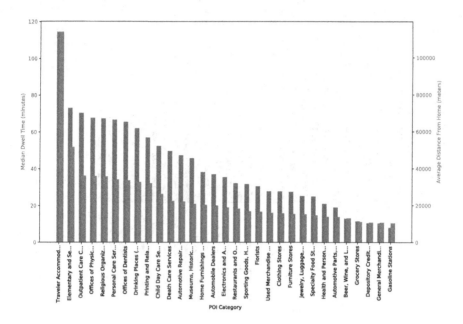

Fig. 5. Comparative Analysis by POI Category: Displaying Median Dwell Time and Average Travel Distance.

5   Discussion

Visitor Temporal Patterns Across Various POI Categories. Our analysis uncovers significant differences in visitor engagement between mid-week and weekends, addressing RQ1. As illustrated in Fig. 3, religious organizations see peak attendance on Sundays in many US regions, consistent with traditional Christian Sunday worship. However, regional variations are evident, as shown in Utah (UT) and South Carolina (SC) (Fig. 3 (a&b)), where Saturdays are less popular for religious activities compared to Sundays. This contrasts with Delaware (DE) and Rhode Island (RI) (Fig. 3 (c&d)), where Saturday gatherings are as prevalent as Sunday ones. This is corroborated by a survey indicating that in Rhode Island, 36% of adults regularly attend religious services, and 48% consider religion very important. Future research could delve into this spatial diversity to further understand these regional differences. Regarding temporal patterns, without accounting for spatial diversity, Figs. 3 (d&e) reveal that weekdays (Monday to Friday) see the highest visitation rates for categories like elementary and secondary schools, and financial institutions. On the other hand, Fig. 3 (f) illustrates that places serving alcohol are most frequented on Fridays and Saturdays, likely for social activities. Additionally, we observe consistent visitation across both weekdays and weekends in categories such as death care services, indicating a steady temporal demand for these services.

In exploring daytime popularity variability across different POI categories, Fig. 4 presents interesting insights into consistent human activity patterns. The

Table 1. Aggregated Level Geographic Divisions of Outpatient Care Centers POIs

Division	Distance(m)	Dwell(min)	Land Area(m^2)	Pop Density
East North Central	13060.09	91.34	6.29e+11	0.000075
East South Central	16670.69	87.88	4.62e+11	0.000042
Middle Atlantic	10318.30	97.12	2.57e+11	0.000165
Mountain	13092.44	86.36	2.22e+12	0.000011
New England	13595.98	103.61	1.62e+11	0.000093
Pacific	20712.28	88.87	2.32e+12	0.000023
South Atlantic	16189.70	92.80	6.87e+11	0.000096
West North Central	12206.47	92.29	1.31e+12	0.000016
West South Central	14655.54	83.51	1.10e+12	0.000037

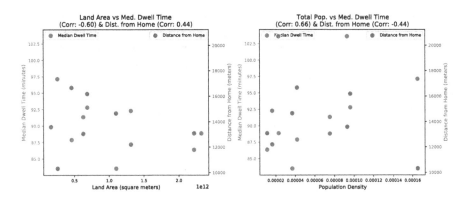

Fig. 6. Left: This scatter plot visualizes the relationship between the land area of a geographic division and median dwell time & the distance from home to outpatient care services. Right: This scatter plot shows the relationships of population density with both median dwell time and distance from home.

figure corroborates previous research findings, such as those in Betancourt (2023) [4], by highlighting low nighttime activities and higher daytime engagements in various POIs. Significantly, morning hours see the highest foot traffic in dentists' offices, physicians' offices, outpatient care centres, and schools, reflecting their alignment with standard daytime schedules for appointments and education. In contrast, morning visits to places serving alcohol and restaurants are noticeably lower, as these venues typically don't attract early-hour social or dining activities. As the day shifts to the afternoon, a notable increase in popularity is observed in social venues, particularly those serving alcohol, aligning with an uptick in leisure activities. Evenings peak activity for these places, aligning with global social nightlife trends and offering relaxation and socialization opportunities. Restaurants remain busy during both lunch and dinner times, highlighting their integral role in daily dining habits. For travel accommodations, nighttime is the prime time for check-ins, likely due to late travel schedules or arrivals, indicating a preference or necessity to settle into accommodations during the night.

Place Sense: Behavior and Engagement. In our analysis of POIs from the perspective of place sense, focusing on two key features-median dwell time and distance from home-we observed patterns that align with the typical routines of city life. Based on Fig. 5, POI category of Traveler Accommodation not only has the highest dwell time but also records the longest average travel distance (approximately 113,856 m). This aligns with the expectation that accommodations for travellers are often destinations in themselves, leading to both extended stays and longer travel distances. Essential and quick-visit categories like Gasoline Stations and Grocery Stores exhibit significantly lower dwell times, around 8 and 11.5 min respectively, indicating brief, purpose-driven visits. Category of Gasoline Stations, despite their brief dwell times, show a surprisingly high average travel distance (around 36,077 m). This could indicate their frequent use as stopovers on longer journeys, rather than just local convenience stops. Category of Grocery Stores presents a shorter average travel distance (about 26,220 m) compared to gasoline stations, which is consistent with their role in fulfilling routine, local shopping needs, leading to shorter, more frequent visits. Category of Educational and Healthcare Institutions, like schools and outpatient care centres, tend to have moderate travel distances, suggesting a balance between accessibility and the specialized nature of their services.

Spatial Analysis of Outpatient Healthcare Accessibility and Dwell Time in the US: Drawing on the insights from Table 1 and Fig. 6, we address RQ2's objectives. The moderate negative correlation (–0.60) between land area and median dwell time at outpatient care POIs suggests a trend where larger geographic divisions often experience shorter visits. Conversely, the moderate positive correlation (0.44) between land area and the distance patients travel from home to access healthcare services indicates that individuals in larger geographic divisions face longer travel distances. Furthermore, the positive correlation (0.66) between population density and median dwell time implies that in more densely populated areas, patients tend to spend more time at healthcare facilities. On the other hand, the negative correlation (–0.44) between population density and the distance from home signifies that patients in denser areas typically enjoy shorter travel distances to reach healthcare services. Based on this, we have gained below insights:

Geographic Size and Travel Distance: The moderate positive correlation between land area and the distance patients travel to access healthcare services aligns with findings by [14,34], who observed similar trends in rural versus urban settings. In larger geographic divisions, such as the Pacific and Mountain divisions, patients typically face longer travel distances, underscoring the challenges in healthcare accessibility in expansive regions.

Population Density and Dwell Time: The positive correlation between population density and median dwell time at healthcare facilities is consistent with the observations of [6], highlighting the impact of higher patient influx in densely populated areas like the Middle Atlantic, South Atlantic and New England regions. This suggests that more populous areas might experience longer wait times and potentially strained healthcare resources.

Travel Distance with Population Density: The negative correlation bebreaktween population density and the distance from home further supports the notion that urban centres, with higher population densities, offer better proximity to healthcare services compared to more sparsely populated regions. These findings have significant implications for healthcare policy and planning, emphasizing the need for tailored approaches to improve healthcare accessibility and efficiency in different geographic and demographic contexts

6 Conclusion and Future Direction

In this study, we developed an innovative preprocessing framework using KNIME, tailored to enhance geospatial analysis by efficiently cleansing datasets associated with an increasing number of POIs. A key aspect of our approach was the integration of POI datasets with census data, allowing for a comprehensive analysis of POIs from both place-based factors and the visitor experience perspective. We introduced two novel metrics - median dwell time and distance from home - providing fresh insights into the nature of POIs in urban settings. To showcase the efficacy of the KNIME framework, we addressed two critical research questions: one examining the temporal variations in POI category engagement and the other exploring spatial analytics across outpatient health centres in the US.

Our analysis revealed distinct patterns in POI utilization, with leisure and non-daily activity locations like Traveler Accommodations and Museums typically involving longer travel distances. Conversely, sites for daily needs such as grocery stores and medical offices tend to be more localized. Also, the popularity of POI types such as travel accommodation and bars at night part of the day. For a better understanding of health disparities across different geographical divisions of the US, we consider the geographic (land area) and demographic (population density) factors with these two new features introduced in our studies. Our findings demonstrate a high correlation between geographic Size and travel distance, population density and dwell time and a negative correlation between land area and dwell time and total population and distance from home. Our findings demonstrate a clear correlation between geographic size and travel distance, as well as population density and dwell time, further elucidating the dynamics of POI accessibility.

Looking forward, our study will include more analyses incorporating additional demographic factors such as age, sex, and origin of visitors, which are vital for understanding health disparities in the context of outpatient care services.

This enhancement has already been initiated in our KNIME framework through the integration of census data, laying the groundwork for more detailed and insightful analysis in future research endeavours. Incorporating finer geographical scales in future research will greatly benefit from the spatial capabilities of KNIME software, enabling precise analysis tailored to the unique characteristics of state, county, and city levels in the US landscape. This approach will enable more localized and specific insights. Additionally, the applicability of our framework to various POI categories offers exciting opportunities to compare urban dynamics across different cities and POIs, potentially revealing unique urban patterns and informing urban planning and policy decisions. Our study not only contributes to the existing body of knowledge on urban POI dynamics but also sets a foundation for future research that can leverage detailed demographic data to uncover deeper insights into POIs in cities.

Framework Availability. The Novel POI Spatiotemporal Framework is publicly available for use and can be accessed at https://github.com/NeginZarbakhsh/Novel-POI-Spatiotemporal-Framework-By-Dwell-Time-and-Travel-Distance.git.

References

1. Agnew, J.A., Shelley, F.M., Pringle, D.G.: Agnew, J.A.: 1987: place and politics: the geographical mediation of state and society. Prog. Human Geogr. **27**(5), 605–614 (2003)
2. Barbosa, H., et al.: Human mobility: models and applications. Phys. Rep. **734**, 1–74 (2018)
3. Berthold, M.R., et al.: Knime-the konstanz information miner: version 2.0 and beyond. ACM SIGKDD Explor. Newsl. **11**(1), 26–31 (2009)
4. Betancourt, F., Riascos, A.P., Mateos, J.L.: Temporal visitation patterns of points of interest in cities on a planetary scale: a network science and machine learning approach. Sci. Rep. **13**(1), 4890 (2023)
5. Chang, T., Hu, Y., Taylor, D., Quigley, B.M.: The role of alcohol outlet visits derived from mobile phone location data in enhancing domestic violence prediction at the neighborhood level. Health Place **73**, 102736 (2022)
6. Cyr, M.E., Etchin, A.G., Guthrie, B.J., Benneyan, J.C.: Access to specialty healthcare in urban versus rural us populations: a systematic literature review. BMC Health Serv. Res. **19**(1), 1–17 (2019)
7. Di Martino, S., Mazzocca, N., Di Torrepadula, F.R., Starace, L.L.L.: Mobility data analytics with KNOT: The KNime mObility Toolkit. In: Mostafavi, M.A., Del Mondo, G. (eds.) Web and Wireless Geographical Information Systems. W2GIS 2023, LNCS, vol. 13912, pp 95–104. Springer, Cham (2023). https://doi.org/10.1007/978-3-031-34612-5_6
8. Du, Z., Zhang, X., Li, W., Zhang, F., Liu, R.: A multi-modal transportation data-driven approach to identify urban functional zones: An exploration based on hangzhou city, china. Trans. GIS **24**(1), 123–141 (2020)
9. Fillbrunn, A., Dietz, C., Pfeuffer, J., Rahn, R., Landrum, G.A., Berthold, M.R.: Knime for reproducible cross-domain analysis of life science data. J. Biotechnol. **261**, 149–156 (2017)

10. Giannopoulos, G., Alexis, K., Kostagiolas, N., Skoutas, D.: Classifying points of interest with minimum metadata. In: Proceedings of the 3rd ACM SIGSPATIAL International Workshop on Location-based Recommendations, Geosocial Networks and Geoadvertising, pp. 1–4 (2019)
11. Hu, Y., Quigley, B.M., Taylor, D.: Human mobility data and machine learning reveal geographic differences in alcohol sales and alcohol outlet visits across us states during covid-19. PLoS ONE 16(12), e0255757 (2021)
12. Jay, J., Heykoop, F., Hwang, L., de Jong, J., Kondo, M.: Effects of the covid-19 pandemic on park use in us cities. medRxiv pp. 2021–04 (2021)
13. Jenkins, P., Farag, A., Wang, S., Li, Z.: Unsupervised representation learning of spatial data via multimodal embedding. In: Proceedings of the 28th ACM International Conference on Information and Knowledge Management. p. 1993-2002. CIKM '19, Association for Computing Machinery, New York, NY, USA (2019). https://doi.org/10.1145/3357384.3358001, https://doi.org/10.1145/3357384.3358001
14. Kirby, J.B., Yabroff, K.R.: Rural-urban differences in access to primary care: beyond the usual source of care provider. Am. J. Prev. Med. 58(1), 89–96 (2020)
15. Lagos, N., Ait-Mokhtar, S., Calapodescu, I.: Point-of-interest semantic tag completion in a global crowdsourced search-and-discovery database. In: ECAI 2020, pp. 2993–3000. IOS Press (2020)
16. Lai, S., Farnham, A., Ruktanonchai, N.W., Tatem, A.J.: Measuring mobility, disease connectivity and individual risk: a review of using mobile phone data and mhealth for travel medicine. Journal of travel medicine 26(3), taz019 (2019)
17. Lefevre, S., Tuia, D., Wegner, J.D., Produit, T., Nassar, A.S.: Toward seamless multiview scene analysis from satellite to street level. Proc. IEEE 105(10), 1884–1899 (2017)
18. Liang, Y., Yin, J., Pan, B., Lin, M.S., Miller, L., Taff, B.D., Chi, G.: Assessing the validity of mobile device data for estimating visitor demographics and visitation patterns in yellowstone national park. J. Environ. Manage. 317, 115410 (2022)
19. Liu, B., Deng, Y., Li, M., Yang, J., Liu, T.: Classification schemes and identification methods for urban functional zone: A review of recent papers. Appl. Sci. 11(21), 9968 (2021)
20. Maláková, K.: A geodemographic view of the accessibility of selected outpatient services in czechia. Int. J. Public Health 67, 1604067 (2022)
21. McKenzie, G., Janowicz, K., Gao, S., Gong, L.: How where is when? on the regional variability and resolution of geosocial temporal signatures for points of interest. Comput. Environ. Urban Syst. 54, 336–346 (2015)
22. Milias, V., Psyllidis, A.: Assessing the influence of point-of-interest features on the classification of place categories. Comput. Environ. Urban Syst. 86, 101597 (2021)
23. Psyllidis, A., Gao, S., Hu, Y., Kim, E.K., McKenzie, G., Purves, R., Yuan, M., Andris, C.: Points of interest (poi): a commentary on the state of the art, challenges, and prospects for the future. Computational Urban Science 2(1), 20 (2022)
24. Seamon, D.: Body-subject, time-space routines, and place-ballets. The human experience of space and place 148, 65 (1980)
25. Srivastava, S., Vargas Munoz, J.E., Lobry, S., Tuia, D.: Fine-grained landuse characterization using ground-based pictures: a deep learning solution based on globally available data. Int. J. Geogr. Inf. Sci. 34(6), 1117–1136 (2020)
26. Sun, Y., Huang, J., Yuan, C., Fan, M., Wang, H., Liu, M., Qin, B.: Gedit: geographic-enhanced and dependency-guided tagging for joint poi and accessibility extraction at baidu maps. In: Proceedings of the 30th ACM international conference on information & knowledge management. pp. 4135–4144 (2021)

27. Talukdar, S., Singha, P., Mahato, S., Pal, S., Liou, Y.A., Rahman, A., et al.: Land-use land-cover classification by machine learning classifiers for satellite observations—a review. Remote Sensing **12**(7), 1135 (2020)

28. Wang, J., Kong, X., Xia, F., Sun, L.: Urban human mobility: Data-driven modeling and prediction. ACM SIGKDD Explorations Newsl **21**(1), 1–19 (2019)

29. Zarbakhsh, N., McArdle, G.: Points-of-interest from mapillary street-level imagery: A dataset for neighborhood analytics. In: 2023 IEEE 39th International Conference on Data Engineering Workshops (ICDEW). pp. 154–161. IEEE (2023)

30. Zarbakhsh, N., Misaghian, M.S., Mcardle, G.: Human mobility-based features to analyse the impact of covid-19 on power system operation of ireland. IEEE Open Access Journal of Power and Energy **9**, 213–225 (2022)

31. Zhang, F., Zu, J., Hu, M., Zhu, D., Kang, Y., Gao, S., Zhang, Y., Huang, Z.: Uncovering inconspicuous places using social media check-ins and street view images. Comput. Environ. Urban Syst. **81**, 101478 (2020)

32. Zhou, J., Gou, S., Hu, R., Zhang, D., Xu, J., Jiang, A., Li, Y., Xiong, H.: A collaborative learning framework to tag refinement for points of interest. In: Proceedings of the 25th ACM SIGKDD International Conference on Knowledge Discovery & Data Mining. pp. 1752–1761 (2019)

33. Zhu, Y., Deng, X., Newsam, S.: Fine-grained land use classification at the city scale using ground-level images. IEEE Trans. Multimedia **21**(7), 1825–1838 (2019)

34. Ziller, E., Milkowski, C.: A century later: Rural public health's enduring challenges and opportunities. Am. J. Public Health **110**(11), 1678–1686 (2020)

Exploring Spatio-temporal Dynamics: A Historical Analysis of Missing Persons Data in Mexico, Revealing Patterns and Trends

Roberto Zagal[1], Christophe Claramunt[2], Carlos Hernandez[3]([⊠]), and Felix Mata[3]

[1] Instituto Politécnico Nacional, ESCOM-IPN, 07320 Ciudad de Mexico, Mexico
[2] Naval Academy Research Institute, Lanvéoc, France
[3] Instituto Politécnico Nacional, UPIITA-IPN, 07340 Ciudad de México, Mexico
hernandez.nava@gmail.com

Abstract. This paper addresses the intricate phenomenon of missing persons, a major problem in Mexico, extending beyond the simple occurrences of disappearances. By developing a historical and spatial data analysis, this research comprehensively examines missing person data from open, official, and social media sources. We apply a data mining framework based on digital media and openly accessible government databases to characterize and visually represent crimes such as enforced disappearances along the temporal and spatial dimensions. The data analysis methodology takes a comprehensive approach, segmenting data by age, sex, nationality, geographic location, and period. This segmentation unveils patterns in space and time, thus contributing to a better understanding of the factors influencing missing person phenomena and valuable insights into the dynamics of missing person incidents that have impacted many states and regions in Mexico over the past decade.

Keywords: spatio-temporal analysis · missing persons · open data analysis

1 Introduction

The phenomenon of adult disappearances in Mexico has become a distressing and intricate phenomenon over the past few years. This intricate issue, which affects individuals in the full exercise of their rights and responsibilities, has generated widespread societal concern, emphasizing the imperative need for a comprehensive and multifaceted scientific approach. Mexico faces distinct challenges in preventing, investigating, and responding to cases of adult disappearance. The lack of an effective response mechanism and the prevailing impunity in many of these cases have fostered an atmosphere of pervasive insecurity and vulnerability among the population. Additionally, identifiable patterns and trends have surfaced, exposing distinct victim profiles, the circumstances surrounding their disappearance, and the locations where these incidents occur most frequently. Scientific inquiry into these aspects becomes crucial to unravel the complexities of this social issue.

M. Lotfian and L. L. L. Starace (Eds.): W2GIS 2024, LNCS 14673, pp. 41–52, 2024.
https://doi.org/10.1007/978-3-031-60796-7_3

In response to this critical need, our research contributes to a better scientific understanding of adult disappearance in Mexico by highlighting the patterns and underlying behaviours that appear in space and time and using data mining and visualization techniques. The approach is experimented with a diverse dataset comprising official records, online news articles, and social media content. The rest of the paper is structured as follows. The next section briefly introduces related work, Sect. 3 gives the background of our research, and a description of the data. Section 4 develops the methodology, while Sect. 5 reports on the results. Finally, Sect. 6 concludes the paper and outlines further work.

2 Related Work

Scientific exploration of the phenomenon of enforced disappearance, particularly within the context of Mexico, has garnered increased attention in recent years due to its significant impact on various states and regions. To address this complex issue, researchers have employed diverse methodologies, with a growing emphasis on social and spatio-temporal data analysis. Several studies have delved into the multifaceted nature of missing persons instances, especially within urban settings like the Valley of Mexico. Furthermore, the complexity of the crime phenomenon requires the involvement of various disciplines, leading to a spectrum of techniques, algorithms, and methods applicable to each aspect found in crime reports. This encompasses descriptive, classifying, predictive, and grouping approaches, each offering local solutions or innovative methods that offer alternative perspectives on the crime phenomenon. A brief overview of recent work and distinctions from the approach presented in this study is provided below.

In [1], the authors evaluate the association between geographic variations and sociodemographic determinants of crime incidence in Nigeria. They employed a mixed Poisson model to account for spatial dependency (clustering) effects and state-specific heterogeneous effects of offences. The findings indicate a positive association between the unemployment rate and rape, kidnapping, and armed robbery, while robbery shows a negative association. Notably, this approach focuses on Bayesian and Markov mechanisms, omitting the utilization of web data. A recent analysis based on fieldwork in diverse localities has been developed along the Greek borderlands [2]. The study contends that death or disappearance, resulting from various causes such as drowning, hypothermia, violence, and deprivation of medical care, has evolved into an intrinsic element of border enforcement in the global north. The paper introduces a pivotal concept, "migrant disappearability," to systematically understand and engage with this form of border violence. The work in [3] analyses the spatial and temporal distribution of sexual crimes in Haining City, focusing on their correlation with urban commercial service facilities. Analysing data from 311 sexual crimes and Point of Interest (POI) data from January 2014 to September 2021, the study identifies a spatial pattern influenced by factors such as the distribution of KTV, Internet cafes, and hotels. Areas with a mix of these facilities exhibit a notable increase in sexual crimes. The findings offer crucial decision-making insights when addressing the prevention of sexual crimes, and introducing effective countermeasures for rectification efforts in Haining. Another contribution examined the criminal offence data of 77 jurisdictions in central Tokyo in 2010–2019

[4]. The pre-weighted counts and post-weighted harm were compared to examine the correlations and time-series changes between them. Analysing pre- and post-weighted harm against counts revealed that, while harm varies more over time and space, high-harm areas exhibit lower clustering tendencies. The findings, including insights from regression analysis on socioeconomic factors, have implications for informing urban policymakers in contexts with low crime rates such as in Japan. The authors in [5] focus on predicting crime hotspots in regions with low population density and unevenly distributed crime, which presents a challenge due to the severe sparsity (class imbalance) in the outcome variable. To address this, machine learning models were developed, specifically tailored for imbalanced class labels. The proposed imbalance-aware hyperensemble increases the hit ratio considerably from 18.1% to 24.6% when aiming for the top 5% of hotspots and from 53.1% to 60.4% when aiming for the top 20% of hotspots. Exploring demographic and immigration data, a study challenged the common belief that immigration heightens crime [6]. Analysing data from Chile over a decade, the researchers investigated the relationship between immigration and crime using a dynamic Durbin Spatial Model. Contrary to the usual expectations, they conclude that there is no statistical evidence linking an increase in the number of immigrants to an escalation in the rate of any crime type.

In our previous work, crime patterns have been explored in relation to the safety of human mobility [7]. The combination of social network data and official crime data favours the identification of safe routes and improves public safety. In a follow-up effort, the determinants of crime activities were further studied by an amalgamation of complementary social and public datasets [8]. The study, centred on Mexico City, provides valuable insights as derived from a solid combination of open crime report data, social data, geographical and socioeconomic data. This article goes further by thoroughly examining the unique geographical and temporal dimensions of the crime patterns as they appear in the city of Mexico, through a combination of machine learning of social and public data, thus providing insight into the complexities of the phenomenon.

3 Research Background and Data Sources Description

Forced disappearances in Mexico constitute a complex and concerning phenomenon that has attracted the attention of researchers and data scientists. This phenomenon is characterized by the deprivation of freedom of an individual, involving the direct intervention of state agents or their acquiescence, and is aggravated by the refusal to acknowledge detention and disclose the fate or whereabouts of the affected person [9]. In Mexico, the National Registry of Persons Disappeared and Unlocated (RNPDNO) [10] is established by the General Law on Forced Disappearance of Persons, Individual Disappearance, and the National Search System for Persons (LGD). The administration and coordination of this tool fall under the purview of the National Commission for the Search of Persons (CNB). Starting in 2019, the CNB implemented a technological strategy to incorporate information in an interoperable manner between federal and state authorities. The public version of the RNPDNO presents statistical data, including the number of persons who disappeared, location and year of disappearance, sex, age, and associated crime.

Our research interest is to identify patterns and trends in these data to better understand the dynamics of forced disappearances. This involves descriptive and clustering techniques applied to each element present in crime reports. This approach allows the revelation of possible relationships with geographic and temporal factors. We use sources from three data categories: 1) open data, 2) official data (government), and 3) social media data. Open data is obtained through the government transparency portal and open data platform (http://datos.edomex.gob.mx/) and from the National Search Commission of Mexico, which contains various crime types from the last three decades, but we centre the study on the last decade to 2023. The data structure is denormalized, comprising fields such as crime, year, date, hour, municipality, suburb, street, and, in certain instances, latitude and longitude. The general structure contains attributes such as state name, gender, age, nationality, and general official reports from ONGs. The second data category is from: The National Institute of Statistics and Geography (INEGI) serves as the primary authority in the country responsible for gathering and disseminating information about Mexico's territory, resources, population, and economy. INEGI presents its databases in CSV format, accompanied by dictionaries, entity-relationship models, metadata, and catalogues. The third data category is retrieved from social media: Facebook pages (in Spanish) "ExtraviadosMx," "Comisión de Búsqueda de Personas CDMX," and "Personas Extraviadas o Desaparecidas."

4 Methodology

The methodology developed represents an adaptation of the widely recognized Knowledge Discovery in Databases (KDD). By implementing this approach, our objective is to discern meaningful patterns and extract valuable insights from news articles and social media content, with a particular focus on those related to forced disappearances. The aggregated data assumes a role in acquiring pertinent and precise information concerning disappearances in the Ciudad de Mexico (CDMX) region. As illustrated in Fig. 1, the framework data flow is composed of six stages that cover data gathering, exploration, identification of spatial and temporal trends and outliers, and the exploration of geographical and temporal patterns associated with adult disappearances. In the subsequent subsections, we elaborate on each of these substeps in detail.

4.1 Data Gathering, Pre-processing, and Cleansing

The first two stages were conducted with open and official data, extracting domains such as crime, date, municipality, street, between streets, neighbourhood, latitude, and longitude. Omitted domains with insufficient data quality for analysis (i.e., containing several nulls and numerous outliers). The stop words were removed and a cluster of all words within the text was generated to identify the top words in each news item. The star model, resembling a normalized database but geared towards statistical queries, was utilized. It includes a fact table and various catalog tables. Catalog generation and fact table creation were performed based on the basis of the obtained values. Data cleaning techniques, including data interpolation and random data insertion, were implemented. These imputation methods were chosen to estimate values and fill in missing data,

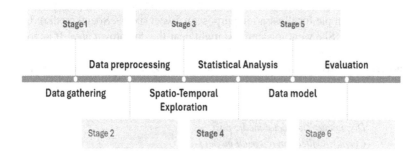

Fig. 1. Principles of the data analysis methodology

thereby increasing the number of records. Among the most relevant attributes found in all datasets were age, date, borough, and neighbourhood. For the official data, no modifications were necessary as they adhere to a specific format, facilitated by forms filled out in a structured manner. Regarding data from news articles and social media, an initial random selection of records was made to understand the composition of the information.

After analysis, essential data such as gender, age, borough, neighbourhood, state, and date were extracted using regular expressions. Given that in most records only the person's name is provided, determining the gender of the missing individual posed a challenge. Consequently, the gender guesser library was used, using a rule-based app-roach to estimate the gender associated with a name. It employs patterns and heuristics based on the frequency of names in different genders in specific regions or languages. The extraction of posts from social media is achieved using a web-scrapper tool: Apify (https://apify.com/) where all pertinent news and posts were successfully retrieved from the Facebook pages using API Facebook the name of pages are (in Spanish): "Extravi-adosMx," "Comisión de Búsqueda de Personas CDMX," and "Personas Extraviadas o Desaparecidas".

We applied the Term Frequency-Inverse Document Frequency algorithm (TF-IDF) [11]. It is a statistical measure that evaluates the importance of a word in a document relative to a collection of documents (i.e., posts, tweets, X messages). The goal is to identify words that are distinctive and relevant to a specific document by weighing them based on their frequency within that document compared to their frequency across the entire corpus. Term Frequency (TF) measures how often a term (i.e., word) appears in a document. Calculated as the ratio of the number of times the term occurs in the document to the total number of terms. The Inverse Document Frequency (IDF) gives how important a term is along the entire corpus. Calculated as the logarithm of the ratio of the total number of documents to the number of documents containing the term. The TF-IDF score gives the product of TF and IDF, indicating the importance of a term in a specific document relative to the entire corpus.

The following algorithm was used to apply, where the following post was adapted (with Mary as a sample for illustration purposes): Tweet (i.e., X Social media): Urgent: Help us find Mary. She went missing last night near the downtown area. If anyone has information, please contact the local authorities.

Algorithm: TF-IDF Calculation for the Term "Mary" in a Social Media Post

Input:

Term: The term for TF-IDF calculation (e.g., "Mary")

Document: The social media post

Corpus: Collection of social media posts

Output: tf_idf_score: TF-IDF score for "Mary" in the post

Procedure:

1. *Count_terms_in_document(document):*
2. *Split document into terms, return total count*
3. *Count_occurrences_of_term(term, document):*
4. *Count term occurrences in document*
5. *Count_documents(corpus):*
6. *Return total social media post count*
7. *Count_documents_containing_term(term, corpus):*
8. *Count posts in corpus containing term*
9. *Calculate_term_frequency(term, document):*
10. *Calculate term frequency in document*
11. *Calculate_inverse_document_frequency(term, corpus):*
12. *Calculate inverse document frequency*
13. *Calculate_tf_idf(term, document, corpus):*
14. *Calculate TF-IDF score for term in document*

4.2 Data Integration, Statistical Analysis, and Exploration

This third stage oversees implementing data integration mechanisms so that it seeks to adapt them in a single standardization scheme, modifying their attribute type and combining the different annual records of each source, obtaining a single unified record. After classifying previously processed data, the growth in incidence and prevalence of crimes is generated through the implementation of classification algorithms or association methods. The fourth stage classifies the data obtained from the previous module, under a geographic and temporal scheme, and provides a record of the areas where there are a greater number of crimes.

The objective is to understand its traceability during the different time intervals. The construction of data cubes commenced using information from the star model as a source in spatio-temporal domain queries for crimes [12]. Data exploration and transformation involved several steps, such as obtaining geographic coordinates from a postal address and subsequently converting the denormalized table to a star model. The smooth model was implemented to classify news items, identifying those with postal addresses, and Geopy for reverse geocoding. The algorithm for data insertion by reverse geocoding is as illustrated below. The denormalized table was manually converted to the star model, involving the creation of respective catalogs and the fact table.

Data Insertion Algorithm

 1. Begin
 2. Extract data from web news and social media.
 3. Process data
 4. Extract geographic information
 5. Process with reverse geocoding
 6. Generate data with coordinates
 7. If the location is within State_name
 8. Store the record in a database table (news_state_coordinates).
 9. End
 10. Else
 11. Discard the record and return to Step 5
 12. End else
 13. End

5   Experimental Results

Let us report on the main insights and statistics obtained. Regarding the complex phenomenon of missing persons, a multifaceted narrative unfolds. This issue goes beyond the mere occurrence of disappearances and then encompasses a spectrum of outcomes that include cases of individuals being located, some found alive, and others unfortunately discovered deceased. In instances where lives are lost, an additional layer of complexity arises; some remain unidentified. Notably, gender identification becomes a challenging task in certain cases, amplifying the intricacies of resolving these incidents. Our data analysis endeavours provide a comprehensive understanding by segmenting data based on various dimensions: age, gender, geographic location, time periods, and even nationality. This segmentation is undertaken with the overarching goal of unveiling patterns that span both geographical spaces and temporal dimensions, shedding light on the intricate web of factors contributing to the phenomenon of missing persons.

 We started with an interesting finding related to age groups. When analysing the data by age ranges, we observe that for women, the most critical age range is between 15 and 19 years, starting at 10 years and decreasing from the age of 30. On the contrary, a different pattern is observed for men. Their critical stage begins at 15 years and starts declining until the age of 40. This means that men experience a more extended period during which they are vulnerable to this crime (Fig. 2). The overall statistics are shown in Fig. 3. The total number of missing persons is highest in the State of Mexico (Estado de Mexico in spanish), with a ratio of 25,182 for men and 28,004 for women.

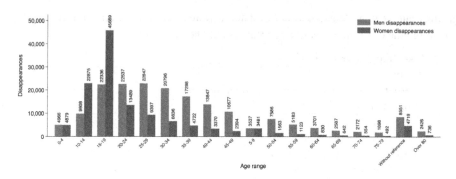

Fig. 2. Historical trend of disappearances in Mexico by age range and gender.

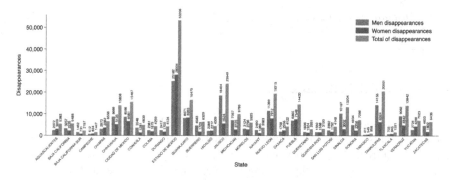

Fig. 3. Missing persons by state and gender.

As illustrated in Fig. 3, the State of Mexico is illustrated as the state with the highest number of cases of disappeared people. It is worth mentioning that the population of the state of Mexico is 17,501,220 people in the year 2023. In the state of Mexico, a noteworthy phenomenon emerges as it registers the highest number of missing persons cases. However, a closer examination reveals a particularly distressing trend: women in most states in Mexico bear the brunt of this crime. It is essential to highlight that an equal number of cases involving women also extends to instances where the gender of the individual could not be identified upon their location. This aspect sheds light on the complexity of the issue, emphasizing the need for a comprehensive understanding of the challenges surrounding disappearances, especially concerning women, and the difficulties in gender identification in certain cases, even upon resolution. Figure 4 shows the maps of missing persons in Mexico by state. States with the darkest colour signifies a higher number of records of missing and non-located persons sourced from comprehensive data across states.

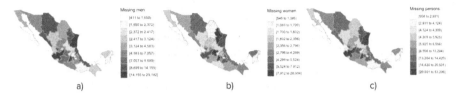

Fig. 4. a) missing for men, b) missing for women, and c) the total of missing persons by state.

As depicted in Fig. 4 a) for women the darkest state are State of Mexico, Guanajuato and Nuevo León; Fig. 4 b) for men the darkest state are State of Mexico, Jalisco and Tamaulipas and Fig. 4 c) for total of missing people, are the same states that for men. Situated in the northeast, west, and central parts of the country, respectively, these states offer a rich landscape for scientific analysis. Identifying key similarities among these states, their topographic diversity is evident, encompassing mountainous terrains, plains, and coastlines, especially notable in Tamaulipas. Beyond geographical features, population density diverges, with Tamaulipas exhibiting a lower density compared to Jalisco and the State of Mexico. The economic landscapes of these regions are intricately related to demographic and geographical factors. Jalisco's renown lies in its agro-industrial and technological sectors, Tamaulipas is linked to the petroleum and maquiladora industries, while the State of Mexico stands out as a significant industrial and commercial centre.

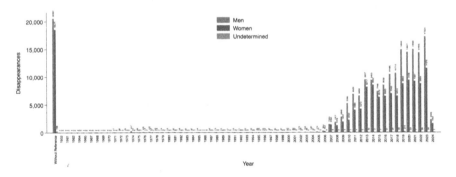

Fig. 5. Trend of disappearances in Mexico by gender.

Our analysis extends to the temporal trends of disappearance phenomena spanning from 1952 to 2024 in Mexico, as illustrated in Fig. 5. This temporal analysis enables a comprehensive understanding of how these phenomena have evolved over the years, contributing valuable insights into the dynamics of missing persons incidents. Figure 5 also shows the historical behaviour of this crime on an annual basis and a clear increase that began in the year 2010. There were continuous increases with an accelerated increase from 2017 to 2018 and a drastic increase from 2018 to 2019. Despite fluctuations, the trend persisted and in 2022, there was another drastic upswing leading into 2023. Generally, the graph illustrates year-over-year growth, with some cases showing a consistent increase. As mentioned earlier, in some instances, the rise is steady, while in others, it is

50 R. Zagal et al.

quite drastic. The initial increase was around 7,000 cases (for 2017 to 2018 year), and the latest represents an upsurge of almost 15,000 cases (for 2022 to 2023 year).

One can observe in Fig. 6 that this crime varies by nationality, with Mexicans being the primary victims for obvious reasons. However, approximately 12,000 cases could not identify nationality, securing the second position on the list. The third position is held by individuals from the United States, followed by Honduran, Guatemalan, Colombian, and Salvadoran nationals. To a much lesser extent, the cases involve individuals from Venezuela, Nicaragua, Cuba, and Ecuador. Figure 7 displays the disappearance reports indicated by private individuals and authorities. Private reports are coloured red, while reports from authorities are coloured blue.

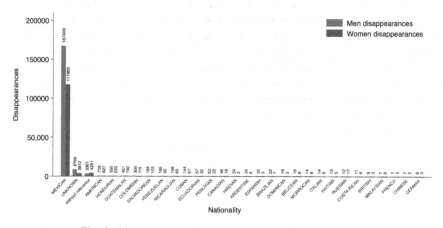

Fig. 6. Disappearances in Mexico by nationality and gender.

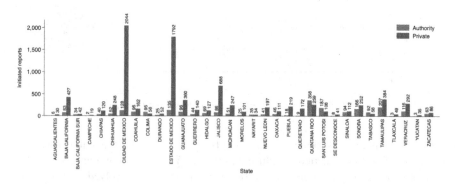

Fig. 7. Disappearance reports initiated from private and authorities. (Color figure online)

The pattern indicates that individuals contribute a larger number of reports, while authorities submit a minor number of reports. However, it should be noted that the authorities play a crucial role in enhancing the completeness of the data, contributing to a more comprehensive representation of the cases.

6 Conclusions

This paper studies the intricate phenomenon of missing persons, which extends beyond the simple occurrences of disappearances. By developing a historical data analysis framework in both space and time, we comprehensively examined missing person data from open, official, and social media sources. The application of a data mining framework, drawing from digital media and accessible government databases, enabled us to characterize and visually represent crimes such as enforced disappearances across various temporal and spatial dimensions. The overarching goal of our study is to contribute to proactive decision-making and improve a better understanding of crime phenomena, employing an open data analysis approach with spatial-temporal criteria. By segmenting data across key dimensions such as age, gender, geography, time spans, and nationality, we aimed to unveil patterns in both spatial and temporal dimensions, enriching our understanding of the factors influencing the missing person's phenomenon.

This research provides a perspective on the scientific exploration of crime data, particularly addressing the critical issue of missing and unlocated people in Mexico. The distinctive contribution lies in shedding light on a matter of significant concern that has profoundly affected various states and regions over the past decade. In conclusion, our study not only provides a comprehensive analysis of missing persons incidents but also underscores the importance of collaborative efforts between individuals and authorities. Although individuals contribute significantly to the reporting of cases, authorities play a crucial role in improving data completeness, ensuring a more accurate and thorough representation of the complex dynamics surrounding disappearances in Mexico.

The approach used enables a comprehensive understanding of crimes. The integration of open data with news information provides a holistic overview of the crime phenomenon, offering an initial glimpse into its behaviour within a ten-year period.

Future work involves identifying criminal patterns at the level of municipalities and streets, incorporating machine-learning approaches for broader-scale analyses, and enhancing granularity in both time and space. Mechanisms to debug and identify potentially fake news are also on the agenda to strengthen the credibility of this ongoing research. Moreover, the categorization of similar datasets has revealed discernible patterns and trends in cases of adult disappearance. The strategic use of utility terms has streamlined data filtering and analysis, while the systematic classification of variables into relational categories has provided a cohesive structure for comprehensive analysis and visualization. This identification of prevalent trends contributes to a nuanced understanding of the multifaceted factors surrounding this social phenomenon. Lastly, the implementation of a static heat map, incorporating official data, serves as a visually compelling tool, offering a clear depiction of the geographic distribution of adult disappearances in Mexico.

Acknowledgements. Authors of this paper want to thank to: IPN, COFAA, SIP Projects 20241571 and 20240707-2284; CONAHCYT PROJECTS: 7051 and CF-2023-G-1170, UPIITA-IPN, and ESCOM-IPN for their support.

References

1. Adeyemi, R.A., Mayaki, J., Zewotir, T.T., Ramroop, S.: Demography and crime: a spatial analysis of geographical patterns and risk factors of crimes in Nigeria. Spatial Stat. **41**, 100485 (2021)
2. Laakkonen, V.: Deaths, disappearances, borders: migrant disappearability as a technology of deterrence. Polit. Geogr. **99**, 102767 (2022)
3. Jiang, X., Mao, Z., Zheng, Z., Lin, Z., Wang, Y., Sheng, S.: Spatio-temporal characteristics of sexual crime and influencing factors of commercial service facilities: a case study of Haining City, China. Int. J. Law Crime Justice **76**, 100647 (2024)
4. Ohyama, T., Hanyu, K., Tani, M., Nakae, M.: Investigating crime harm index in the low and downward crime contexts: a spatio-temporal analysis of the Japanese Crime Harm Index. Cities **130**, 103922 (2022)
5. Kadar, C., Maculan, R., Feuerriegel, S.: Public decision support for low population density areas: an imbalance-aware hyperensemble for spatio-temporal crime prediction. Decis. Support Syst. **119**, 107–117 (2019)
6. Leiva, M., Vasquez-Lavín, F., Oliva, R.D.P.: Do immigrants increase crime? Spatial analysis in a middle-income country. World Dev. **126**, 104728 (2020)
7. Mata, F., Claramunt, C.: A mobile trusted path system based on social network data. In: Proceedings of the 23rd SIGSPATIAL International Conference on Advances in Geographic Information Systems, pp. 1–4 (2015)
8. Carrillo-Brenes, F., Vilches-Blázquez, L.M., Mata, F.: A proposal for semantic integration of crime data in Mexico City. In: Mata-Rivera, M.F., Zagal-Flores, R., Arellano Verdejo, J., Lazcano Hernandez, H.E. (eds.) GIS LATAM 2020. CCIS, vol. 1276, pp. 30–48. Springer, Cham (2020). https://doi.org/10.1007/978-3-030-59872-3_3
9. Instituto Nacional de Estadística y Geografía. Encuesta Nacional de Victimización y Percepción sobre Seguridad Pública 2021 (2023). https://www.inegi.org.mx/rnm/index.php/catalog/698/variable/F21/V1833?name=AP6_14. Accessed 10 Mar 2024
10. Inter-American Court of Human Rights (IACtHR). Case of Radilla Pacheco: Preliminary Objections, Merits, Reparations, and Costs Judgment of November 23, 2009. Series C No. 209. https://www.corteidh.or.cr/docs/casos/articulos/seriec_209_esp.pdf. Accessed 10 Mar 2024
11. Jalilifard, A., Caridá, V.F., Mansano, A.F., Cristo, R.S., da Fonseca, F.P.C.: Semantic sensitive TF-IDF to determine word relevance in documents. In: Thampi, S.M., Gelenbe, E., Atiquzzaman, M., Chaudhary, V., Li, K.-C. (eds.) Advances in Computing and Network Communications. LNEE, vol. 736, pp. 327–337. Springer, Singapore (2021). https://doi.org/10.1007/978-981-33-6987-0_27
12. Kasprzyk, J.-P., Devillet, G.: A data cube metamodel for geographic analysis involving heterogeneous dimensions. ISPRS Int. J. Geo-Information **10**, 87 (2021)

Assessing and Managing Soil Quality with Geodata: The IQS Project

Maryam Lotfian[1]([✉])[iD], Jens Ingensand[1][iD], Karine Gondret[2],
Fabienne Favre-Boivin[3], Géraldine Bullinger[3], Guillaume Raymondon[4],
and Pascal Boivin[2]

[1] Institute INSIT, School of Business and Engineering Vaud, University of Applied Sciences and Arts Western Switzerland, 1401 Yverdon-les-Bains, Delémont, Switzerland
{maryam.lotfian,jens.ingensand}@heig-vd.ch
[2] Institut inTNE, University of Applied Sciences Western Switzerland (HEPIA), Route de Presinge 150, 1254 Genève, Jussy, Switzerland
{karine.gondret,pascal.boivin}@hesge.ch
[3] Institut iTEC, University of Applied Sciences Western Switzerland (heia-fr), Boulevard de Pérolles 80, 1700 Fribourg, Switzerland
{fabienne.favre,geraldine.bullinger}@hefr.ch
[4] Région Morges, Rue Dr. Yersin 1, 1110 Morges, Switzerland
guillaume.raymondon@regionmorges.ch

Abstract. Despite its soil protection regulation, ongoing land sealing and soil loss have continued over the past three decades and Switzerland lacks a comprehensive soil map. Soil quality is affected by land use which is challenging to map because it may change on the short-time, and also soil functions are controlled by soil properties that are not necessarily taken into account in soil mapping, such as organic matter content. Moreover, stakeholders seldom integrate soil information in their projects, since the data is scarce and the soil awareness is poor. To address these challenges, we developed a user-oriented framework assessing the soil functions based on expert predictions from land use, which are corrected with available soil data. The framework was applied to estimate soil quality in the Morges region. It takes into account all available digital information such as land-use layers, aerial imaging, geological maps etc. to split the area into polygons of predicted soil quality associated with an estimated accuracy, and integrates in a second step all available information on the soils, such as soil analysis, soil depth, polluted sites etc. Two complementary tools based on open-source software allow refining the estimated scores of the polygons and simulating the impact of development projects on soil quality. A semi-automated process was implemented to model input parameters and generate maps. Workshops involving experts, decision-makers, and soil specialists from the region allowed to improve and validate the soil mapping and the interface. The framework, named IQSM, allows to generate and update maps inexpensively, this can be replicated in any Swiss location. The open-source methods and the user-oriented interface raised a strong interest among stakeholders.

© The Author(s), under exclusive license to Springer Nature Switzerland AG 2024
M. Lotfian and L. L. Starace (Eds.): W2GIS 2024, LNCS 14673, pp. 53–63, 2024.
https://doi.org/10.1007/978-3-031-60796-7_4

Keywords: Soil quality · Soil functions · Soil mapping · Geo-spatial data · Urban planning

1   Introduction

Soil is a non-renewable natural resource that fulfills a number of functions, such as biomass production, habitat for biodiversity and flood regulation [1]. Soil undergoes very long processes of formation [2]. In Switzerland, large areas have been permanently sealed over the last 30 years. Despite the tightening of the Swiss Spatial Planning Act in 2014, high-quality soil continues to be destroyed. Between 1985 and 2018, residential and infrastructure land in Switzerland increased by 776 km2, mainly at the expense of cultivated land [3]. According to the Federal Office for the Environment (FOEN), there is no longer any intact soil in Switzerland, and its use is unsustainable [3].

Soil quality assessment is crucial for evaluating the health and functionality of soil in any given region [4]. Soil quality encompasses the capacity of soil to sustain biodiversity, enhance water and air quality, and support human health and habitation [5]. Assessing soil quality involves measuring various soil parameters, including highly dynamic ones such as pH, organic matter content, surface permeability, available water capacity, and porosity. These measurements are then used to evaluate soil quality in each of its essential functions. To effectively combat soil degradation, soil quality must be considered in land use planning. This requires defining soil quality indices, mapping these indices, and monitoring their evolution over time. However, Switzerland lacks a comprehensive soil map. Moreover, soil mapping is mostly based o static soil properties, thus failing to capture soil quality and its changes. As soil quality is primarily influenced by land use practices, there is an urgent need to provide decision-makers with tools that enable them to visualize and manage land use with a focus on preserving and improving soil quality [6].

The objective of the IQS Morges project is to use existing spatial data layers such as land cover, buildings, and orthoimages to predict soil properties and related functions. The predictions will be used to calculate a soil function index for each targeted soil function and generate corresponding maps. Additionally, we developed interactive tools that enable users to manually update the predicted soil quality in specific areas. The soil functions are recalculated in the polygons where additional information was provided, ensuring quick map updates. Another key goal is to simulate the future state of soil based on proposed land use planning projects. This will allow urban planners to evaluate the potential impact of these projects on soil quality and make informed decisions. While the tools developed are currently accessible to experts, the project envisions expanding public participation by allowing individuals to submit their observations of soil conditions and contribute to the validation of the computed soil quality maps.

2 Study Area

The Morges region, located in the canton of Vaud, Switzerland (Fig. 1), is facing the issue of soil sealing resulting from the densification of urban areas. In response, the region has opted to implement a straightforward and effective tool to incorporate soil quality considerations into development projects, ensuring sustainable soil management practices. To develop a prototype for this tool, the Morges region has embarked on a collaborative project involving three universities: HEIA-FR (Freiburg) and HEIPA (Geneva) for soil expertise and HEIG-VD (Yverdon-les-Bains) for geospatial analysis.

Considering that the implementation of a soil quality index necessitates a comprehensive soil quality map, and that existing soil data is inadequate, project partners propose constructing a model leveraging all available geospatial and remote sensing data and technologies.

The project area encompasses the following municipalities: Denges, Echandens, Echichens, Lonay, Lully, Lussy-sur-Morges, Morges, Préverenges, St-Prex, and Tolochenaz. It extends across the entire territory, including public domains, built-up areas, agricultural and forestry lands, and natural environments.

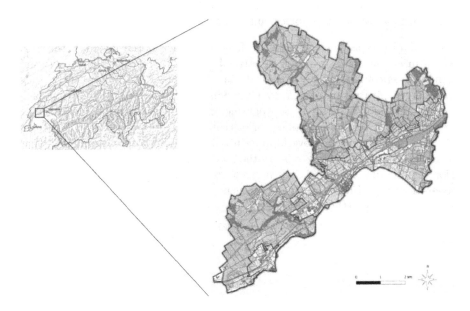

Fig. 1. Study area of IQS Morges project

3 Input Data and Pre-processing

As the assessment of soil quality involves a complex procedure, particularly challenging for non-experts, the objective of IQS Morges is to establish a grading system that is comprehensible to non-pedologists and, most importantly, urban planners. To determine the scores for soil parameters, we utilized the attributes of geospatial layers, such as identifying permeable and impermeable surfaces, buildings with or without green roofs, railways, and so on. The geospatial layers used in this study are as follows (all in Swiss reference system CH1903+LV95):

- **Official surveying layer**: Includes information like above-ground buildings, underground buildings, hard surfaces, water bodies, and so on (vector format).
- **Land use**: A vector layer representing the various land uses in the study area.
- **Agricultural surfaces**: A vector layer including agricultural land and its subtypes (e.g., arable land, pasture, etc.).
- **Soil types**: A vector layer classifying the various soil types present in the study area.
- **Green spaces**: A vector layer identifying areas designated as green spaces (e.g., parks, gardens).
- **Ortho images (RGB + NIR)**: A raster layer of high-resolution aerial images (10 cm pixel size) with bands representing visible (RGB) and near-infrared (NIR).
- **Digital Elevation Model (DEM)**: A raster layer representing the terrain height information, used for calculating slope.

The data pre-processing workflow, from input geospatial layers to the final layer utilized for soil scoring, is illustrated in Fig. 2. Initially, the layers were cropped to encompass solely the study area's boundaries. Subsequently, they were merged into a single layer by preserving only those attributes from each layer that are employed in the soil parameters scoring procedure. To merge the layers, a priority logic was applied, prioritizing the more precise layer's features when merging layers with overlapping attributes. This approach ensures that the merged layer accurately reflects the spatial distribution of soil parameters. Prior to assigning scores to each polygon, we conducted three additional data preparation steps. First, we calculated the normalized difference vegetation index (NDVI) using the orthoimages. NDVI was used to differentiate between green

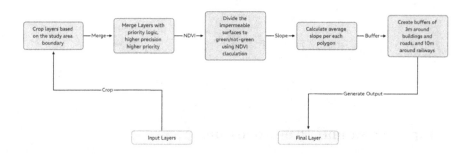

Fig. 2. A summary of data pre-processing steps

(0.2 < NDVI <= 1) and non-green (-1 <= NDVI <=0.2) areas within impermeable surfaces. This information is crucial for accurately assessing soil quality
in these areas (Fig. 3).

Second, we calculated the average slope per polygon using the DEM. The
slope was classified into six categories: less than 5%, between 5 and 10%, between
10 and 15%, between 15 and 18%, between 18 and 30%, and greater than 30%.
This information is used to adjust soil quality scores based on the slope gradient.

In the final step of data preparation, we generated buffer layers around buildings, roads, and railways. The buffer widths were 3 m for buildings and roads,
and 10 m for railways. These buffers were created to account for the negative
impact of these structures on soil quality and to reduce the soil quality score
and reliability score in their vicinity.

Once the data preparation was complete, we were ready to assign scores to
each polygon based on a combination of attributes from the merged layer and
the additional data generated during data preparation.

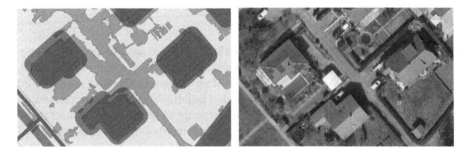

Fig. 3. Example of the calculation of NDVI for extracting green spaces in the impermeable surfaces (light orange green, and dark orange not green) (Color figure online)

4 Methodology

In this project, our methodology comprised three main steps: the generation of
base maps detailing the quality of soil functions, real-time adjustment of these
base maps through additional information, and the simulation of future soil
conditions based on an urban planning project.

4.1 Base Map Generation

To establish a comprehensive foundation, the team of pedologists implemented
a hierarchical framework. This framework assigned distinct levels (ranging from
level 1, the most general, to level 3, the most detailed) to various layer attributes.
A scoring system, spanning from 1 to 6, was employed to evaluate each soil
parameter, with 1 denoting very poor quality (e.g., impermeable surfaces) and

6 representing the highest quality. These scores were paired with a reliability index, also on a scale of 1 to 6, reflecting the confidence in the assigned score (1 being less reliable, and 6 highly reliable). All this information was stored in a Postgres/PostGIS database.

To generate the base maps, a Python script was developed. This script initially assigned levels 1–3 to each polygon based on their attributes using the heirarchical framework. Subsequently, it assigned soil scores for each parameter using the information provided by pedologists. Following this, the script calculated soil functions and generated maps depicting the quality score and reliability of the score. The calculation of each function was based on specific formulas (See Table 1). These formulas are derived from the Soil Management Assessment Framework (SMAF) methodology [7]. Pedologists contributing to the project determined the coefficients through an iterative process, resulting in the final formulas for each soil function as showcased in Table 1. In total, two maps were produced for each function: one indicating the quality score and the other illustrating the reliability of the score (Fig. 4).

4.2   Adjustment Tool

The aim of the adjustment tool is to refine the IQS base map through a three-step process for progressively refining the soil quality map. At the end of each stage, the project manager assesses the relevance of moving on to the next stage, based on the results obtained and the desired goal. The adjustment tool is implemented using QGIS for the user interface, and Python script to manipulate the user input and generate the new map. The three steps implemented in the adjustment tool are as follows:

Step 1: Aims to correct the segmentation errors or any missing information on the IQS base map (e.g. unidentified or modified roads and buildings) by observing the current aerial photos or by a quick field visit.

Step 2: Aims to identify, through additional documentation research such as historical maps, or municipality archives, objects that are difficult to be observed through aerial images or field visit (such as an old building which does not exist anymore, or backfilled areas.)

Step 3: Aims to improve the reliability of the map by adding pedological information collected in the field and, if necessary, measured in the laboratory. This is the most time- and resource-intensive stage.

Irrespective of the step in progress, users are required to first digitize the polygon where information needs updating. Subsequently, based on the type of information to be added, they utilize the relevant step. For Step 1, users specify the main three levels through drop-down menus (e.g., built area » above ground building » with green roof). The selected categories are then sent to the database, linked to the Python script for calculating soil functions, and the score and reliability are updated accordingly (Fig. 5).

Table 1. Equations defined by the pedologists teams to calculate each soil function based on soil properties

Functions	Soil Properties	Equation
Habitat for Living Organisms	Permeability (perm)	$0.2 \cdot$ 'perm_score'$+0.1 \cdot$'dep_score'$+$ $0.4 \cdot$ 'poro_score'$+0.3 \cdot$ 'om/c_score'
	Depth (dep)	
	Porosity (poro)	
	Organic matter-clay (OM/C)	
Biomass Production	Permeability (perm)	$0.2 \cdot$ 'perm_score'$+0.2 \cdot$ 'dep_score'$+0.1 \cdot$ 'poro_score'$+$ $0.2 \cdot$ 'om/c_score'$+0.3 \cdot$ 'pH_score'
	Depth (dep)	
	Porosity (poro)	
	Organic matter-clay (OM/C)	
	pH	
Flood Regulation	Permeability (perm)	$0.6 \cdot$ 'perm_score'$+0.2 \cdot$ 'dep_score'$+0.2 \cdot$ 'poro_score'
	Depth (dep)	
	Porosity (poro)	

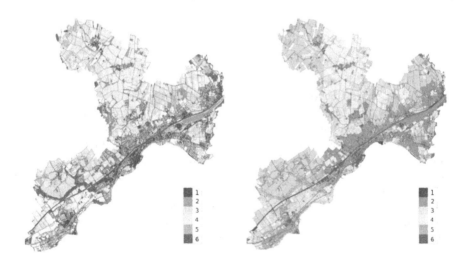

Fig. 4. Example of base maps (score on the left, and reliability on the right) for the flood regulation function

Similarly, for information in Step 2, drop-down menus are used to select the old state of the soil, allowing modification of reliability and score based on historical information. For example, if an old building has been replaced by a green space, this change is factored into the soil quality score for that zone.

Fig. 5. A screenshot of adjustment tool

For pedological data in Step 3, text boxes enable users to directly input measured soil parameters. In this case, hierarchical levels are not used, and soil functions are calculated directly from the field measures.

4.3   Simulation Tool

The primary objective of this tool is to provide project managers with insights into the impact of development projects on soil quality. It serves as a means to identify strategies that optimize soil functions within the development area. Specifically designed to assess and compare various urban development project scenarios, the tool evaluates their influence on critical soil functions, including "water infiltration/storage," "habitat for life," and "biomass production." Functioning as a decision-making aid, it provides project-specific recommendations to enhance soil quality.

The simulation tool, like the adjustment tool, is designed with a user-friendly interface using QGIS. It is linked to a PostGIS database, which is updated on a regular basis as new projects are added. A Python script also handles these database updates, calculating the scores and reliability of soil functions for each individual development project.

When the simulation is finished, a map representing soil functions is generated. This map illustrates where soil quality has improved or decreased as a result of the construction project. Figure 6 summarizes the complete procedure, from generating base maps to calculating footprints after simulation per soil function. This detailed image highlights the core concept of the approach, demonstrating the tool's ability to guide decision-making and provide significant insights for maximizing soil quality in the context of different development projects.

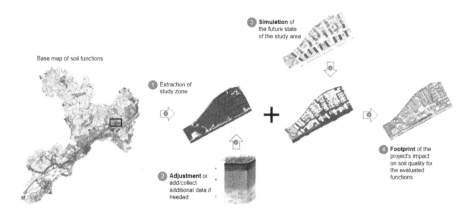

Fig. 6. An overview of IQS project core steps

5   Conclusion and Future Perspectives

Soil degradation is a crucial environmental concern, needing a thorough assessment of soil quality in order to limit the impact of human activities. Given different soil function, which are critical not only for human well-being but also for the broader environment and biodiversity, assessing soil quality involves evaluating its varied functions. Considering the resource-intensive process of measuring properties of soil, the IQS Morges project proposes a simple and easily understandable grading system to assign soil quality scores using information from existing geospatial layers. As a result, it generates maps showing representing scores for soil functions quality as well as maps indicating the reliability of these scores.

Through the developed adjustment and simulation tools, users can interact with the generated soil quality maps to either enhance them, as facilitated by the adjustment tool, or to simulate potential future states of soil function maps, as offered by the simulation tool. This project assists urban planners, policymakers, and municipal authorities in evaluating diverse scenarios for development projects. It enables them to visualize the impact of each development project on soil quality and choose options that minimize adverse effects.

The project has undergone thorough discussions with stakeholders across six interactive workshops, and has received positive feedback and interest. Notably, there is a growing interest from other regions seeking to replicate the analysis for their respective areas. The stakeholders greatly appreciated the implementation of a grading system for soil quality, as it facilitated easy comparison of maps across diverse development projects. As previously highlighted in the abstract, this analysis can be extended to additional regions, provided that the necessary spatial layers are available for those areas. However, a centralized database encompassing all regions has not yet been established. Creating such a database remains a task to be accomplished, aiming to simplify the replication of this analysis for other regions and countries. This promising approach can be extended to other domains, effectively simplifying complex concepts, such as in environmental monitoring projects, for broader applicability. Despite its success, the project acknowledges areas for improvement:

1) Web GIS application development: While the tools are powerful and user-friendly in QGIS, their utilization is limited by the requirement for QGIS installation and familiarity with its functions. An enhancement strategy involves developing the tools as a web GIS application, simplifying accessibility by enabling users to contribute from any device with internet access. This approach also simplifies field data collection.
2) Public contribution to soil observations: Another perspective involves expanding data sources beyond experts by allowing public contributions to soil quality observations. Volunteered Geographic Information (VGI) and Citizen Science projects, proven effective in ecological and environmental fields, and they encourage the public to contribute valuable data for scientific analysis [8,9].
3) Consideration of additional factors: The current simulation project evaluates future development project states without incorporating factors such as climate change scenarios. Including such considerations would provide additional information for generating more comprehensive future soil function maps.
4) Improved compatibility with existing databases (for example, with NABO-DAT database [10] which handles soil analysis in Switzerland)
5) Improved automating of the process to generate updated maps.

By addressing these future perspectives, the project aims to improve the accessibility, inclusivity, and overall effectiveness of soil quality assessment tools, resulting in more informed decision-making in the fields of urban development and environmental sustainability.

References

1. Evans, D., et al.: Sustainable futures over the next decade are rooted in soil science. Eur. J. Soil Sci. **73**, e13145 (2022). https://bsssjournals.onlinelibrary.wiley.com/doi/abs/10.1111/ejss.13145
2. Van Breemen, N., Buurman, P.: Soil formation. (Springer Science and Business Media) (2002)
3. Federal Office for the Environment (FOEN), F. Soil: In brief - bafu.admin.ch. https://www.bafu.admin.ch/bafu/en/home/topics/soil/in-brief.html. Accessed 11 Jan 2024
4. Mamehpour, N., Rezapour, S., Ghaemian, N.: Quantitative assessment of soil quality indices for urban croplands in a calcareous semi-arid ecosystem. Geoderma **382**, 114781 (2021). https://www.sciencedirect.com/science/article/pii/S0016706120325362
5. Nabiollahi, K., Golmohamadi, F., Taghizadeh-Mehrjardi, R., Kerry, R., Davari, M.: Assessing the effects of slope gradient and land use change on soil quality degradation through digital mapping of soil quality indices and soil loss rate. Geoderma **318**, 16–28 (2018). https://www.sciencedirect.com/science/article/pii/S0016706117314003

6. Montanarella, L., et al.: World's soils are under threat. Soil. **2**, 79–82 (2016). https://soil.copernicus.org/articles/2/79/2016/
7. Andrews, S., Karlen, D., Cambardella, C.: The soil management assessment framework. Soil Sci. Soc. Am. J. **68**, 1945–1962 (2004). https://acsess.onlinelibrary.wiley.com/doi/abs/10.2136/sssaj2004.1945
8. Moradi, M., Roche, S., Mostafavi, M.: Evaluating OSM building footprint data quality in Quebec province, Canada from 2018 to 2023: a comparative study. Geomatics **3**, 541–562 (2023). https://www.mdpi.com/2673-7418/3/4/29
9. Lotfian, M., Ingensand, J., Brovelli, M.: An approach for real-time validation of the location of biodiversity observations contributed in a citizen science project. In: The International Archives of the Photogrammetry, Remote Sensing and Spatial Information Sciences. XLVIII-4/W1-2022, pp. 271–278 (2022). https://isprs-archives.copernicus.org/articles/XLVIII-4-W1-2022/271/2022/
10. Agroscope National Soil Information System NABODAT - agroscope.admin.ch. https://www.agroscope.admin.ch/agroscope/en/home/topics/environment-resources/soil-bodies-water-nutrients/nabo/nationale-bodeninformation/nabodat.html. Accessed 21 Mar 2024

Open Data and Reproducible Research

Publication of Satellite Earth Observations in the Linked Open Data Cloud: Experiment Through the TRACES Project

Daniela F. Milon-Flores[1]([✉]), Camille Bernard[1], Jérôme Gensel[1],
Gregory Giuliani[2], Bruno Chatenoux[3], and Hy Dao[4]

[1] Univ. Grenoble Alpes, CNRS, Grenoble INP, LIG, Grenoble, France
`{daniela.milon-flores,camille.bernard,`
`jerome.gensel}@univ-grenoble-alpes.fr`
[2] Institute for Environmental Sciences, University of Geneva, Geneva, Switzerland
`gregory.giuliani@unige.ch`
[3] GRID-Geneva, United Nations Environment Program, Geneva, Switzerland
`bruno.chatenoux@unige.ch`
[4] Department of Geography and Environment, University of Geneva, Geneva, Switzerland
`hy.dao@unige.ch`

Abstract. Environmental pressures, such as overexploitation of natural resources and pollution, are urgent concerns affecting the Earth's global system. Both experts and non-expert stakeholders need access to meaningful Open Data to analyze the environmental impact of global warming in an area of interest, and thus implement effective environmental policies. A large and free collection of Earth observation (EO) data from satellites is currently available. However, EOs are sensor data whose interpretation is reserved for specialists due to the lack of semantic contextualization (e.g., definition of satellite-derived data, metadata, etc.). Moreover, although several resources are already accessible on the Web, most EO data remain isolated, whereas linking them together would provide a comprehensive understanding of environmental changes over time. In this paper, we present the Linked Earth Observation Data Series (LEODS) framework that leverages Semantic Web (SW) technologies for the integration and publication of EO data in the Linked Open Data (LOD) Cloud. LEODS relies on a spatio-temporal modeling approach which complies with SW standards and ensures future semantic enrichment of EO data. Precisely, LEODS is the first step towards the main objective of the French-Swiss collaborative project called TRACES, that is, to build a Knowledge Graph (KG) integrating EO data with various data sources (socio-economic, urban, legislative texts, etc.) to monitor the environmental evolution of areas of interest. To highlight the advantages of our proposal, we present and explore, through SPARQL queries and visualizations, the results of implementing LEODS with data relevant to the TRACES project.

Keywords: Spatiotemporal data · Knowledge Graph · Semantic Enrichment

© The Author(s), under exclusive license to Springer Nature Switzerland AG 2024
M. Lotfian and L. L. L. Starace (Eds.): W2GIS 2024, LNCS 14673, pp. 67–85, 2024.
https://doi.org/10.1007/978-3-031-60796-7_5

1   Introduction

The overexploitation of natural resources such as forests and seas, as well as the pollution of air, soil, and water are urgent concerns affecting the Earth's global system and leading to climate change and loss of biodiversity. The Intergovernmental Panel on Climate Change (IPCC)[1] constantly reports the drastic consequences of inappropriate human behavior against the environment. To improve decision-making and implement effective environmental policies that counteract these negative trends, expert and non-expert stakeholders, *e.g.,* policy-makers, citizens, associations, researchers, analysts, etc., need access to meaningful Open Data to enhance their understanding of the environmental changes of an area of interest.

Earth monitoring programs such as US Landsat[2] and European Copernicus Sentinel[3] provide a free and open collection of satellite data depicting the Earth, also known as Earth Observation (EO) data. Due to the enormous amount of EO data, most state-of-the-art works [1,11,23] propose to organize EO data into Data Cubes. An Earth Observation Data Cube (EODC) is a multidimensional array typically composed of four dimensions: time, latitude, longitude, and spectral bands [4]. Current EODCs have emerged as a technological solution for storing, managing, accessing, and analyzing large EOs [11]. Experts can calculate indices from satellite images that assess various environmental characteristics of an area of interest, *e.g.,* calculating the Normalized Difference Vegetation Index (NDVI) to measure the vegetation cover of a given area [1]. Currently, management platforms such as EVER-EST[4] and RELIANCE[5] and some countries such as Australia[6], Switzerland[7] and Brazil[8] are making a great effort to adopt this approach. However, traditional EODCs have two major limitations: (1) their interpretation is usually reserved for specialists even when metadata is available to explain the satellite derived indices [2], (2) their relative isolation from available Web resources supplied by the Open Data Initiative [36] complicates the proper contextualization and investigation of a study area [12,25]. Consequently, the expert-oriented and non-contextualized data available in EODCs are insufficient to adequately understand environmental changes over time and their underlying causes.

To ensure the semantic enrichment of data, guarantee its understanding by a wider audience, and break down data silos while introducing causal links between different datasets, it is pertinent to adopt Semantic Web (SW) technologies. SW is an umbrella term encompassing standards and specifications, typically developed by the World Wide Web Consortium (W3C), to represent and exchange

---

[1] https://ipcc.ch.
[2] https://landsat.gsfc.nasa.gov.
[3] https://copernicus.eu/en.
[4] https://ever-est.eu.
[5] https://reliance-project.eu.
[6] https://dea.ga.gov.au/about/open-data-cube.
[7] https://swissdatacube.org.
[8] https://brazildatacube.org/.

data in the Linked Open Data (LOD) Cloud [15, 28, 32] while following the FAIR principles (*i.e.,* findable, accessible, interoperable, and reusable). Under the vision of the LOD paradigm, data are published on the Web as a network of Knowledge Graphs (KG) that increase data accessibility for both humans and machines [9], provide adequate support for data integration [35], and facilitate the inference of implicit facts and knowledge [13]. To publish data as KG, well-known modeling languages such as Resource Description Framework (RDF) and Web Ontology Language (OWL) are used to define ontology models (or vocabularies) in the form of RDF triples (*i.e.,* subject, property, and object) that describe domain-specific concepts and their relationships.

Among the possible candidates ontologies for publishing EO data in the LOD Cloud, the RDF data cube (QB) is of particular interest in the context of EODCs. QB is a W3C-standard ontology, aligned with OLAP (Online Analytical Processing) concepts, that focuses on publishing data according to a multidimensional model, in the form of open-linked data cubes [29]. This approach gives the QB vocabulary significant potential to integrate heterogeneous data that share standard dimensions, such as time and space, as well as, to semantically enrich EO data by linking it to various LOD resources. Because QB is compatible with the SDMX (Statistical Data and Metadata eXchange) standard model[9], it is widely used by national and international statistical agencies such as those in Scotland[10] and France[11] to publish and exchange socioeconomic data. However, it is surprising that the QB vocabulary is not widely used for publishing EO data, with notable exceptions such as the joint initiative of the Open Geospatial Consortium (OGC) and W3C that focus on the representation of dense raster-level EO data in the SW using the QB vocabulary [7]. Nevertheless, high data storage cost is to be expected in this approach. In turn, the lack of research focused on the effective representation of spatiotemporal EO data as RDF data cubes leads to flawed modeling of their components and the creation of silos of cubes that cannot be reused on the LOD Cloud [16].

Our research aims to efficiently leverage the QB vocabulary in conjunction with several SW technologies to investigate their benefits within the EO domain. Therefore, we present the Linked Earth Observation Data Series (LEODS) framework, specifically designed for integrating and publishing EO data on the LOD Cloud. LEODS provides and implements a processing chain focused on converting EO data into what we call EO-RDF data cubes. Essentially, it aggregates the satellite imagery at the lowest administrative division level to be as close as possible to the stakeholders. Note that for uniformity in this study, the term "municipality" is hereafter adopted as the denomination of the lowest division level[12]. The framework then adopts the standard ontologies of W3C RDF

---

[9] https://sdmx.org/.

[10] https://statistics.gov.scot/home.

[11] https://rdf.insee.fr/def/index.html.

[12] The lowest administrative division level term varies among regions, *e.g.,* "commune" in France and Switzerland and "municipality" in Great Britain.

Data Cube and OWL Time[13] as well as GeoSPARQL[14] of OGC and Territorial Statistical Nomenclature (TSN)[15] for the spatio-temporal modeling of the cubes ensuring their semantic enrichment and integration with various available Web resources such as socio-economic, urban, climatic, legislative text, etc., which are essential for the proper contextualization of a municipality.

To demonstrate the advantages of our proposal, we present and explore, through SPARQL queries and visualizations, the results of implementing LEODS with data relevant to the TRACES project[16]; an international collaborative research program between France and Switzerland. As a result, three EO-RDF data cubes with hierarchical dimensions: spatial (municipalities, departments, countries), temporal (daily, monthly, seasonal, annual), and indices (vegetation, water, snow, and urbanization) are now available in a SPARQL endpoint[17], provided with a set of predefined queries to facilitate data exploration by users.

The structure of the article is organized as follows: Sect. 2 presents the related work, Sect. 3 introduces the LEODS framework and the entire processing chain it supports. The case study and results obtained with LEODS are presented and discussed in Sect. 4. Finally, Sect. 5 concludes the article and presents perspectives associated with our work.

2 Related Work

As noted by [2], EO data from satellites are sensory data lacking semantic meaning. To properly interpret EO data, it is necessary to follow a semantic enrichment process that enhances EOs with additional information that provides context. The enrichment can be performed at a low level, where symbols are associated with semantic concepts (*e.g.,* color information), or at a high level, where associations refer to explicit expert knowledge (*e.g.,* land cover interpretations) [33]. Typical approaches to perform semantic enrichment in EO data are content-based, where extracted features from images (*e.g.,* time retrieval or land cover type) are utilized for the enrichment, and ontology-based approaches, where SW models are leveraged to represent and enrich EO data in the LOD Cloud. Below, we outline the research relevant to our proposal.

In [2,33,37], the authors argue that traditional EODCs lack semantics and propose to add a semantic layer to improve information retrieval in satellite images. Thus, using the Satellite Image Automatic Mapper™ (SIAM™) expert system software and a thesaurus ontology to organize the features extracted from the imagery, they semantically enrich the EODCs. The result is a semantic EODC that is defined as *a data cube where, for each observation, at least one*

---

[13] https://w3.org/TR/owl-time/.

[14] https://opengeospatial.github.io/ogc-geosparql/geosparql11.

[15] https://lig-tdcge.imag.fr/tsn/index.html#anchor-924051221.

[16] TRACES project PRCI Franco-Suisse. Funded by ANR and FNS. Website: https://traces-anr-fns.imag.fr/.

[17] The TRACES repository at: https://steamerlod.imag.fr.

nominal interpretation (i.e., categorical) is available [...]. The authors demonstrate improvement in information retrieval by querying the enriched EODCs. However, it is important to note that neither the semantics added to the EODCs nor the thesaurus ontology used have been published in the LOD Cloud, which would be of great value to end users to better interpret the EO data. Other work also focuses on the analysis and exploration of satellite imagery to extract useful information for end users involved in tasks such as environmental monitoring and land use planning. [31] proposes an open-source R package for satellite image time series analysis using Machine Learning. [10] presents a prototype of a system produced to manage and explore large volumes of remote sensing image data. Both approaches focus on extracting land cover features (*e.g.,* mountains, grasslands, water, etc.) from satellite imagery and enhance the search for information in large EO data. However, once again, the results of semantic image analysis are not published in the LOD Cloud, which keeps leading to the semantic isolation of the EO data.

Continuing, during our research, we identified several vocabularies/ontologies designed to facilitate the publication of EO data on the LOD Cloud, the most relevant ones are:

1. The Observations and Measurements (O&M)[18] is an OGC standard designed to describe observations and measurements in the geospatial and environmental domains, *e.g.,* the relationships between the target spatial objects, the measured properties, the measurement procedure, and the captured data resulting from those observational events. Although O&M is versatile within its intended scope, there are certain areas where it may not provide complete coverage, *e.g.,* Social Sciences and Economics.

2. The joint W3C and OGC Spatial Data on the Web (SDW) Working Group developed a set of ontologies to describe sensors, actuators, samplers as well as their observations, actuation, and sampling activities [14]. A first module called SOSA (Sensor, Observation, Sampler, and Actuator)[19] and an extension module called SSN (Semantic Sensor Network)[20] describe systems of sensors and observations, the used procedures, the subjects being observed, samples and the process of sampling. Although both ontologies can be easily integrated to support in-depth descriptions related to sensors, the ontologies may be too complex if a simple sensor description is needed.

3. The W3C RDF Data Cube Vocabulary (QB)[21] is a W3C recommendation for the publishing of multidimensional data beyond the EO domain in the form of open-linked data cubes. The QB vocabulary is aligned with OLAP concepts, allowing efficient storage, management, and accessibility of the data. Although the vocabulary is widely used in socio-economic domains, a mismodeling of its components (*e.g.,* dimensions, measures, and attributes) can

---

[18] https://ogc.org/standards/om.
[19] https://w3.org/ns/sosa/.
[20] https://w3.org/ns/ssn/.
[21] https://w3.org/TR/vocab-data-cube/.

lead to silos of cubes that cannot be reused in LOD Cloud resulting in major isolation problems.

4. The Agricultural Information Model (AIM) is an ontology developed in the framework of the Horizon 2020 DEMETER project [27]. The goal of AIM is to enable information interoperability between data domains such as agricultural data, Earth observation data, and meteorological data by using state-of-the-art ontologies such as SNN/SOSA, GeoSPARQL, and OWL-Time. At the moment AIM remains under development and is expected to be approved as an OGC standard in the future.

Later, with or without relying on the ontologies above, several initiatives to publish EO data in the LOD Cloud were proposed, including those of TELEIOS and LEO projects [19]. In both studies several tools, such as Geotriples and Sextant [20,26], and ontologies such as stRDF [17] were developed to manage big EO data. Specifically in [18], the authors propose to use the stRDF ontology to publish satellite image data in the LOD Cloud. However, their approach is limited to using SW technologies to publish only satellite image metadata (*e.g.*, time of acquisition and geographical coverage) as LOD, while ignoring the publication of other relevant information such as environmental indices that can be calculated from the imagery. In the work of [34,35], the authors argue that raster data is not human-readable and that SW ontologies can be used for the integration of data calculated from raster, *e.g.*, land cover indices, change indicators, etc. Thus, as a first contribution, they propose a network of ontologies that allows the representation of such data in the LOD Cloud. Among the ontologies, they reuse the SOSA vocabulary to describe raster observations, and the TSN (Territorial Statistical Nomenclature Ontology)[22] and OWL-Time ontologies to associate spatiotemporal concepts. Subsequently, a methodology is introduced to extract features from the pixel data and map them to the semantic model. Although a network of ontologies seems to be the most appropriate approach to comply the LOD vision, this specific work does not use the QB ontology despite being a standard recommendation suitable for modeling and integrating heterogeneous spatio-temporal data. QB has already been used to organize data of various natures in the LOD Cloud, such as medical data [8,22,30], historical data [5] and especially socio-economic data[23] due to its compatibility with the SDMX model. However, despite the benefits of the QB vocabulary, it is rarely used in the field of EO data. In the following, we describe the limited works found in the literature that adopt an ontology network approach involving QB to publish and enrich EO data in the LOD Cloud.

In [7], the W3C and the OGC consortia introduced a method for publishing EO raster data using ontologies such as QB, SNN, and GeoSPARQL. The proposal describes how dense geospatial raster data can be organized in the dimensions of the cube: latitude, longitude, and time, and also specifies how pixel metadata and their provenance can be attached to their components. However,

---

[22] https://lig-tdcge.imag.fr/tsn/index.html.

[23] Scotland: https://statistics.gov.scot/home and France: https://rdf.insee.fr/def/index.html.

within this approach, data is published pixel by pixel, which is very costly in terms of data storage. Furthermore, it would be more appropriate to publish aggregated data at the lowest administration level, e.g., municipalities, which are meaningful to stakeholders and enable an adequate contextualization of a given area with complementary resources such as socio-economic ones. The works of [3,21] describe a similar approach to represent meteorological data such as temperature and humidity as LOD to monitor climate variability and capture its behavior. Among the reused ontologies, the QB vocabulary is used to create spatiotemporal slices of meteorological observations enriched with statistical attributes. In addition, both methods leverage the SSN ontology to perform a more tailored description of the observations, such as sensor-related features and data collection methodology. Although this procedure granularly and technically contextualizes the EOs, the result is a data cube restricted to represent only meteorological data. We believe that this part of their approach diverges from our objective, since non-expert stakeholders are not concerned with such a low level of granularity description of the observations and the lack of such data does not affect the interpretation of the environmental evolution.

In our work, we are interested in opening up EO data for wide audiences by reusing standard semantic models including the RDF data cube. Unlike most of the related work described above, our focus is neither on the simple representation of metadata as LOD nor on the treatment of EO data at the raster level. Instead, we focus on publishing spatially aggregated EO data at the lowest administrative division level, to be as close as possible to expert and non-expert stakeholders interested in the environmental aspects of their municipalities. In addition, to ensure that expert-oriented and non-contextualized data become more understandable and meaningful, we aim for a higher level of semantic enrichment beyond the EO domain by contextualizing the data with available Web resources of different nature, such as socio-economic ones. Therefore, a specific framework is needed to describe how to preprocess, model, publish, and explore EO spatio-temporal data on the LOD Cloud. The approach should adopt a multidimensional modeling generic enough (a) to be applicable to any globally measured EO data and (b) to ensure the integration, through shared spatiotemporal dimensions, with data cubes published in domains other than EO.

3   The LEODS Framework

In this section, we present the LEODS framework, which supports the transformation of EO data into RDF data cubes, while assuring its future integration and enrichment with several Web resources. As illustrated in Fig. 1, LEODS covers a processing chain that: (1) aggregates EO data, initially at the pixel level, to the municipality level, (2) designs a multidimensional model that gives structure to the data cubes, (3) instantiates the model and publishes the data as EO-RDF data cubes on the LOD Cloud, and (4) provides users with predefined SPARQL queries to explore the open-linked data cubes. In the following subsections, each step of the LEODS framework is explained.

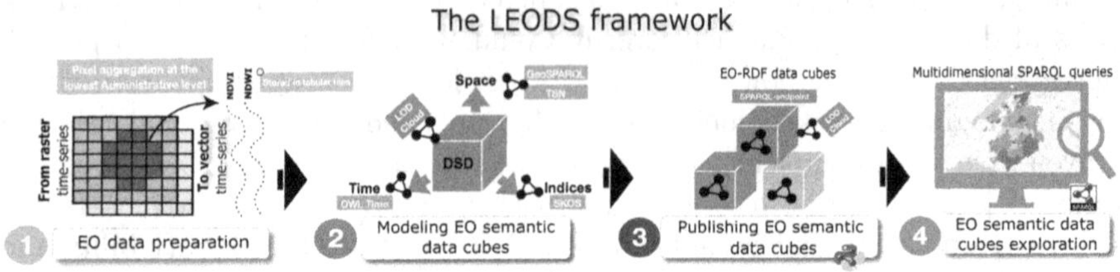

The LEODS framework

Fig. 1. Pipeline of the LEODS framework.

3.1 Step 1: EO Data Preparation

The initial phase managed by our framework aims to aggregate EO data, initially at the pixel level, to the municipality level in order to (1) be as close as possible to the stakeholders, (2) ensure municipalities contextualization with available local Web resources, and (3) manipulate multidimensional structured data. This process starts with the acquisition of satellite images for a given study area and a desired observation period, followed by essential preprocessing steps such as geometric correction and denoising. The processed pixels are then spatially aggregated at the lowest administrative division level (*i.e.,* at the municipality level), and derived environmental indices (such as NDVI) with various temporal aggregations (*e.g.,* seasonal, annual) can be calculated from them. Additionally, it is useful to apply zonal statistical methods (*i.e.,* statistical calculation of all pixels within a given municipality), such as the calculation of mean and standard deviation (std), to summarize the data for each indice. Finally, the preprocessed data are delivered in the form of vector time-series stored in tabular files. This step of the framework is considered optional if the user is working directly with time series of EO vectors.

3.2 Step 2: Modeling EO Semantic Data Cubes

The second step of the LEODS framework involves modeling the Data Structure Definition (DSD) of the QB ontology to embody the essential characteristics of EO data into the RDF data cubes. The first objective is to associate the EO vector time-series values, obtained in the previous step, with the components of the DSD. The essential components are: (1) *observations*, representing the observed values in the data set. (2) Observations can be organized along two or more *dimensions.* Given the nature of EO data, space and time are two standard dimensions that must be included in the data cube. Beyond spatiotemporal dimensions, specific dimensions relevant to the subject of the dataset should also be included. For example, in the TRACES project, we focus on environmental aspects, so an additional dimension is the set of environmental indices derived from the satellite imagery. A good practice to determine if tabular values can be mapped as dimensions is to review the list of standard dimensions[24] provided by

---

[24] https://purl.org/linked-data/sdmx/2009/dimension.

the SDMX statistical model. Furthermore, we suggest defining the dimensions with a hierarchical structure to allow essential SPARQL queries when exploring the data. (3) An *attribute* (or unit) provides context to an observation. For example, the value 50 becomes meaningful when associated with the attribute hectares (HA). The QUDT vocabulary[25] contains several attributes ready to be reused. (4) The *measure* refers to the specific phenomenon observed and is closely related to the attribute. In the EO data domain, typical measures include zonal statistics (*e.g.*, men, std), land cover surface, and land surface temperature. As with the dimensions, SDMX provides a list of standard measures[26] that facilitate the recognition of this component. Once the DSD components have been identified, it is advisable to explore standard ontologies that can be reused for the instance of the components. For example, the time dimension can be linked to the OWL-Time ontology since it already contains the necessary elements to represent the time concept in the LOD Cloud. Similarly, the spatial dimension can be described using the TSN ontology, which represents concepts about geographic territories at different administration division levels, such as municipalities. Moreover, it is coupled to the TSN-Change ontology; focused on capturing the changes undergone by territories from one version to another [6].

The DSD modeling is a crucial step and some criteria should be considered during the process: (a) the model must be generic enough to ensure integration with heterogeneous data sharing standard dimensions such as time and space and to be applicable to any globally measured EO data beyond environmental indices, and (b) the cube components should be properly defined and reusable as possible to mitigate the silos of RDF data cubes.

3.3   Step 3: Publishing EO Semantic Data Cubes

After modeling the structure of the RDF data cubes, the next step consists of the semi-automatic transformation of the EO vector time-series into EO-RDF data cubes following the modeled DSD. This process can be facilitated using tools such as the RDFlib library[27], the RDF mapping language[28], and the command-line tool Tarql[29]. Open Refine supports the RDF language as an extension, allowing the instance of basic components of the model. However, we recommend using it for an initial interaction process with QB components and RDF syntax, as the tool can be restrictive during implementation. For greater flexibility, we suggest using the RDFlib library to instantiate the full conceptual model of the cubes (*i.e.*, the DSD) in RDF triples using Python; which simplifies the RDF syntax. Then, ad-hoc Tarql scripts can be implemented to automatically convert the observations, in tabular files, to RDF files following the DSD cube model. Subsequently, both the instantiated model and the observations files can

---

[25] https://qudt.org/vocab/unit/.
[26] https://purl.org/linked-data/sdmx/2009/measure.
[27] https://rdflib.readthedocs.io/en/stable/.
[28] https://rml.io/specs/rml/.
[29] https://tarql.github.io/.

be concatenated into a single file containing EO-RDF data cubes. Then, to fully comply with the vision of the LOD paradigm, the produced linked cubes must be published and made accessible to interested stakeholders through a SPARQL endpoint, a Web service that enables the querying of RDF data.

3.4 Step 4: EO Semantic Data Cubes Exploration

Finally, once the EO-RDF data cubes are accessible, it is crucial to initiate the exploration phase, demonstrating how to extract meaningful information from these cubes. For this aim, we propose to use the GraphDB tool[30], which, in addition to storing triples, includes a LOD graph visualization module. This visualization is essential for discovering and navigating through the cube components. GraphDB also supports SPARQL and GeoSPARQL queries, essential for manipulating and retrieving information from EO-RDF data cubes. Thus, to facilitate analysis and interpretation, we suggest providing users with a set of predefined queries that exploit the advantages of the implemented cube model. Greater diversity in the queries enhances the chances for interested users, experts or non-experts, to comprehend the breadth of information that can be extracted from the EO-RDF data cubes.

4 Implementing the LEODS Framework: A Case Study

4.1 Production of EO-RDF Data Cubes

In this section, we describe the results of implementing the LEODS framework with data from selected study areas of the Swiss Data Cube (SDC). Precisely, the TRACES project partners are the creators of the SDC, a well-known EODC providing analysis-ready data on the geographical extent of Switzerland and part of France since 1984 [11]. Therefore, as described in the first step of the framework, we started by selecting three study areas within the SDC, namely the communities (*i.e.*, groups of municipalities) of Evian in France, Fribourg in Switzerland, and Grand-Geneva located on the border of both countries. Subsequently, as a result of the preprocessing and spatial aggregation of the selected images at the municipality level, a total of 365 municipalities were obtained for the three study areas, 37 municipalities belonging to Evian, 127 to Fribourg, and 201 to Grand-Geneva. Furthermore, three families of environmental indices were calculated: (a) the Landsat land cover characterization indices (LIS), (b) the Landsat land surface temperature indice (LST), and (c) the Land cover indices according to the standard Corine nomenclature (CLC) (See Table 1). On the one hand, LIS and LST indices are available as seasonal data over the period 1985 to 2022 (*i.e., aprox. 4 observation per year × 38 years = 152 observations per indice*), and, zonal statistics such as mean, std, and accuracy features such as data quality were calculated for both indices families. On the other hand, due to the different provenance of the CLC data, only 5 observations are available

---

[30] https://graphdb.ontotext.com/.

Table 1. Three families integrate the selected environmental indices for our case study: LIS, LST and CLC. A detailed description of the calculated indices is available in [24].

Environmental indices				
Indice family	Application domain	Indice	Name	Total number of indices
LIS	Vegetation	NDVI	Normalized Difference Vegetation Index	20
			...	
	Water	NDWI	Normalized Difference Water Index	
			...	
	Urbanization	NDBI	Normalized Difference Built-Up Index	
			...	
	Snow	NDSI	Normalized Difference Snow Index	
			...	
LST	Temperature	st	Surface Temperature	1
CLC	Land cover	clc-11	Urban fabric	15
			...	

for the years 1990, 2000, 2006, 2012, and 2018. In addition, although it does not include zonal statistics, it does calculate land cover area occupation in units such as HA and percentage (%). Posteriorly, the data was delivered as EO vector time-series in CSV files.

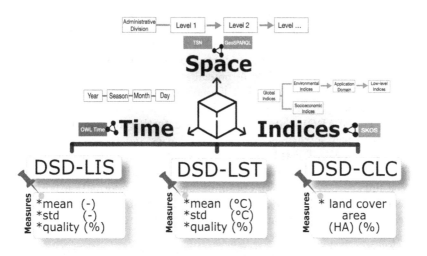

Fig. 2. Final DSD design of the three EO-RDF data cubes.

Then, the second phase of the framework leads to the modeling of the structure of the EO-RDF data cubes. As shown in Fig. 2, among the three study areas, we identified three shared dimensions: Time, Space, and Indices, where "Indices" is a specific dimension related to the topic of our dataset. To ensure integration and enrichment in the cubes, we decided to reuse well-known ontologies and introduce hierarchical elements in the dimensions. Concretely, we reused the TSN and OWL-Time ontologies for the representation of the spatio-temporal dimensions, while for the Indices, we modeled our own concept using the SKOS (Simple Knowledge Organisation System)[31] ontology. Furthermore, the choice of TSN to describe the spatial dimension was not an arbitrary decision. Typically, the boundaries of municipalities change over time, so the complementary TSN-Change ontology can be used in the future to model these spatial dynamics. Subsequently, we tailored each dimension to be hierarchical, meaning the Spatial dimension is organized as "municipalities, departments and countries", the Temporal dimension is organized as "daily, monthly, seasonal, and annual", and the Thematic indices as "low-level indices, application domain, environmental indices, and global indices". Note that we paid special attention to the design of this latter dimension to make it generic enough to include indices beyond the scope of the EO, such as population, sensing instruments, etc. Regarding the identification of measures and attributes, for CLC, we easily identified the Land cover area measure with two units (HA and %) whereas, for LIS and LST, we identified the same three measures: mean, std, and data quality, with various attributes such as celsius degrees ($^\circ C$), percentage (%) and unitless attributes (-)[32]. Therefore, three DSDs were instantiated to preserve the different units in the same cube. Next, metadata and LOD connections were added to enrich and contextualize the cube components. In this regard, a significant contribution is the provided metadata on the indices. There is not much information about expert-oriented indices such as NDBI on the Web, so descriptions, calculation formulas, and bibliographic citations were added to semantically enrich each indice. A similar process was conducted for the municipalities by connecting them to LOD resources available in official statistical agencies such as INSEE (National Institute of Statistics and Economic Studies)[33] in France and FSO (Federal Statistical Office)[34] in Switzerland. In the specific case of FSO, they reused the GeoSPARQL ontology to describe further information about the municipalities such as their geographic boundaries and their highest administrative division levels. For this reason, it was not necessary to design a detailed hierarchy in our spatial dimension. Therefore, in addition to enriching the EO data, the linkage process allows obtaining meaningful information not present in the original dataset. Finally, Python and Tarql scripts were implemented and executed enabling the semi-automatic production of three EO-RDF data cubes. These open-linked cubes, in addition to preserving all the advantages of traditional EODCs, organize now multidimensional Linked Data that integrates basic semantics, such as metadata and connections to LOD resources, contributing to

---

[31] https://w3.org/2004/02/skos/core.

[32] LIS measurements are unitless because they are calculated as a ratio of differences between two spectral bands, and the units are canceled during the calculation.

[33] insee.fr/fr/accueil.

[34] bfs.admin.ch/bfs/en/home.html.

their enrichment and reuse. The cubes were later stored in a GrahphDB triple store, where users can access them through a SPARQL endpoint[35].

4.2 Spatio-Temporal SPARQL Queries for Linked Data Exploration

The last step of the framework is the data exploration of the produced EO-RDF data cubes. SPARQL and GeoSPARQL queries can be used to retrieve relevant information from them. As part of our methodology, we aim to provide stakeholders with predefined SPARQL queries that facilitate the exploration of the open-linked cubes. Although our current focus in this study is on spatio-temporal queries, we implemented different types of queries currently accessible in a GitHub repository [24]. The repository hosts basic queries to retrieve cube components such as dimensions, measures, and attributes, as well as more essential queries exploiting the hierarchical components of the cubes to perform OLAP operations such as Drill-down and Roll-up. Regarding the implemented spatio-temporal queries, in Listing 1.1, we present a specific query to demonstrate the strengths of our final EO-RDF data cube design by manipulating all dimensions and retrieving geo-spatial information not present in the original dataset.

```
SELECT ?name ?code ?mean ?geometry
WHERE {
  ?obs rdf:type qb:Observation;
       qb:dataSet :Seasonaly-LIS-dataset;
       :dimensionArea   ?area;
       :dimensionTime   ?time;
       :dimensionIndice codelist:NDVI;
       :measureMeanUnitless ?mean;
  ?area sett:studyArea traces-geo:Fribourg;
       tsn:hasName ?name;
       tsn:hasIdentifier ?code;
       owl:sameAs ?bounderies.
  ?time time:year "2022"^^xsd:gYear;
       sett:seasonOfYear sett:Spring.

  SERVICE <https://geo.ld.admin.ch/query>
  {
    ?bounderies geo:hasGeometry ?coor.
    ?coor geo:asWKT ?geometry.
  }
}
ORDER BY DESC(?mean)
LIMIT 3
```

Code Listing 1.1. SPARQL query that retrieves geographic coordinates and NDVI values of certain municipalities in Fribourg in 2022.

---

[35] The TRACES repository at: https://steamerlod.imag.fr.

Table 2. Output of the SPARQL query presented in Listing 1.1.

name	code	mean	geometry
"Val-de-Charmey"	"CH2163"	"0.295"^^xsd:float	"POLYGON ((7.2370203970318..))
"Plaffeien"	"CH2299"	"0.292"^^xsd:float	"POLYGON ((7.2370203970318..))
"Jaun"	"CH2138"	"0.279"^^xsd:float	"POLYGON ((7.2370203970318..))

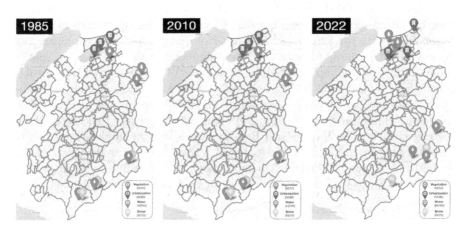

Fig. 3. Municipalities in Fribourg with the highest mean values over the years 1985, 2010, and 2022 respectively. Representative indices were chosen: Vegetation (green), Urbanization (red), Water (blue), and Snow (light blue). (Color figure online)

Specifically, we performed a slice-type query in which the spatial dimension was fixed on the community of Fribourg, the temporal dimension was fixed on the year 2022, and the indice dimension was fixed at NDVI to retrieve the top three municipalities with the highest NDVI-mean values of the selected slice. As shown in Table 2, because we enriched each municipality with official LOD resources, we were able to connect to FSO's SPARQL endpoint and run a federated GeoSPARQL query to extract the spatial coordinates of the boundaries of the top municipalities. The reader should note that this information was not present in the original dataset and that, due to the LOD connections, the data is no longer isolated. This is one of the fundamental principles of the LOD paradigm. Subsequently, using the Python Folium library[36], it was possible to plot the coordinates of the retrieved municipalities on a map. Then, to achieve the final chart in Fig. 3, we repeated the previous query several times varying the year value *i.e., 1985, 2010, and 2022*, and varying the indice value. The indices were not chosen arbitrarily, instead, representative indices were chosen from each Application domain (See Table 1) to provide more comprehensible results. Thus, we show in the plot, the top three municipalities with the highest mean NDVI values in green (Vegetation), NDBI in red (Urbanization), NDWI

---

[36] https://python-visualization.github.io/folium/latest/#.

in blue (Water), and NDSI in light blue (Snow). The first insights suggest that the areas more populated by citizens are located in the northern part of Friburg, where Urbanization and Vegetation indices predominate, while the mountainous area is located in the south due to the predominance of Snow and Water indices.

```
SELECT ?name ?code (AVG(?mean) AS ?avgmean)
WHERE {
  ?obs rdf:type qb:Observation;
       qb:dataSet  :Seasonaly-LST-dataset;
       dimensionArea ?area;
       :dimensionTime ?time;
       :dimensionIndice codelist:st;
       :measureMeanDegCel ?mean.

 ?area sett:studyArea traces-geo:Fribourg;
       tsn:hasName ?name;
       tsn:hasIdentifier ?code.
  ?time time:year "2022"^^xsd:gYear.

}
GROUP BY ?name ?code
ORDER BY ?name
```

Code Listing 1.2. SPARQL query that calculates the average Surface Temperature in the municipalities of Fribourg in 2022.

Next, we decided to implement a query (Refer Listing 1.2) that takes advantage of the LST indice. Thus, similar to the previous slice-type query, we decided to focus on the Fribourg study area during the same periods to enable a correlation between the results. Then, the average surface temperature was calculated for each year. The results are illustrated in Fig. 4. In the plot, the areas colored in dark blue represent the municipalities with the lowest temperatures, while those colored in dark red represent the highest temperatures. Thus, there is a clear increase in temperature over the years, with an evident reduction of the dark blue colored areas in 2022. Furthermore, it is possible to make a correlation with the results of query in Listing 1.1, We can observe that the municipalities with higher temperatures match those where the Urbanization indices were located in Fig. 3 . While those municipalities with the lowest temperatures are correlated with the Water and Snow indices. However, to better understand how Vegetation is related to the average temperature (areas colored in orange and yellow), a more detailed analysis needs to be conducted. Different types of queries can be performed by exploiting the spatio-temporal model of the produced EO-RDF data cubes. In addition, as a result of the enrichment process with metadata and links to LOD resources, the study areas are now more contextualized. This greatly enhances the knowledge gained and facilitates its understanding.

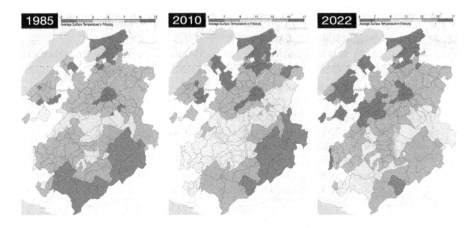

Fig. 4. Average surface temperature in the Fribourg study area.

5   Conclusions and Future Work

In this paper, we presented the LEODS framework, focused on the integration and semantic enrichment of EO data in LOD Cloud. Through a processing chain, our framework describes how to embody EO data into open-linked data cubes. During the process, EO data, originally at the pixel level, was aggregated at the lowest administrative division level to be closer to stakeholders and ensure its contextualization with other local Web resources. Subsequently, a careful multidimensional modeling of the cubes was conducted generically enough to ensure their future integration with heterogeneous data sharing spatiotemporal dimensions and with various indices beyond the EO domain. To illustrate the advantages of our approach, we have implemented the LEODS framework with data relevant to the TRACES project. As a result, three EO-RDF data cubes, not longer isolated but enriched with metadata, connected to various LOD resources, following FAIR principles, and preserving the advantages of traditional EODCs are now available to stakeholders in a SPARQL endpoint. The structure of the cubes incorporates a model generic enough to guarantee its integration with other resources through its spatio-temporal dimensions, as well as to ensure the inclusion of indices beyond the scope of the EO. Furthermore, predefined queries were provided to stakeholders to facilitate their exploration and analysis of the data. We expect that both expert and non-expert users can benefit from our approach. In future work, we intend to use the EO-RDF data cubes as a first step in the creation of a KG describing the environmental trajectories of municipalities. Finally, we aim to add more indices, such as population, to our existing EO-RDF data cubes and to continue to enrich them with new LOD resources.

A   Appendix

A.1   Glossary

AIM Agricultural Information Model
CLC Corin Land Cover
DSD Data Structure Definition
EO Earth Observation
EODC Earth Observation Data Cube
FAIR Findable, Accessible, Interoperable, and Reusable
FSO Federal Statistical Office
HA Hectares
INSEE National Institute of Statistics and Economic Studies
IPCC Intergovernmental Panel on Climate Change
KG Knowledge Graph
LEODS Linked Earth Observation Data Series
LIS Landsat land cover indices
LOD Linked Open Data
LST Landsat land surface temperature indices
NDBI Normalized Difference Built-Up Index
NDVI Normalized Difference Vegetation Index
NDWI Normalized Difference Water Index
NDSI Normalized Difference Snow Index
OGC Open Geospatial Consortium
OWL Web Ontology Language
QB RDF data cube
RDF Resource Description Framework
SDC Swiss Data Cube
SDMX Statistical Data and Metadata eXchange
SDW Spatial Data on the Web
SIAM Satellite Image Automatic Mapper
SKOS Simple Knowledge Organisation System
SOSA Sensor, Observation, Sampler, and Actuator
SSN Semantic Sensor Network
ST Surface Temperature
SW Semantic Web
TSN Territorial Statistical Nomenclature Ontology
W3C World Wide Web Consortium

References

1. Appel, M., Pebesma, E.: On-demand processing of data cubes from satellite image collections with the gdalcubes library. Data **4**(3), 92 (2019)
2. Augustin, H., Sudmanns, M., Tiede, D., Lang, S., Baraldi, A.: Semantic earth observation data cubes. Data **4**(3), 102 (2019)

3. Ayadi, N.Y., Faron, C., Michel, F., Gandon, F., Corby, O.: A model for meteorological knowledge graphs: application to météo-france data. In: ICWE 2022-22nd International Conference on Web Engineering (2022)

4. Baumann, P.: The datacube manifesto (2017). http://earthserver.eu/tech/datacube-manifesto

5. Bayerl, S., Granitzer, M.: Data-transformation on historical data using the rdf data cube vocabulary. In: Proceedings of the 15th International Conference on Knowledge Technologies and Data-driven Business, pp. 1–8 (2015)

6. Bernard, C., Villanova-Oliver, M., Gensel, J., Dao, H.: Modeling changes in territorial partitions over time: ontologies TSN and TSN-change. In: Proceedings of the 33rd Annual ACM Symposium on Applied Computing, SAC 2018, pp. 866–875. ACM (2018). https://doi.org/10.1145/3167132.3167227

7. Brizhinev, D., Toyer, S., Taylor, K., Zhang, Z.: Publishing and using earth observation data with the rdf data cube and the discrete global grid system. In: W3C Working Group Note and OGC Discussion Paper W3C 20170928, pp. 16–125 (2017)

8. Casey, S., Doody, P., Shields, A.: An ontology-based system for cancer registry data. In: 2022 33rd Irish Signals and Systems Conference (ISSC), pp. 1–6 (2022). https://doi.org/10.1109/ISSC55427.2022.9826197

9. Cyganiak, R., Wood, D., Lanthaler, M.: RDF 1.1 Concepts and Abstract Syntax (2014). https://www.w3.org/TR/rdf11-concepts/

10. Datcu, M., et al.: Information mining in remote sensing image archives: system concepts. IEEE Trans. Geosci. Remote Sens. **41**(12), 2923–2936 (2003). https://doi.org/10.1109/TGRS.2003.817197

11. Giuliani, G., et al.: Building an earth observations data cube: lessons learned from the swiss data cube (sdc) on generating analysis ready data (ard). Big Earth Data **1**(1–2), 100–117 (2017)

12. Giuliani, G., Masó, J., Mazzetti, P., Nativi, S., Zabala, A.: Paving the way to increased interoperability of earth observations data cubes. Data **4**(3) (2019). https://doi.org/10.3390/data4030113. https://www.mdpi.com/2306-5729/4/3/113

13. Hamdani, Y., Xiao, G., Ding, L., Calvanese, D.: An ontology-based framework for geospatial integration and querying of raster data cube using virtual knowledge graphs. ISPRS Int. J. Geo Inf. **12**(9), 375 (2023)

14. Hitzler, P., et al.: The modular SSN ontology: a joint w3c and OGC standard specifying the semantics of sensors, observations, sampling, and actuation (2019). https://doi.org/10.3233/SW-180320

15. Hogan, A.: The semantic web: two decades on. Semant. Web **11**(1), 169–185 (2020)

16. Kalampokis, E., Zeginis, D., Tarabanis, K.: On modeling linked open statistical data. J. Web Semant. **55**, 56–68 (2019)

17. Koubarakis, M., Kyzirakos, K.: Modeling and querying metadata in the semantic sensor web: the model stRDF and the query language stSPARQL. In: Aroyo, L., Antoniou, G., Hyvönen, E., ten Teije, A., Stuckenschmidt, H., Cabral, L., Tudorache, T. (eds.) ESWC 2010. LNCS, vol. 6088, pp. 425–439. Springer, Heidelberg (2010). https://doi.org/10.1007/978-3-642-13486-9_29

18. Koubarakis, M., et al.: Managing big, linked, and open earth-observation data: Using the teleios\/leo software stack. IEEE Geosci. Remote Sens. Maga. **4**(3), 23–37 (2016)

19. Koubarakis, M., et al.: Linked earth observation data: the projects teleios and leo. In: Proceedings of the Linking Geospatial Data Conference (2014)

20. Kyzirakos, K., et al.: Geotriples: transforming geospatial data into rdf graphs using r2rml and rml mappings. J. Web Semant. **52**, 16–32 (2018)

21. Lefort, L., Bobruk, J., Haller, A., Taylor, K., Woolf, A.: A linked sensor data cube for a 100 year homogenised daily temperature dataset. In: SSN, pp. 1–16 (2012)
22. Leroux, H., Lefort, L.: Using cdisc odm and the rdf data cube for the semantic enrichment of longitudinal clinical trial data. In: SWAT4LS (2012)
23. Lewis, A., Oliver, S., Lymburner, L., Evans, B., Wyborn, L., Mueller, N., Raevksi, G., Hooke, J., Woodcock, R., Sixsmith, J., et al.: The australian geoscience data cube-foundations and lessons learned. Remote Sens. Environ. **202**, 276–292 (2017)
24. Milon-Flores, D.F., Bernard, C., Gensel, J., Giuliani, G., Chatenoux, B., Dao, H.: Leods framework repository. https://github.com/DanielaFe7-personal/Traces-EO-RDF-data-cubes
25. Nativi, S., Mazzetti, P., Craglia, M.: A view-based model of data-cube to support big earth data systems interoperability. Big Earth Data **1**(1–2), 75–99 (2017)
26. Nikolaou, C., et al.: Sextant: visualizing time-evolving linked geospatial data. J. Web Semant. **35**, 35–52 (2015)
27. Palma, R., et al.: Agricultural information model. In: Bochtis, D.D., Sorensen, C.G., Fountas, S., Moysiadis, V., Pardalos, P.M. (eds.) Information and Communication Technologies for Agriculture-Theme III: Decision, pp. 3–36. Springer, Heidelberg (2022). https://doi.org/10.1007/978-3-030-84152-2_1
28. Patel, A., Jain, S.: Present and future of semantic web technologies: a research statement. Int. J. Comput. Appl. **43**(5), 413–422 (2021)
29. Richard Cyganiak, D.R., Tennison, J.: The RDF data cube vocabulary. W3c recommendation, W3C (2014). https://www.w3.org/TR/vocab-data-cube/
30. Rodriguez, T.N., Hogan, A.: Covidcube: an RDF data cube for exploring among-country COVID-19 correlations. In: CEUR Workshop Proceedings, vol. 2980. CEUR-WS.org (2021). http://ceur-ws.org/Vol-2980/paper395.pdf
31. Simoes, R., et al.: Satellite image time series analysis for big earth observation data. Remote Sens. **13**(13), 2428 (2021)
32. de Sousa, L.M.: Spatial Linked Data Infrastructures. Zenodo (2023)
33. Sudmanns, M., Augustin, H., van der Meer, L., Baraldi, A., Tiede, D.: The Austrian semantic EO data cube infrastructure. Remote Sens. **13**(23), 4807 (2021)
34. Tran, B.H., Aussenac-Gilles, N., Comparot, C., Trojahn, C.: An approach for integrating earth observation, change detection and contextual data for semantic search, pp. 3115–3118. IEEE (2020)
35. Tran, B.H., Aussenac-Gilles, N., Comparot, C., Trojahn, C.: Semantic integration of raster data for earth observation: an RDF dataset of territorial unit versions with their land cover. ISPRS Int. J. Geo Inf. **9**(9), 503 (2020)
36. Ubaldi, B.: Open government data: towards empirical analysis of open government data initiatives (2013)
37. Van Der Meer, L., Sudmanns, M., Augustin, H., Baraldi, A., Tiede, D.: Semantic querying in earth observation data cubes. Int. Arch. Photogram. Remote Sens. Spat. Inf. Sci. **XLVIII-4/W1-2022**, 503–510 (2022). https://doi.org/10.5194/isprs-archives-XLVIII-4-W1-2022-503-2022. https://isprs-archives.copernicus.org/articles/XLVIII-4-W1-2022/503/2022/

Geospatial Webservices and Reproducibility of Research: Challenges and Needs

Maxime Collombin[2]([✉]) [iD], Massimiliano Cannata[3] [iD], Olivier Ertz[2] [iD],
Gregory Giuliani[4] [iD], Jens Ingensand[1] [iD], Claudio Primerano[3] [iD],
and Daniele Strigaro[3]

[1] University of Applied Sciences Western Switzerland (HEIG-VD), INSIT Institute,
Canton of Vaud, Switzerland
[2] University of Applied Sciences Western Switzerland (HEIG-VD), MEI Institute,
Canton of Vaud, Switzerland
maxime.collombin@heig-vd.ch
[3] University of Applied Sciences Southern Switzerland (SUPSI), IST Institute,
Canton Ticino, Switzerland
[4] University of Geneva (UNIGE), Institute for Environmental Sciences, Geneva,
Switzerland

Abstract. This article investigates challenges and requirements related to the reproducibility of geospatial research using geospatial webservices. Several researchers have identified hinders related to technology on the one hand, as well as challenges regarding existing well-known standards that respect FAIR principles (findable, accessible, interoperable, reusable). Therefore four hypotheses are established regarding reproducibility using geospatial webservices. These four hypotheses are addressed in an online survey. The results shows correlations between academic affiliations, open standards, and reproducibility in geospatial research.

Keywords: open science · geospatial web services · reproducibility · FAIR · interoperability · reproducible research

1 Introduction

In the era of cloud computing, big data and Internet of Things, research is very often data-driven: based on the analysis of data, increasingly available in large quantities and collected by experiments, observations or simulations [3]. These data are very often characterized as being dynamic in space and time and as continuously expanding or changing. Modern spatial data infrastructures (e.g. national and international spatial data infrastructures such as Swisstopo or INSPIRE), are based on interoperable web services which expose and serve large quantities of data on the Internet using widely accepted open standards defined by the Open Geospatial Consortium (OGC) and the International Organization for Standardization commonly (ISO) [7]. These standards mostly comply with

M. Lotfian and L. L. L. Starace (Eds.): W2GIS 2024, LNCS 14673, pp. 86–92, 2024.
https://doi.org/10.1007/978-3-031-60796-7_6

FAIR principles [2] but do not offer any capability to for instance retrieve a dataset for a defined instant, to refer to its status in that specific instant and to guarantee its immutability. These three aspects hinder the replicability of research based on such a kind of services.

2   Challenges and Hypotheses: Bridging Open Science, Interoperability, and Reproducibility

Cannata et al. [1] emphasize the crucial link between Open Science concepts and the challenges of interoperability and time-varying data management. The ability to achieve results consistent with prior studies enhances scientific transparency, fosters a deeper understanding of research, amplifies the impact of studies, and ultimately strengthens the credibility of scientific endeavors [4,5]. This alignment with Open Science principles is denoted as reproducible research, a paradigm that demands availability of the same source code, dataset, and configuration used in a study. However, for geospatial data, existing OGC standards, despite respecting FAIR-principles [2] and modern data sharing, fall short in fully supporting the reproducibility concept as envisioned by Open Science. Specifically, these standards lack a guarantee that geodata accessed at a given moment can be persistently and immutably accessed in the future, particularly concerning system-time considerations.

This observation is reinforced by Nüst and Pebesma [6], who offer a comprehensive summary of reproducibility in the geospatial domain. They acknowledge the limited body of work on reproducibility within this domain, highlighting the necessity of physical, logical, and cultural components for achieving reproducibility. The authors identify the primary challenge as the general lack of knowledge regarding reproducibility practices among researchers. They also enumerate barriers, including the utilization of proprietary software, challenges posed by a multitude of tools in a single research project, dependencies on geospatial infrastructure relying on online services, difficulties in accessing original datasets due to potential changes, and potential inconsistencies in free platforms offering scripting capabilities.

In light of these challenges, we have established four hypotheses regarding the significance of standardization and reproducibility within research organizations:

- **H1** Organizations in the academic sector, harbouring highly specialized data management profiles, exhibit a stronger emphasis on standardization, thereby fostering research reproducibility.
- **H2** The utilization of open standards is correlated with enhanced reproducibility, driven by practical needs. Standardization and interoperability are intertwined themes that converge to meet a shared objective.
- **H3** Spatial databases (DBMS) play a pivotal role in promoting reproducibility. However, challenges associated with managing raster data, large datasets, and objectives such as data validation or archiving can hinder reproducibility.

– **H4** Technical expertise and a profound understanding of standardization contribute to both interoperability and reproducibility. The integration of technology watch further influences these factors.

As we delve deeper into the geospatial research landscape, these hypotheses provide a foundation for refining our understanding and advancing the state of the art in reproducibility practices within the domain.

3 Survey

To explore and validate the aforementioned hypotheses, a survey was conducted using the Open Source Lime Survey software (https://www.limesurvey.org). This survey contained 50 questions categorized into 9 themes and covering aspects such as organization, data utilization, web services, standards and reproducibility, challenges and needs, tools and software, collaboration, recommendations, and additional comments. For the sake of transparency, all resources relating to the configuration of the survey and the results, with the exception of personal information, are accessible at the following GitLab repository: https://gitlab.com/geo-ord/osires_surveys.

The survey targeted key research organizations in Switzerland renowned for their expertise in the geospatial field as well as NGOs and geospatial data providers such as the Swiss state and Swiss cantons. The survey remained open for a duration of two weeks to allow ample time for participation.

Out of the 75 institutions contacted, 59 organizations accessed the survey. Notably, 15 organizations responded to the survey in its entirety.

4 Results

Given the modest response rate to the survey, the collected responses provide insights into certain discernible trends rather than yielding statistically significant findings.

The results suggest that there is evidence in support of the first hypothesis **H1**: organizations affiliated with the academic sector prioritize standardization, thereby fostering the reproducibility of research outcomes. Upon reviewing respondent profiles, a considerable proportion of the participating entities originate from the academic sector, alongside representation from the public sector and NGOs. These entities express a clear interest in standardization and ensuring the reproducibility of their data management processes.

It is worth noting that out of the 12 respondents who indicated the importance of standardisation in their research, 25% were from academic institutions, 33% were from the government sector and 25% were from NGOs. Similarly, when assessing the importance of reproducibility in research, 25% of the 8 participants who responded favourably to the question were affiliated with academic institutions, 38% were from the public sector and 38% were associated with NGOs.

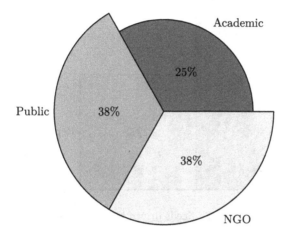

Fig. 1. Importance of reproducibility by type of organisation

The survey revealed that the main data management requirements are to ensure data quality control and accuracy. Integration with GIS software and other platforms, version management and change tracking are other important requirements. Participants responded that essential steps in ensuring reproducible results are the continuous flow of data within business systems, as well as improving data discoverability.

The analysis of the participants' responses showed that 80% consider standardization to be essential to meet the specific needs of their research processes. Similarly, 53% of the respondents stressed the importance of reproducibility.

These observations provide evidence to affirm the hypothesis **H2** that the use of open standards promotes reproducibility and responds to specific needs. Standardization and interoperability are linked themes that converge towards a common goal, reinforcing the robustness and transparency of geospatial research processes.

The answers also provide support of hypothesis **H3**, according to which the use of spatial databases (DBMS) favours reproducibility. One reason are the possibilities these systems offer for versioning, as described by Cannata et al. [1].

In particular, 50% of respondents stated that they use a DBMS in their organisation. In addition, 50% of respondents indicated the importance of reproducibility in their research, which corresponds to the supposed positive impact of spatial databases on reproducibility.

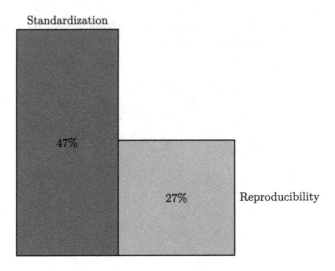

Fig. 2. Needs driven by uses-cases

The management of raster data appears to be more difficult, since these data are more difficult to store in a DBMS. The use of standardized geoservices such as OGC-WFS poses performance constraints for large volumes of data. Other constraints linked to data management and publication, such as quality control and archiving, do not appear to significantly hinder reproducibility.

There is also evidence in support of hypothesis **H4**, according to which technical expertise and knowledge of standardization promotes interoperability and reproducibility. Technical limitations in the software and programming languages used have a negative impact on reproducibility. The only respondent who answered that standardization does not play an important role in his research, expressed a lack of knowledge or was confronted with technical problems, notably the absence of dedicated software, which hinders the application of standardization in his research. This respondent also indicated a low importance of reproducibility in his research, which corresponds to the identified challenges, thus reinforcing the importance of technical expertise and knowledge in addressing concerns about standardisation and reproducibility.

By highlighting challenges such as the limitations of proprietary software and the complexity associated with the use of a variety of tools, our survey confirms that academic bodies put particular importance to standardization, thereby supporting our first hypothesis. Our study also highlights more detailed aspects of data management requirements, underlining the significant role of standardization and interoperability for the robustness and transparency of geospatial research processes.

The results of our study also confirm the importance of spatial databases (DBMS) in improving reproducibility, despite persistent challenges, particularly in the management of raster data. In addition, technical expertise and a thorough knowledge of standardization emerge as determining factors in promoting interoperability and reproducibility, thus complementing the perspective of Nüst and Pebesma [6].

It is essential to note that these findings remain preliminary, and future iterations of our investigation will aim at refining these observations. This will contribute to a better understanding of the dynamic interplay between standardization, interoperability and reproducibility in the field of geospatial research.

5   Conclusions and Perspectives

This study highlights significant challenges in the field of geospatial research, particularly in the area of reproducibility of results using geospatial webservices. The identified trends underline the central role of standardization, open science principles and technical expertise in promoting the reproducibility of research. As we move forward, we argue that future initiatives should prioritize reproducibility issues in collaboration with the geospatial community. Improving spatial data infrastructures to align them more closely with open science principles and raising awareness of reproducibility practices among researchers are key steps in advancing the transparency and credibility of geospatial studies. Another important point is the readiness of current standards for reproducible research. As [1] have pointed out, commonly used OGC standards do not guarantee the immutable access to a dataset in its status at a specific time of consumption. We therefore suggest that reproducibility should emphasized in the establishment of new standards and the adaptation of existing standards.

In light of this, we plan a subsequent iteration of the survey, aiming at expanding participation and gathering more comprehensive data from stakeholders.

References

1. Cannata, M., et al.: The challenges of reproducibility for research based on geodata web services (2023). https://doi.org/10.20944/preprints202312.2316.v1
2. Giuliani, G., Cazeaux, H., Burgi, P.Y., Poussin, C., Richard, J.P., Chatenoux, B.: SwissEnvEO: a fair national environmental data repository for earth observation open science. Data Sci. J. **20**, 22 (2021). https://doi.org/10.5334/dsj-2021-022
3. Hamdi, A., Shaban, K., Erradi, A., Mohamed, A., Rumi, S.K., Salim, F.D.: Spatiotemporal data mining: a survey on challenges and open problems. Artif. Intell. Rev. **55**(2), 1441–1488 (2021)
4. Kedron, P., Li, W., Fotheringham, S., Goodchild, M.: Reproducibility and replicability: opportunities and challenges for geospatial research. Int. J. Geogr. Inf. Sci. **35**(3), 427–445 (2020). https://doi.org/10.1080/13658816.2020.1802032
5. Konkol, M., Kray, C.: In-depth examination of spatiotemporal figures in open reproducible research. Cartography Geogra. Inf. Sci. **46**(5), 412–427 (2018). https://doi.org/10.1080/15230406.2018.1512421

6. Nüst, D., Pebesma, E.: Practical reproducibility in geography and geosciences. Ann. Am. Assoc. Geogr. **111**(5), 1300–1310 (2020)

7. Simoes, J., Cerciello, A.: Serving geospatial data using modern and legacy standards: a case study from the urban health domain. In: The International Archives of the Photogrammetry, Remote Sensing and Spatial Information Sciences, vol. XLVIII-4/W1-2022, pp. 419–425 (2022). https://doi.org/10.5194/isprs-archives-XLVIII-4-W1-2022-419-2022

Geospatial Technologies and Tools

TAME II: A Modern Geographic Text Annotation Tool

Jochen L. Leidner[1,2(✉)] ⓘ and Luca Jung[1]

[1] Information Access Research Group, Center for Research in Responsible Artificial Intelligence (CRAI), Coburg University of Applied Sciences and Arts, Friedrich-Streib-Straße 2, 96459 Coburg, Bavaria, Germany
[2] Department of Computer Science, University of Sheffield, Regents Court, 211, Portobello, Sheffield S1 4DP, UK
leidner@acm.org

Abstract. Toponym resolution can be defined as the process of mapping each toponyms in a document or corpus unambiguously to an associated spatial footprint corresponding to the location intended by the writer of a document. Various toponym resolution methods have been proposed that use the latitude and longitude of the centroids as the spatial representation, but arguably large cities regions or countries are poorly represented by a single point.

Two decades ago, Leidner presented TAME, the first geo-annotation tool described in the literature, but it (a) lacked extensibility (such as support for multiple users and multiple gazetteers), (b) it is not publicly available, and (c) it did not support polygon footprints. As a consequence, to date, in all annotated text collections, place names are associated exclusively using gazetteers with centroid geographic footprint representations.

In this paper, we present TAME II, a more flexible system for creating labeled corpora for the training of and evaluation of toponym resolvers, which supports multiple kinds of geographic footprint types (polygons, centroids and bounding rectangles. It has been implemented as a modern Web-based application that is available for the public on the Web. To the best of our knowledge, TAME II is the first text annotation tool that supports gazetteers with polygon footprints, and the first Web-based tool generally available.

1 Introduction

Since geographic space permeates all of human cognition and narration (everything happens *somewhere*), extracting spatial/geographic information from text

The authors gratefully acknowledge the funding provided by the Free State of Bavaria under its "Hitech Agenda". All views are the authors' and do not necessarily reflect the views of any funding agencies or affiliated institutions. We would like to thank Tim Menzner for helping with the cloud deployment of our system and the feedback of our three anonymous reviewers that improved the presentation of our paper.

M. Lotfian and L. L. L. Starace (Eds.): W2GIS 2024, LNCS 14673, pp. 95–104, 2024.
https://doi.org/10.1007/978-3-031-60796-7_7

has long been recognized as an important goal. Computing the mapping from mentions of toponyms (named places like urban dwellings or countries) to spatial footprints has been is called *toponym resolution* [11,12], and there have been many recent proposals for methods that use it to link so-called "unstructutred" textual prose to geographic representations, or rather, to make the geographies implicit in text collections explicit and therefore also computable: for instance, once we have latitude and longitude information available for mentions of `Berlin` and `Zürich` in an email, respectively, we can easily compute the travel distance between the two places mentioned or index them in a spatial search engine. The field of digital humanities can also benefit from the automated geo-spatial analysis by relating historic documents to geographic maps [7].

Many alternative methods for toponym resolution have been proposed in the literature, including heuristic algorithms [12,16], statistical correlation based methods [17], unsupervised [4,10], self-supervised [2,8] and supervised machine learning models [19]. To evaluate all of these methods and to train (induce the parameters of) the methods using machine learning, textual datasets are required in which named mentions of places are annotated by manual coders with spatial footprint information from a gazetteer [9].[1] For example, such an annotation could be the latitude/longitude of the centroid, given a text span that mentions the name of place (Fig. 1).

In this paper, we describe TAME II, a new Web-based annotation software tool that permits the annotation of multiple collections by multiple groups of annotators over the WWW. Specifically, it goes beyond the state of the art in that it supports the annotation of toponyms not just with centroids, but also with Minimum Bounding Boxes (MBRs) and polygons.

The remainder of this paper is structured as follows: Sect. 2 describes relevant related work. Section 3 describes the design and implementation of our system. Section 5 provides a qualitative (comparative) comparison with past work, and 6 summarizes and concludes with some suggestions for further research.

The TAME II software tool was developed as part of a long-term research program by the Information Access Research group directed by the first author to advance the state of the art in cross-walking the textual and geographical dimensions.

2   Related Work

In this section, we review several groups of past work: first, directly comparable systems for the annotation of text collection with geographic footprints, general annotation tools for text documents, and, last but not least, temporal annotation tools. See [12–14] for detailed surveys of toponym resolution and [6,15] for related technologies such as postal address geocoding.

---

[1]   A gazetteer is a geographic database consisting of triples $(t; f; g)$, where t is a toponym (place name), f is a feature type (such as dwelling, mountain, lake, human artifact etc.), and g is a geographic footprint, such as a centroid, bounding box or polygon representing the place in geographic space [9].

He took the noon flight from London to Toronto.
Because he had some time to kill, he had coffee
next to the cathedral dedicated to St. Peter.

He was glad to be on the DLR after landing in London on
time at City airport. Not only had his luggage
arrived, but also he succeeded in avoiding Heathrow;
he said down in a small cafe opposite St. Paul's.

Fig. 1. Mapping Toponym Mentions to Geographic Footprints: Two Londons (modified, Mercator map by Ste81 used under Creative Commons CC BY 3.0 – Source: Wikimedia Commons)

Annotation Tools for Text Documents. There is an abundance of general-purpose annotation tools that permit enriching a span of text with a class label (such as "LOCATION"), and associating further meta-data with it. For example, BRAT[2] is a configurable, Web-based open source text annotation tool [20]. The General Architecture for Text Engineering (GATE) [3] also has an integrated editor to highlight pieces of text and to associate arbitrary key-value pairs with it. However, such generic tools are ill-suited for annotating toponym mentions with spatial footprints: for instance, there are over 1600 "Santa Ana"s on earth, so looking up manually the right one from a list to enter it by hand would not be efficient – we need tool support for selecting the right referent among the set of candidates.

Existing Annotation Tools for Text Collection and Geo-Footprints. The first dedicated annotation tool for the toponym resolution task was TAME, the Toponym Annotation Markup Editor, as described in [11] and Sect. 4 of Leidner's Ph.D. thesis [12,13] (2007, 2008). In particular, pp. 126-130 are concerned with the TAME annotation tool and its use to create the TR-CoNLL and TR-MUC4 annotated datasets.[3] He also introduced the Toponym Resolu-

---

[2] not an acronym.

[3] CoNLL is the Conference for Natural Language Learning; in its 2003 edition the CoNLL dataset was released as part of a shared task for named entity tagging. MUC4 is the dataset reseased for the 4th Message Understanding Contests. The versions prefixed with "TR-" were additionally annotated with centroid footprint information as part of the first author's Ph.D. thesis, i.e. in addition to markup where a location name begins and ends, it was included what places with that name exist on earth, which latitude/longitude they correspond to, and which one is the one most likely intended by the author of the story.

tion Markup Language (TRML), an application of XML (the eXtensible Markup Language). Using TAME is very straight-forward Technically, TAME comprises of two scripts and a set of static XHTML pages, and has many drawbacks: it can only handle one particular (hardwired) gazetteer, it only permits centroid footprints and it has no user or collection management.

To the best of our knowledge, to date TAME is still the only toponym resolution-specialized tool described in the literature. However, it is neither flexible nor even available; therefore, our aim is to construct a superior replacement in the form of an application that can be deployed on the cloud.

Temporal Annotation of Text Documents. In our current four-dimensional world model of space-time, geographic space occupies three axes; complementary is the time axis, and therefore extracting temporal information from text ought to be discussed as related research for completeness' sake. TimeML[4] is a markup language, also based on XML. to enrich text with temporal information. It has been accepted as an ISO standard [18]. Callisto and TANGO (TimeML Annotation Graphical Organizer) are publicly shared tools developed as part of the ARDA AQUAINT question answering research initiative to annotate news stories with temporal information [21].

3   TAME II: The System

Figure 2 shows a sample news story being annotated in TAME II. In this section, we will describe the design, implementation and user interface of the system.

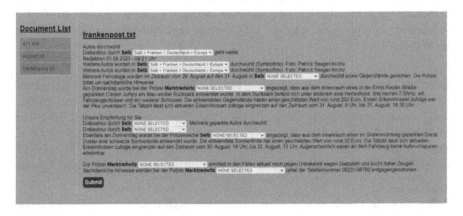

Fig. 2. Annotating a (German-language) Sample Document in TAME II

---

[4]   see https://timeml.github.io/site/publications/specs.html for the specification (accessed 2024-01-08).

3.1 Design

Whereas TAME was stateless, a collection of static Web pages held together by a common frame page rather than a real application, TAME II maintains state in its database, and provides application-typical functions like user management, dataset (collection) management, assignment of coders (annotators) to collections, access logging and – important for project management – a progress monitoring dashboard.

We adopted the TRML markup language due to its simplicity and because it has been adopted by several research groups, but extended it slightly to permit the representation of MBR and polygon footprints.

3.2 Implementation

We implemented TAME II in Python using the Flask[5] dynamic Web application framework, which provides convenient template mechanism to deal with boilerplate text automatically. The application offers standard user management and document collection management, including import of plain text, HTML, XTRML and export of XTRML files. The application also permits the assigning of work to users (coders) and keeps track of the degree of completion. The toponym lookup is implemented using the fast marisa library[6], which is a Python wrapper around an efficient C++ trie implementation [5]. The trie structure re-generation can be triggered automatically or manually from the GUI after gazetteers have been added or removed or the database has been modified manually, respectively.

4 User Interface

Figure 3 shows some functions available in the Web-based Graphical User Interface (GUI) of TAME II. Shown are the main menu and various dialogs to create new (initially empty) collections, to import sets of files into a collection (the only way to get data into the system; there is no editor for inputting files from scratch, as this tends not to be needed), assignment of collections to groups of annotators (coders), as well as deleting collections and re-building the trie.

The user does not have (nor need to have) direct contact with the footprints associated with a place: the annotation process happens by TAME II (as with TAME before) showing a HTML drop down menu with a set of choices distinguished from one another via textxual description of places. For instance, to choose that a "Paris" is in Texas rather than in France, simply select the second option out of a list:

```
Paris > France > Europe
Paris > TX > USA > North America
...
```

---

[5]   see https://flask.palletsprojects.com/en/3.0.x/ (accessed 2024-01-10) and https://github.com/pallets/flask (accessed 2024-01-10).

[6]   see https://github.com/pytries/marisa-trie (accessed 2024-01-10).

Internally, the right centroid, bounding box or polygon are then associated with the specific mention of Paris in the document.

5 Qualitative Comparative Evaluation

In this section, we compare TAME [11], the main existing geo-annotation tool described in the literature, with our novel system. While the purpose of both tools is the same, they are quite different from each other, so we present a qualitative comparison in Table 1 below.

Since between the implementation of TAME and TAME II, there was a twenty year timeframe, not surprisingly we were able to make the assumption of more powerful servers, and we used a different technology stack as mentioned above. TAME created static XHTML pages by one Perl script that were served by a second Perl (CGI) script, and annotations were written in the file system. In contrast TAME II uses Python's Flask framework and a modern relational database with user management, logging etc., so it can be hosted in the cloud and be used by multiple parallel projects with different datasets and users.

Compared to the original implementation of TAME, TAME II's gazetteers are not hardwired; new datasets can be imported at run-time, and the association between gazetteers and document collections is $m \times n$ and can be changed dynamically; in fact, the number of different gazetteers is only limited by RAM and the size of the integer type in Python.

The tool permits the selection of a CSV column as the key (e.g. toponymm), the footprint type, MBR lat/lons and/or the points making up polygons.

The selection of the "true" (correct, intended) referent from a set of candidates is done based on human-readable path descriptions like in the original TAME ("Dresden > Kreisfreie Stadt Dresden > Sachsen > Germany > Europe > Earth"), but where multiple footprint types are available a prefix indicating the Gazetteer name is added (e.g. "GN" → polygon, Geonames → centroid). The type of footprint (*footprint type*) can be either CENTROID, MBR, or POLYGON. TAME II also has a notion of reference type and feature type: a reference type is the type of a linguistic unit referring to a location (e.g. TOPONYM, ZIPCODE), whereas the feature type specifies the kind of geographic thing that is referred to (e.g. POPULATED_PLACE, ZIPCODE, OTHERS such as mountains, lakes). Finally, while TAME is not available, TAME II was designed to be hosted in the cloud for use by potentially multiple teams.

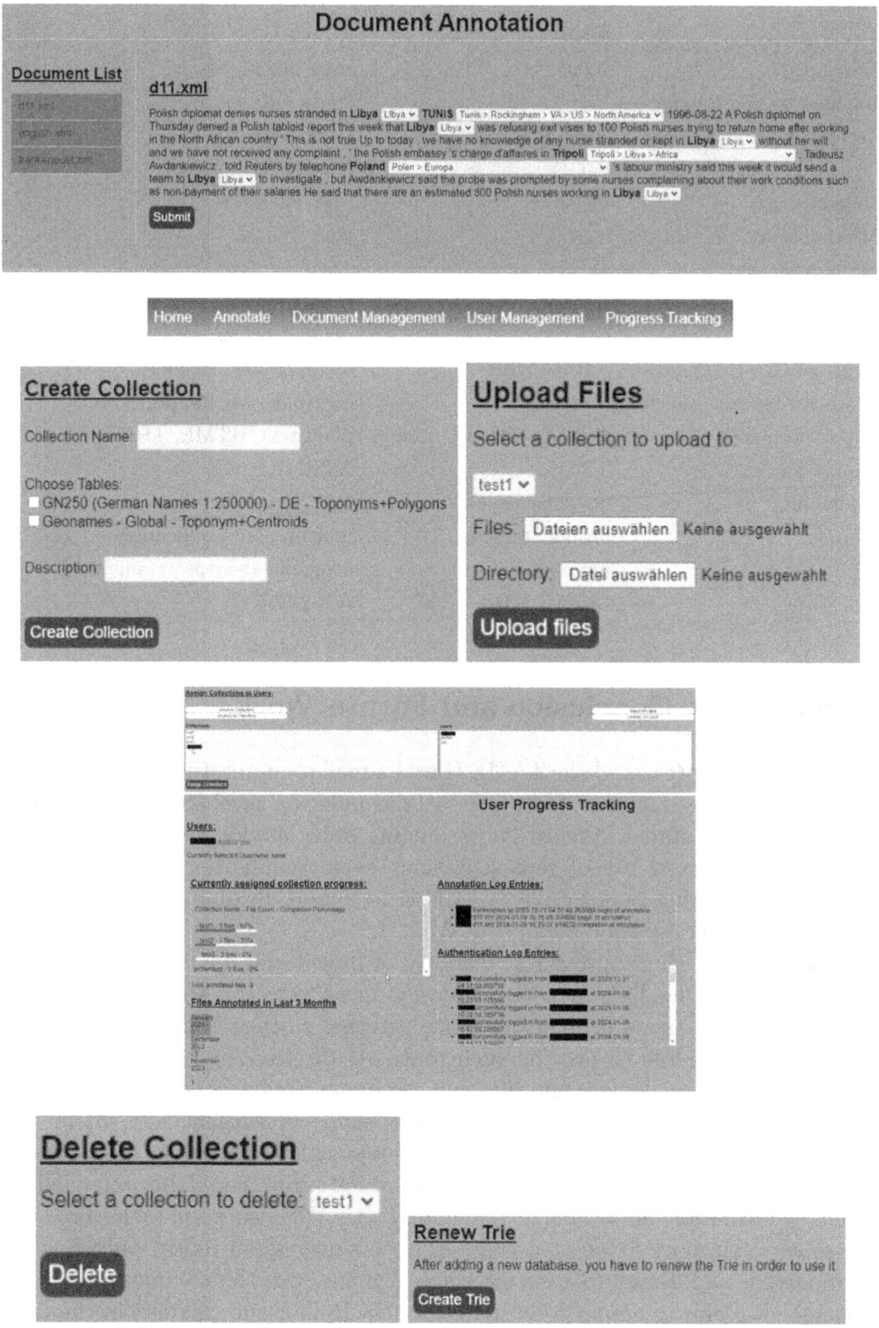

Fig. 3. A Selection of the Web-Based User Interface of TAME II

Table 1. Qualitative Evaluation: A Comparison between TAME and TAME II

	TAME	TAME II
Developed	2004	since 2023
Implementation language	Perl 5	Python 3
Technology	Web/XML	Web/XML
	(CGI)	(Flask)
Data storage	file store	SQL RDBMS
Multi-collection?	no	yes
Multi-gazetteer	no	yes
Gazetteers	1 (hardwired)	∞ (dynamically extensible)
Mixed representations	n/a	yes (>1 repres. type in same doc.)
Types of Geo-References	1 (toponyms)	3 (toponyms, zipcodes, others)
Footprint types supported	centroids only	centroids, MBRs, polygons
Import format(s)	CoNLL+TR BIO format	plain text/HTML, TRML/XTRML
Export format	TRML	XTRML
Availability	no/disposable	Web-accessible
	un-maintained,	multi-tenant application
	not available	available at https://tame2.org
Reference	Leidner [11]	*this paper*

6   Summary, Conclusion and Future Work

In this paper, we presented the TAME II tool aimed at annotating text document collections with geographic footprints at the mention level. Scientifically, our work extends the state of the art by permitting polygon footprints in gazetteers, by permitting mixed use of representations even within the same document. From an engineering perspective, TAME II is a more flexible and robust tool, which we are making available on the Web.

In conclusion, the improved availability of linked and open data, especially in the GIS space leads to new demands for more powerful software that uses it. Thankfully, progress in main memory, external storage and compute power have made it possible to provide such tools. *At the time of writing, TAME II is, to the best of our knowledge, the only geo-annotation tool generally available online, and the first annotation software that supports polygon footprints.*

In future work, we aim to improve the support for alternative ways to tokenize the input text. Spatial footprint representations could be extended to include information about fuzzy boundaries [1]. We also plan to localize the tool so as to support different user interface languages (currently, only English is supported, and standard user interface elements use the computer's default language - we aim to support German, French, Italian and Spanish in the near future) and improve keyboard shortcuts. Support for further markup formats is another possible venue for future work. Finally, small geographic maps depicting candidate locations potentially mentioned in the document shown at annotation time could facilitate and speed up the work of the human annotators.

References

1. Cadorel, L., Overal, D., Tettamanzi, A.G.B.: Fuzzy representation of vague spatial descriptions in real estate advertisements. In: Proceedings of Workshop on Location-Based Recommendations, Geosocial Networks and Geoadvertising Held at the 6th ACM SIGSPATIAL International. LocalRec '22, Association for Computing Machinery, New York, NY, USA (2022). https://doi.org/10.1145/3557992.3565994

2. Cardoso, A.B., Martins, B., Estima, J.: A novel deep learning approach using contextual embeddings for toponym resolution. ISPRS Int. J. Geo-Inf. **11**(1), 28 (2022). https://doi.org/10.3390/ijgi11010028

3. Cunningham, H., Humphreys, K., Gaizauskas, R., Wilks, Y.: GATE - a general architecture for text engineering. In: Fifth Conference on Applied Natural Language Processing: Descriptions of System Demonstrations and Videos, pp. 29–30. Association for Computational Linguistics, Washington, DC, USA (1997). https://doi.org/10.3115/974281.974299

4. DeLozier, G., Baldridge, J., London, L.: Gazetteer-independent toponym resolution using geographic word profiles. In: Proceedings of the Twenty-Ninth AAAI Conference on Artificial Intelligence, pp. 2382–2388. AAAI '15, AAAI Press (2015)

5. Fredkin, E.: Trie memory. Commun. ACM **3**(9), 490–499 (1960). https://doi.org/10.1145/367390.367400

6. Goldberg, D.W.: Geocoding. In: Castree, N., Goodchild, M.F., Kobayashi, A., Liu, W., Marston, R.A. (eds.) International Encyclopedia of Geography. People, the Earth, Environment and Technology, vol. 15, pp. 1–12. Wiley, New York, NY, USA, 1st edn. (2017).https://doi.org/10.1002/9781118786352.wbieg1051

7. Grover, C., et al.: Use of the edinburgh geoparser for georeferencing digitized historical collections. Philos. Trans. R. Soc. A: Math. Phys. Eng. Sci. **368**(1925), 3875–3889 (2010)

8. Haltermann, A.: Mordecai: Full text geoparsing and event geocoding. J. Open Source Softw. **2**(9), 91 (2017). https://doi.org/10.21105/joss.000911

9. Hill, L.L.: Georeferencing: The Geographic Associations of Information. MIT Press, Cambridge, MA, USA (2006)

10. Kamalloo, E., Rafiei, D.: A coherent unsupervised model for toponym resolution. In: Proceedings of the 2018 World Wide Web Conference, pp. 1287–1296. WWW '18, International World Wide Web Conferences Steering Committee, Republic and Canton of Geneva, CHE (2018). https://doi.org/10.1145/3178876.3186027

11. Leidner, J.L.: An evaluation dataset for the toponym resolution task. Comput. Environ. Urban Syst. **30**(4), 400–417 (2006). https://doi.org/10.1016/j.compenvurbsys.2005.07.003, geographic Information Retrieval (GIR)

12. Leidner, J.L.: Toponym Resolution in Text: Annotation, Evaluation and Applications of Spatial Grounding. Ph.D. thesis, School of Informatics, University of Edinburgh, Edinburgh, Scotland, UK (2007)

13. Leidner, J.L.: Toponym Resolution in Text: Annotation. Evaluation and Applications of Spatial Grounding. Universal Press, Boca Raton, FL, USA (2008)

14. Leidner, J.L.: Georeferencing: From texts to maps. In: Castree, N., Goodchild, M.F., Kobayashi, A., Liu, W., Marston, R.A. (eds.) International Encyclopedia of Geography. People, the Earth, Environment and Technology, vol. 15, pp. 1–10. Wiley, 1st edn. (2017).https://doi.org/10.1002/9781118786352.wbieg0160

15. Leidner, J.L.: A survey of textual data & geospatial technology. In: Werner, M., Chiang, Y.-Y. (eds.) Handbook of Big Geospatial Data, pp. 429–457. Springer, Cham (2021). https://doi.org/10.1007/978-3-030-55462-0_16

16. Leidner, J.L., Sinclair, G., Webber, B.: Grounding spatial named entities for information extraction and question answering. In: Proceedings of the Workshop on Analysis of Geographic References Held at HLT-NAACL 2003, pp. 31–38. ACL, Edmonton, Alberta, Canada (2003). https://aclanthology.org/W03-0105

17. Overell, S., Rüger, S.: Using co-occurrence models for placename disambiguation. Int. J. Geogr. Inf. Sci. 22(3), 265–287 (2008). https://doi.org/10.1080/13658810701626236

18. Pustejovsky, J., Lee, K., Bunt, H., Romary, L.: ISO-TimeML: an international standard for semantic annotation. In: Calzolari, N., (eds.) Proceedings of the Seventh International Conference on Language Resources and Evaluation (LREC'10). European Language Resources Association (ELRA), Valletta, Malta (2010)

19. Speriosu, M., Baldridge, J.: Text-driven toponym resolution using indirect supervision. In: Schütze, H., Fung, P., Poesio, M. (eds.) Proceedings of the 51st Annual Meeting of the Association for Computational Linguistics, pp. 1466–1476. Association for Computational Linguistics, Sofia, Bulgaria (2013)

20. Stenetorp, P., Pyysalo, S., Topić, G., Ohta, T., Ananiadou, S., Tsujii, J.: BRAT: a web-based tool for NLP-assisted text annotation. In: Segond, F. (ed.) Proceedings of the Demonstrations at the 13th Conference of the European Chapter of the Association for Computational Linguistics, pp. 102–107. Association for Computational Linguistics, Avignon, France (2012)

21. Verhagen, M., et al.: Automating temporal annotation with TARSQI. In: Nagata, M., Pedersen, T. (eds.) Proceedings of the ACL, pp. 81–84. Association for Computational Linguistics, Ann Arbor, MI, USA (2005). https://doi.org/10.3115/1225753.1225774

Towards OGC API - Features Centric GIS Applications Controlled by Object Relational Mapping

Olivier Monod[1(✉)] and Denis Rouzaud[2]

[1] Ville d'Yverdon-les-Bains, 1400 Yverdon-les-Bains, Switzerland
`sit@yverdon-les-bains.ch`
[2] OPENGIS.ch GmbH, 7031 Laax, Switzerland

Abstract. Most common GIS applications are composed of a spatially enabled database and a desktop client directly connected to it. In this configuration the business logic is often found either in the client application with custom plugins or in the database where many triggers are defined. When it comes to web GIS applications, a cartographic server is added in between the database and a web client. In this paper, we present an alternative setup where the data-model and the business logic are both defined in Python programming language using the Django web framework ORM. Both desktop and web clients exchange data through OGC services. In addition, the business logic is implemented in a middleware in a Django application. While mitigating the issues we face in standard PostGIS-based solutions, the Django ecosystem also comes with powerful tools offering interesting perspectives for such applications.

Keywords: Geographic Information Systems · OGC API - Features · Object Relational Mapping · QField · QGIS · PostGIS · Geo Data · Infrastructure · Django web framework

1 Introduction

Geographic Information System applications (GIS) developers and integrators face the challenge of keeping a good operation to new feature development ratio. The operations cost can rapidly climb due to the ever increasing number of data synchronization and code maintenance tasks. Despite well documented, good infrastructure design and performant Extract Transform Load softwares (ETL), it soon gets hard to keep operation overhead under control, lost in a sea of multiformat file based data exchanges and database models propagation procedures. In this paper, we detail one possible design that can help to keep operations costs under control. We illustrate the whole discussion with a real life example of gas and water network components in situ controls application on which we plan to apply this design in the future.

We compare the current architecture used with the future design that we imagine, based on tightly coupled Object Relational Mapping (ORM) [2], "a programming technique for converting data between a relational database and

M. Lotfian and L. L. L. Starace (Eds.): W2GIS 2024, LNCS 14673, pp. 105–113, 2024.
https://doi.org/10.1007/978-3-031-60796-7_8

the heap of an object-oriented programming language" [1] and OGC API - Features standard. This Open Geospatial Consortium (OGC) standard is defined as "a multi-part standard that offers the capability to create, modify, and query spatial data on the Web and specifies requirements and recommendations for APIs that want to follow a standard way of sharing feature data" [3].

In the end we acknowledge that GIS applications can take advantage of keeping as close as possible to web standards, creating specific tools only where absolutely necessary.

2   GIS Tools for Utility Management in Yverdon-les-Bains

For a long time, periodic controls of the fluid network infrastructure have been done using paper forms that were then reported into a digital solution manually, inducing a significant and useless overhead. In order to digitize this work, looking for an Open Source solution, the QField [7] option was high on the list of potential candidates. QField is an Open Source, mobile, multi-platform (Android, iOS, Windows) GIS application based on QGIS [8], a very popular Open Source desktop GIS application. QField allows fast and seamless fieldwork. The usual setup would have been:

- Setup an offline project, including local geodata.
- Send the field workers do the job with offline devices.
- Synchronize the new data back into the Geographic Data Infrastructure (GDI) using USB connection for data download and ETL script or sync plugin for data insertion into the database.

While this would have been easy to build for the GIS specialists, it wouldn't have been as convenient as wished for the field workers due to the operations required back at the office to ensure new geodata ends at the right place. That is why the choice was made to use OGC Services as data sources for every layer on Global System for Mobile Communications (GSM) connected devices, assuming full mobile network coverage over the working area. The resulting architecture removes all usual synchronization tasks.

It turns out that the solution worked well and that users adopted the new way of working quite easily. In 2023, a total of 4929 field controls of the water and gas valves were conducted by 4 technicians in charge of the pipe network infrastructure (Fig. 1).

2.1   Results

The good adoption of the solution and motivation of the field workers resulted in an impressive data collection over the three last years, reaching a total of 9344 field controls for the 2021–2023 years. This emphasizes also the excellent User Experience (UX) proposed by Open Source mobile mapping solution QField [7] (Fig. 2).

Fig. 1. Map of in situ controls for gas and water network components in 2023

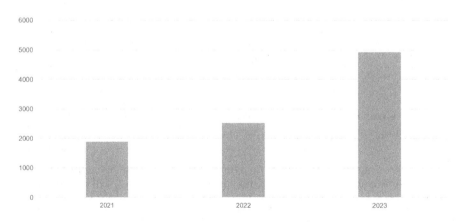

Fig. 2. Number of in situ controls per year

2.2 Current Architecture

Description. A quite usual architecture was designed at this time: Web Feature Service (OGC WFS 2) [6] is deployed using QGIS [7] server connected to the postGIS database. Authentication and user management is done in Geomapfish Open Source geoportal [4] in which a OAauth2 backend have been implemented

(Fig. 3). The project was setup on the Geomapfish instance in Yverdon-les-Bains: Géoportail du Nord vaudois [5].

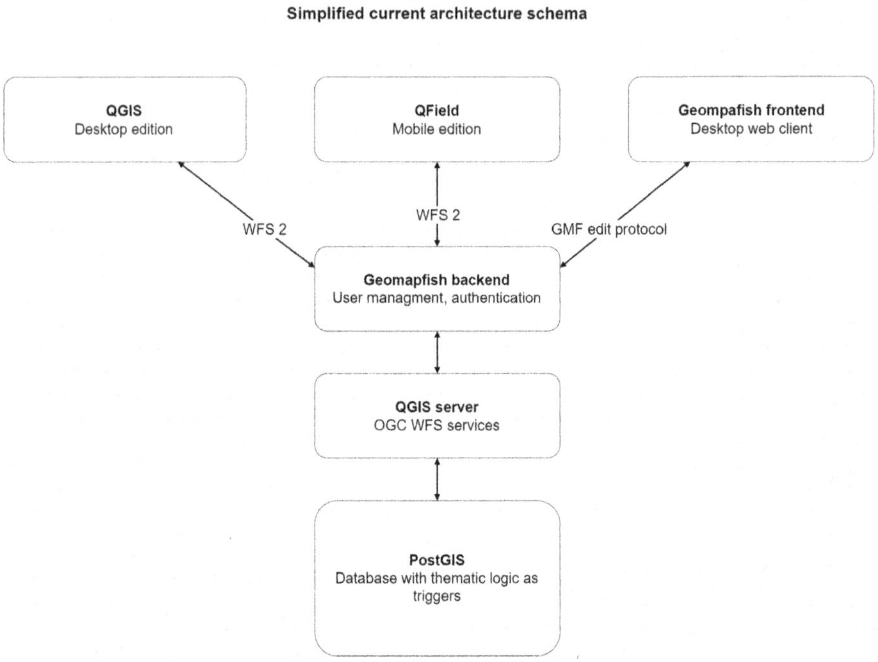

Fig. 3. Simplified current architecture schema

Pros and Cons of the Current Architecture. After a few years in production following advantages and drawbacks are identified.

    Pros

- Low operations costs as almost no synchronizations tasks are required.
- Usual approach for development, no special programming skill needed.

    Cons

- Limited support for debug tools. It is often not trivial to identify which layer of the stack causes problems.
- When adding new fields, value lists, etc. Many manual operations are required: edit database models, adapt the web services, adapt the qgis project.
- Very limited possibilities to implement unit tests.
- Even minor configuration (ex: adding a value to a list) task have to be done by the GDI administrators.
- The propagation of database models changes requires manual work for each instance. Manual adaptations of ETL scripts are also needed and no automation exists to notice the changes to dependent applications.

3   The Object Relational Mapping Proposal with Django

Django is one of the most popular web frameworks written in Python that embrace the Don't Repeat Yourself (DRY) programming principle: "Django makes it easier to build better web apps more quickly and with less code" [9]. The most important difference that distinguishes Django from other Python frameworks is its integrated Object Relational Mapping which makes it particularly easy to work with complex data models and to manage models changes (migrations) efficiently. Furthermore as for the whole framework, the ORM documentation is of very high quality. Besides, Django ships with lots of features that can be useful in any GIS application:

- Integrated security.
- Out-of-the-box administration interface with user management.
- Authentication.
- Popular and well maintained packages such as: multi-tenant; simple historization; oauth clients, oauth backend.
- And last but not least to us: GIS enabled data model with the Geospatial Data Abstraction Library (GDAL) and GEOS integration.
- Spatial extension of Django Rest Framework.

3.1   Controlling a Geo Data Infrastructure with an Object Relational Mapping: What's the Benefit?

Django ORM and migration tools offer a structured, controlled way to manage the database models and maps these models with corresponding Python classes. Thus, the models definition is done in Python using Django syntax. Any model change will then have to be made on the Python class and will be then materialized in the database using the migration tool. Introducing middleware between the webservice and the database allows the developers to implement business logic without the need of adding triggers in the database or developing specific plugins in the client. As an example, for electric network GIS, the application has to ensure that when a tube linestring is divided, related cables linestrings also get divided in a coherent manner.

Many Open Source solutions support OGC API - Features service deployment, among them: QGIS server; mapserver; geoserver; and for Python enthusiasts: pygeoapi. At this point, one could question the rational for a new development.

Without this new tool we would miss some interesting features: easy way to work with complex database relations; easy resolution of value list; avoid writing raw SQL that is difficult to maintain.

But the most important aspect with the perspective of building complex GIS applications is that if we connect one cartographic server directly to the Postgis backend, we are losing the entire business logic offered by our middleware approach, making it a bad solution for applications that do more than publishing layers or editing basic data models.

3.2   The Django-Oapif Package: Single Liner OGC Service Deployment

With the objective of replacing complex network management solutions in the future, a Proof of Concept [10,11] has been realized by OPENGIS Gmbh in 2023. The goal was to validate the direct deployment of a Django model as an OGC service and identify potential limitations.

Development. The result is very efficient in terms of coding simplicity. The new Django package allows to deploy an OGC API - Features service with a single line of code placed on top of the model definition as illustrated in Listing 1.1. With such a tool, it is quite easy to build a new infrastructure (Fig. 5).

```
from django.contrib.gis.db import models
from django_oapif.decorators import register_oapif_viewset

@register_oapif_viewset(crs=2056)
class SwissMunicipalities(models.Model):
id = models.UUIDField(
  primary_key=True,
  default=uuid.uuid4,
  editable=False)
name = models.CharField()
geom = models.MultiPolygonField(srid=2056)
```

Listing 1.1. Python code sample

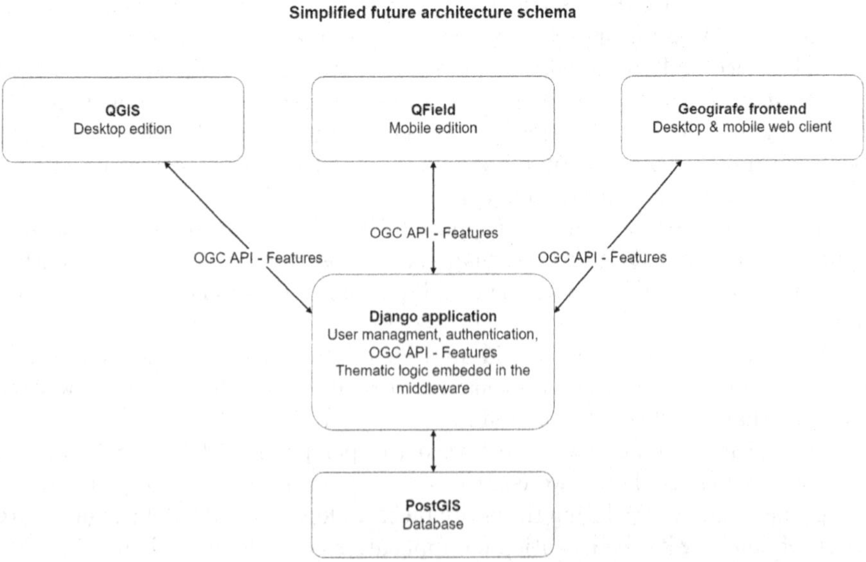

Simplified future architecture schema

Fig. 4. Benchmark of feature fetching time

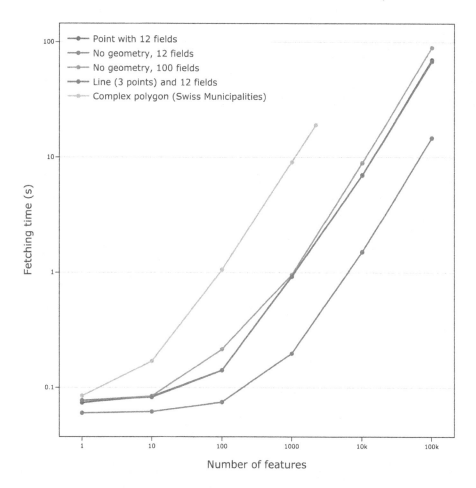

Fig. 5. Simplified future architecture schema

Performance. Since the start of this project, we have been expecting some poor performance in terms of reading time. Fetching a complete layer (known as a collection in Django) might take quite some time (Fig. 4).

As we could have expected, the fetching time is becoming linear after a certain threshold, between 10 to 1000 features depending on the complexity of the serialization.

Profiling showed the serialization of the geometry was a significant part of the cost. Here serialization consists in turning the binary geometry representation into, roughly, a JSON list of coordinates. Instead of achieving this in Django, we tried to delegate this process to Postgis by using one of its native function. This gave very satisfying results (Fig. 6).

Depending on the number and type of features, the gain is within 50 to 200%.

Geometry serialization

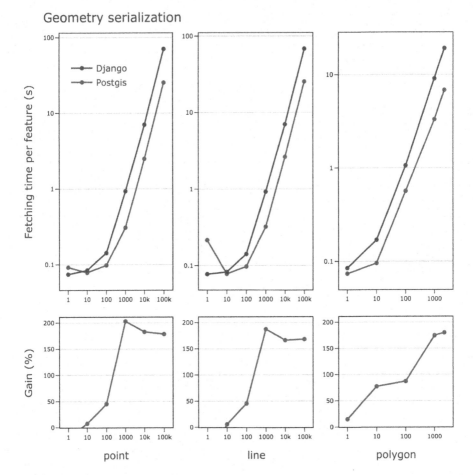

Fig. 6. Benchmark of geometry serialization

4 Conclusion

Using an ORM and django-oapif will require a little more coding literacy from GIS application integrators than before. But in return, maintenance costs of business logic that is distributed in plugins or in the database will sink. Furthermore, GDI administrators will gain better control over the data structures and their evolution making it more robust and understandable. Introducing this middleware approach in GIS applications enable the centralized implementation of complex business logic in a well defined manner and simplifies update process. With the emergence of this architecture design, we hope the gap between advanced desktop GIS solution and web GIS or mobile applications will reduce. The next step will be in the near future to implement a real world GIS application for underground utility network management. Confronting the key concepts mentioned in this article with down-to-earth operational challenges will for sure require new evolutions. The important advantage here is that the proposed here will be easy to adapt to new requirements, and in that sens, is particularly future proof.

Acknowledgment. Django-oapif Proof Of Concept development was funded by: Ville d'Yverdon-les-Bains, Ville de Morges, Ville de Nyon.

References

1. Wikipedia contributors, Wikipedia ORM definition. https://en.wikipedia.org/wiki/Object-relational-mapping. Accessed 18 Jan 2024
2. Torres, A., Galante, R., Pimenta, M.S., Martins, A.J.B.: Twenty years of object-relational mapping: a survey on patterns, solutions, and their implications on application design. Inf. Softw. Technol. **82**, 1–18 (2017)
3. Open Geospatial Consortium, OGC API Features definition. https://ogcapi.ogc.org/features/. Accessed 18 Jan 2024
4. Geomapfish Project Steering Committee, Geomapfish project presentation. https://geomapfish.org. Accessed 18 Jan 2024
5. Ville d'Yverdon-les-Bains, Géoportail du Nord vaudois plateforme. https://mapnv.ch. Accessed 5 Feb 2024
6. Open Geospatial Consortium, OGC Web Feature Service definition. https://www.ogc.org/standard/wfs/. Accessed 18 Jan 2024
7. OPENGIS.ch GmbH, QField application presentation. https://qfield.org. Accessed 18 Jan 2024
8. QGIS community, QGIS application presentation. https://ggis.org. Accessed 18 Jan 2024
9. Django community, The Django web framework presentation. https://www.djangoproject.com/. Accessed 18 Jan 2024
10. OPENGIS.ch GmbH, Django OGC API - Features by OPENGIS repository. https://github.com/opengisch/django-ogcapif. Accessed 18 Jan 2024
11. OpenWisp, Django DRF GIS repository. https://github.com/openwisp/django-rest-framework-gis. Accessed 18 Jan 2024
12. Django community, Geodjango contribution presentation. https://docs.djangoproject.com/en/5.0/ref/contrib/gis/. Accessed 18 Jan 2024

Advanced Computing and GIS Applications

Smooth Building Footprint Aggregation with Alpha Shapes

Stefan Funke[1(✉)] and Sabine Storandt[2]

[1] University of Stuttgart, Stuttgart, Germany
funke@fmi.uni-stuttgart.de
[2] University of Konstanz, Konstanz, Germany
storandt@inf.uni-konstanz.de

Abstract. We propose a method to continuously aggregate building footprints into generalized polygons. This enables smooth zooming that preserves information about dense built-up areas even in coarse-grained views. The goal is to compute a set of polygons for each zoom level that describe the built-up areas well. At the same time, the complexity of the polygons should be low to allow for efficient rendering and easy visual comprehension. Previous approaches for building footprint generalization are quite involved and often come with handcrafted rules for different building shapes and aggregation steps. We show that α-shapes, a generalization of convex hulls, can be elegantly instrumented to retrieve suitable outline polygons for clustered building sets at any desired level of detail. To form clusters, we use the proximity information obtained from a Delaunay triangulation of the buildings exterior. The clusters are then approximated by α-shapes (which are themselves based on Delaunay triangulations). We conduct an experimental evaluation on buildings extracted from OSM up to a country-sized data set containing more than 30 million building footprints. We show that our new method efficiently produces concise polygons for all zoom levels that capture the shape of the built-up areas well.

Keywords: Delaunay triangulation · Alpha shape · Map generalization

1 Introduction

Map generalization is a well-studied problem in cartographic visualization [15,17]. Given a set of input geometries, the goal is to find a sensible visual abstraction that still conveys the important spatial information. Reduced visual complexity helps to avoid visual clutter and allows for more efficient storage and rendering. One prominent use case is spatial object visualization on zoomable digital maps. Here, not just a single generalization of the input objects is needed, but a series of generalizations that cater to the different zoom levels. Continuous zooming is achieved if the generalization sequence does not only consist of an

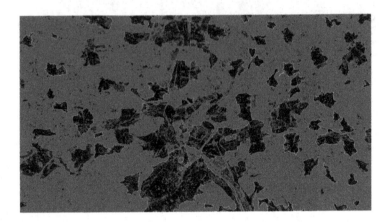

Fig. 1. Example map. The original building footprints are drawn in black, the colored polygons correspond to identified clusters and their respective approximations.

a priori fixed number of zoom levels but allows smooth level of detail selection for arbitrary zoom levels. There exist many different generalization concepts that potentially allow for continuous zooming, including shape simplification and feature elimination, object fading or shrinking, as well as object growing and clustering or aggregation of different objects [3,5,12].

In this paper, we focus on building footprints as input objects. Without proper generalization, buildings quickly disappear in zoomed out views, as their size becomes too small with respect to the total view area. However, the information about the location of dense built-up areas might be of interest also in coarser views. Thus, the generalization concepts of object growing, clustering and aggregation are useful in this context. Indeed, there are already several generalization methods for building footprints that use one or more of these concepts [2,14,18,19]. However, most of them require the application of rather complicated rules for different building types and also a suitable selection of multiple parameters in order to achieve visually pleasing results.

We propose a new framework for building footprint generalization that makes use of general methods for polygon clustering and simplification. Our framework scales to large input sizes and allows for smooth zooming and level of detail selection. Figure 1 shows example maps generated with our approach.

1.1 Related Work

The problem of generalizing a given collection of regions on a map to ensure their visibility on coarse views was discussed thoroughly in [8]. They propose to grow the region polygons when zooming out, while maintaining the topology, area-ratios, and relative positions of the input polygons. However, the approach is not ideal for large sets of small polygons as e.g. building footprints, as no aggregation happens and thus on zoomed out views still thousands of individual polygons need to be drawn.

In [18], methods to simplify individual polygons were introduced. The proposed framework consists of various steps and algorithms, including a classification of buildings based on their local structures, applying rule-based simplification for each building class, and template matching. Shape preservation and area preservation are discussed as quality measures of the obtained results. Another approach for individual building simplification was described in [19], here with a special focus on maintaining existing orthogonal substructures of the building footprints. In [4], buildings and other polygons were simplified iteratively by conducting so called edge-move operations. The method maintains in the simplification a subset of the orientations of the input polygon to enhance visual similarity. They also describe how to make their algorithm topology- and area-preserving. While approaches for individual building simplification help to reduce the drawing complexity on smaller scales significantly, they are not suitable to produce meaningful zoomed out views due to missing aggregation.

In [14], an approach based on individual simplification, growing and aggregation was presented. Here, buildings close to one another are connected with artificial bridges, and the resulting bridged building complexes then grow with respect to the zoom level, and form new bridges when growing close to each other. The growing process is realized by buffering the building complex polygons with miter joins of different shape. Then, dilation and erosion operations are used to smooth the polygon before applying polyline simplification to reduce its complexity further. All these operations require some thresholds or parameters to be chosen appropriately. Finally, holes are removed from polygons and too small polygons are pruned. The running time of the approach is in $\mathcal{O}(n^3)$ where n denotes the number of edges used to describe the input building footprints.

Another approach for building generalization that incorporates aggregation was proposed in [2]. Similar to our method, they first construct a constrained Delaunay triangulation on the building footprints. On this basis, they compute a so called triangle skeleton that is somewhat similar to a Voronoi diagram on the input polygons but might contain non-convex cells. Based on the triangle skeleton, distribution density and proximity between the polygons is measured. Then an involved merging process is conducted based on these statistics. Building aggregation relies on first rastering the buildings and then filling up empty rows and columns between the individual buildings. Another algorithm that relies on Delaunay triangulation for neighborhood detection and building clustering was described in [1]. Sophisticated methods for displacing and aggregating buildings based on this neighborhood information are discussed there. The approach was shown to compare favorably to the basic polygon aggregation algorithm implemented in ArcGIS with respect to the constructed built-up area sizes.

1.2 Contribution

In this paper, we present a novel approach for smooth building footprint aggregation and generalization. It relies on first clustering buildings and then computing outline polygons of low complexity for each cluster. Both steps are based on Delaunay triangulating the input polygons' exterior corners. In the clustering step, buildings that are connected with Delaunay edges up to a certain length are combined. Based on Kruskal's algorithm, the clusters for all edge length bounds can be computed in time $\mathcal{O}(n \log n)$ in total. Then, for each cluster, we compute the α-shape of the contained buildings to produce a polygon that represents their aggregation. The concept of α-shapes generalizes the notion of a convex hull. The choice of α allows trade-offs between the size of the enclosed area and the complexity of the polygon. α-shapes can be computed efficiently based on a given Delaunay triangulation. We demonstrate the scalability and output quality of our framework on real-world building footprint data from OSM.

2   Building Generalization Pipeline

In this section, we describe the steps of our building generalization pipeline in detail and discuss how to derive suitable visualizations for any desired zoom level. The input is assumed to be a set of polygons that describe building footprints. Each polygon is given as a closed sequence of points in the plane specified by their spatial coordinates. Building polygons may not self-intersect but they are allowed to have holes that are described by sets of internal polygons. We use n to describe the total complexity of the input polygons, that is, n is the number of polygon edges used to describe all building footprints. For the whole of Germany, we have around 36 million buildings mapped in OpenStreetMap and $n \approx 183$ million. See Fig. 2, left, for an example of downtown Stuttgart.

2.1   Delaunay-Based Clustering

Our pipeline crucially relies on the computation of Delaunay triangulation (DT) on the vertices of the building footprints. For a set of points in the Euclidean plane, a DT is a triangulation of the point set where no point is inside the circumcircle of any triangle. DTs maximize the minimum angle of all the triangles. There are many application realms of DTs, for example, in the context of computer vision or routing [10,13]. Furthermore, DT edges usually connect close-by points and therefore the DT is well-suited as a basis for proximity computation and clustering [9]. It is also possible to Delaunay triangulate a set of polygon edges in a so-called constrained Delaunay triangulation (CDT) ([6]), yet for our purposes a simple triangulation of all building vertices suffices. Both DT as well as CDT can be computed in time $\mathcal{O}(n \log n)$ and result in a data structure of size $\mathcal{O}(n)$. Figure 2, right, shows the Delaunay triangulation of the building vertices on the left.

Given the DT, a simple way of clustering the building polygons is to select an edge length threshold β and to put all buildings that are connected with a DT edge of length at most β into one cluster. For fixed β, the clustering can be computed in time $\mathcal{O}(n)$ by first iterating over all edges, marking the ones that are sufficiently short, and then extracting the connected components of the graph that consist of a node for each building footprint and the set of marked edges between them. However, as our goal is to support continuous zooming,

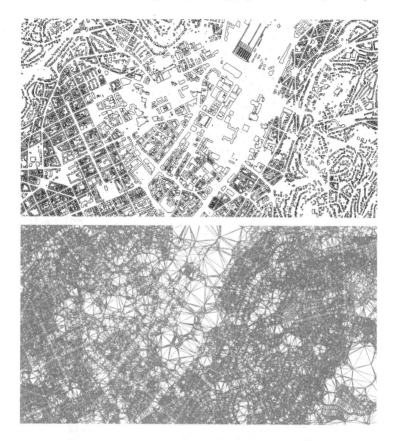

Fig. 2. Top: Raw building data from OpenStreetMap, Bottom: Delaunay triangulation of building vertices. Visualized are all Delaunay edges falling below a selected length threshold β.

we would like to compute the clustering for each possible β, that is, for each edge length occurring in the DT. As there are $\mathcal{O}(n)$ such edges, conducting the above described algorithm for each edge length individually would take time $\mathcal{O}(n^2)$. But we can do much better by leveraging Kruskal's minimum spanning tree algorithm. Here, we first sort the edges increasingly by length and consider each node (in our application each building) as cluster of their own. Then, the edges are considered one-by-one in that order. Whenever an edge connects two distinct clusters, the clusters are combined into one. The running time of the algorithm depends on the efficiency of a dynamic union-find data structure that determines whether an edge is between nodes within one cluster or between two nodes from different clusters, and then updates the clusters accordingly. Using a proper union find data structure, the total running time of the clustering is in $\mathcal{O}(n \log n + n\alpha(n))$ where the first part stems from the initial sorting step. Here,

$\alpha(n)$ denotes the very slow growing inverse Ackermann function. Thus, we can compute the set of all clusters for all β threshold in $\mathcal{O}(n \log n)$ in total.

Note that with increasing β the clusters can only get new members but never evict buildings. This is important to ensure visual consistency between different zoom levels. See Fig. 3 for an example in the suburbs of Stuttgart. For smaller values of β, many villages are clusters themselves (top) whereas for larger values of β, nearby villages merge to larger clusters (bottom).

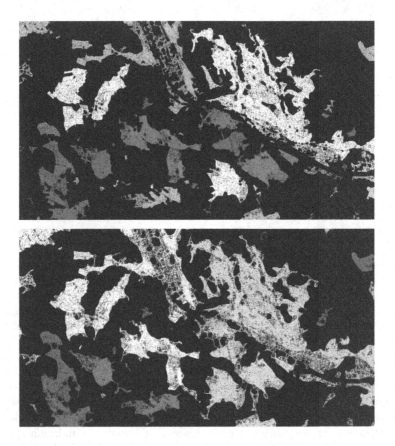

Fig. 3. Two different clusterings based on the Delaunay triangulation.

2.2   Aggregation and Simplification with α-Shapes

Given the input building polygons and the set of clusters for one particular edge threshold, the goal is now to aggregate the polygons in each cluster to derive a suitable visualization. A simple way of aggregation is to compute for each cluster the bounding box or the convex hull of its members. These naive approaches lead to cluster polygons of low complexity, which is beneficial for rendering. But by enforcing convexity, it is very likely that these polygons cover large areas which do not contain any cluster members. This distorts the perception of the built-up area size and also makes the visualization very sensitive to the location of individual buildings.

In order to achieve better trade-offs between the area of the cluster polygons and the complexity, the notion of α-shapes [11] can be instrumented. For a set of points P in the Euclidean plane, an edge between $p, q \in P$ is part of the α-shape, if there exists a circle of radius α with p and q on its boundary and no other point of P inside this circle. Clearly, the set of α-shape edges is a subset of the Delaunay edges, and indeed, for a given α one can determine the set of α-shape edges in linear time.

See Fig. 4 for a schematic illustration of α-shapes for decreasing values of α. For very large values of α we simply obtain the convex hull of the point set. By decreasing α, we increase the complexity of the shape approximation and also outline concavities; for too small values of α, though, the resulting shape becomes disconnected.

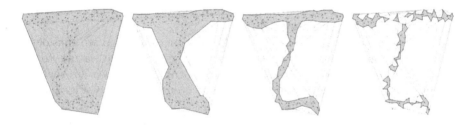

Fig. 4. The α-shape for decreasing values of α.

2.3 Visualization Pipeline

Depending on the application scenario, our computation can be partitioned into a preprocessing phase and and an online phase.

Preprocessing. In any case, construction of the Delaunay triangulation as well as the Delaunay clustering can take place at preprocessing time.

On-Demand Aggregation and Simplification. In an map rendering context, one is typically interested in rendering of the map at a certain level-of-detail and a certain geographic region. In terms of building data, the desired level-of-detail is determined by a clustering (i.e., a β-value) as well as α-values for the individual cluster approximations).

For a given geographic region one determines all the clusters intersecting the region and computes for each of those clusters their *alpha*-shape approximation. Then, for each cluster one starts with a large α (corresponding to the convex hull of the cluster) and decreases α (increasing the complexity of the cluster approximation) depending on the desired quality of the cluster approximation, also see Fig. 4. α can be decreased as long as the resulting set of edges forms a single closed loop to avoid disconnectedness as in Fig. 4, right.

This approach is feasible for small, i.e., very zoomed-in geographic regions. For very large regions like a whole country, the time to construct the α-shape on demand might be prohibitive for interactive response times. Alternatively, we can also precompute data for a small set of different levels of detail. Note that unfortunately we cannot simply use the DT of the complete point set (as computed in the preprocessing phase), as the DT of a set of points corresponding to a cluster is not necessarily a subset of the complete DT.

Precomputed Aggregation and Simplification. To avoid the running time overhead of constructing α-shapes for the clusters on demand, we can define certain levels-of-detail and precompute the α-shapes for the complete map. This is even feasible for a rather large number of levels-of-detail, since the size of the α-shape approximations is almost negligible in size compared to the building data itself as we will see in our experimental section. How would one choose parameters for such a level-of-detail?

As a first step one should decide at what distance buildings are considered to be in the same cluster. In Fig. 5, left the respective β value was set to the equivalent of around 200 m. There, most settlements in the area are separate clusters. When increasing β to an equivalent of around 500 m, see Fig. 5, right, nearby settlements are merged into the same cluster resulting in fewer and larger clusters. Note, that very small clusters are ignored on purpose. By choosing a larger α we can also get a coarser approximation of each individual cluster shape. In Fig. 5, right, we chose an α about twice the size of the left.

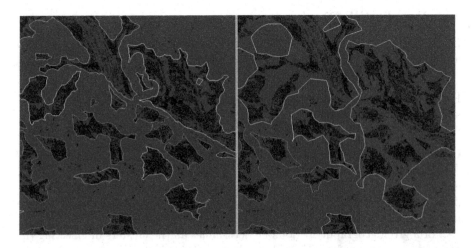

Fig. 5. Variation of Level-of-Detail by varying β and α.

For each of the chosen levels-of-detail one would compute the α-shapes for all clusters in the complete map and store the respective edges in a suitable indexing data structure for quick retrieval and rendering.

3   Experimental Evaluation

Our (single-threaded) C++ implementation was benchmarked on a desktop system with an AMD Ryzen 5600x runnning Ubuntu 22.04. We used three different data sets extracted from the OpenStreetMap project to assess scalability, see Table 1. Extraction time denotes the time to extract the building data using libosmium ([7]). Delaunay time is the running time for constructing the Delaunay triangulation using CGAL ([16]). We see that these preparatory stages of our pipeline can easily be executed even on a country-level scale (probably also on a planet-scale with a sufficiently powerful server or workstation as the the running times scale near-linearly). On average a building footprint is a polygon with around 5 vertices (most buildings are simple rectangles).

3.1   Levels-of-Detail

We have three key parameters to guide the aggregation process: the *clustering distance* β which determines which buildings will end up in the same cluster, the *shape approximation Parameter* α which determines how an individual cluster is approximated, and the *minimum cluster size* μ which determines what clusters are considered too small (in terms of number of points) to be represented at all. Instead of choosing a fixed α, our routine first computes the smallest α_min for which the cluster approximation is still a simple closed polygon. We then multiply α_{min} with a factor α_{mul} to decrease the complexity of the α-shape, i.e., $\alpha := \alpha_{min} \cdot \alpha_{mul}$.

For simplicity we considered 5 parameter choices which we deem sufficient for most application scenarios:

VillageFine: city districts are still represented as distinct clusters; $\beta = 125$, $\alpha_{mul} = 7$, $\mu = 250$

VillageCoarse: city districts typically merge into one cluster while different cities remain distinct clusters; $\beta = 250$, $\alpha_{mul} = 10$, $\mu = 1{,}000$

MetroFine: cities within a metropolitan areas merge, medium sized cities are still present; $\beta = 500$, $\alpha_{mul} = 10$, $\mu = 4{,}000$

Table 1. Data sets from OpenStreetMap

	Regierungsbezirk Stuttgart	Baden-Württemberg	Germany
buildings	1.6 M	4.7M	36.2M
vertices	7.9M	23.1M	183.3M
extraction time	7.8 s	23.8 s	195.8 s
Delaunay time	5.0 s	16.5 s	153.9 s

MetroCoarse: metropolitan areas merge and are coarsely approximated; medium sized cities are pruned; $\beta = 500$, $\alpha_{mul} = 40$, $\mu = 40,000$

CountryView: only metropolitan areas survive and are coarsely approximated; $\beta = 500$, $\alpha_{mul} = 160$, $\mu = 400,000$

All these parameters are monotonously increasing as we want larger and larger clusters which are approximated more and more coarsely. In Table 2 we show details about the precomputation time as well as the complexity of the resulting aggregation. For example, precomputing aggregations for the whole of Germany at the MetroCoarse level took less than 9 min and resulted in 50,218 α-shape segments. Compared to the around 183M vertices of all buildings in Germany, storing the five aggregations is negligible in terms of space consumption (around 6 million edges, represented by two vertex IDs each).

Table 2. Precomputation time and resulting number of edges.

	Regierungsbezirk Stuttgart		Baden-Württemberg		Germany	
	precomp. time	# edges	precomp. time	#edges	precomp. time	# edges
VillageFine	21.5 s	142,802	63.0 s	437,401	537.5 s	3,859,933
VillageCoarse	25.8 s	56,427	75.2 s	182,124	642.0 s	1,507,124
MetroFine	37.3 s	17,585	91.0 s	60,081	730.8 s	447,698
MetroCoarse	27.8 s	2,079	59.4 s	6,772	510.8 s	50,218
Country	18.1 s	261	30.6 s	491	342.9 s	4,592

To give a visual impression of the results, in Fig. 6 we have depicted three different levels of detail for the Karlsruhe-Stuttgart region. In practice, the first one would certainly only be used for close-up renderings within that region, whereas the third is suitable also for country-wide renderings. In Fig. 7, we have shown three aggregations for the whole of Germany. For a rendering of such a large area, probably MetroCoarse would be the right choice, for a continent-wide rendering, Country seems suitable.

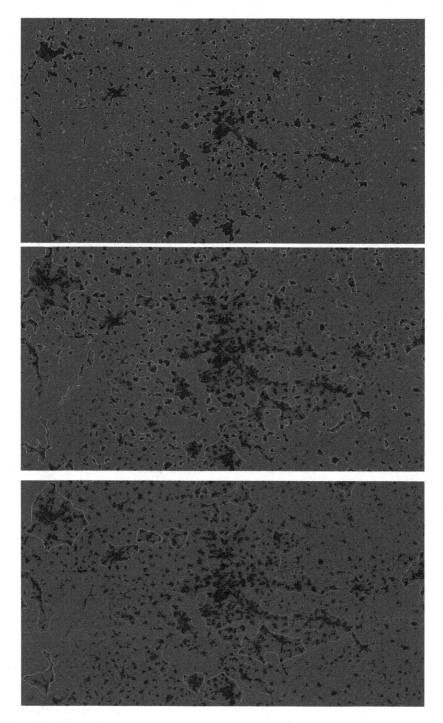

Fig. 6. Building aggregation for the Karlsruhe-Stuttgart Region in three levels of detail: VillageFine, MetroFine, MetroCoarse

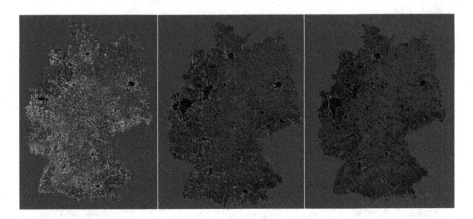

Fig. 7. Building aggregation for Germany in three levels of detail: VillageCoarse, MetroCoarse, Country.

4   Conclusions and Future Work

In this paper we proposed the instrumentation of *Delaunay clustering* as well as α-shapes to aggregate building footprints for map rendering purposes. In our prototypical implementation we used the scheme to precompute 5 different levels-of-detail aggregations which can then be used for efficient map rendering on demand. While this seems sufficient for most purposes, it might be interesting to allow for a truly continuous, on-demand scheme. While our Delaunay clustering scheme already provides for that, the on-demand computation of α-shapes for the respective clusters cannot guarantee response times in the millisecond range. In future research we want to explore the concise computation and storage of all alpha shapes for truly continuous on-demand aggregation of building footprints.

References

1. Ai, T., Yin, H., Shen, Y., Yang, M., Wang, L.: A formal model of neighborhood representation and applications in urban building aggregation supported by delaunay triangulation. PLoS ONE **14**(7), e0218877 (2019)
2. Ai, T., Zhang, X.: The aggregation of urban building clusters based on the skeleton partitioning of gap space. In: The European Information Society: Leading the Way With Geo-Information, pp. 153–170 (2007)
3. Bereuter, P., Weibel, R.: Algorithms for on-the-fly Generalization of Point Data using Quadtrees. University of Zurich, Tech. rep. (2012)
4. Buchin, K., Meulemans, W., Speckmann, B.: A new method for subdivision simplification with applications to urban-area generalization. In: Proceedings of the 19th ACM SIGSPATIAL International Conference on Advances in Geographic Information Systems, pp. 261–270 (2011)
5. Cao, H., Wolfson, O., Trajcevski, G.: Spatio-temporal data reduction with deterministic error bounds. In: Proceedings of the 2003 Joint Workshop on Foundations of Mobile Computing, pp. 33–42 (2003)

6. Chew, L.P.: Constrained delaunay triangulations. In: Proceedings of the Third Annual Symposium on Computational Geometry, pp. 215–222 (1987)
7. libosmium contributors: Osmium library. https://osmcode.org/libosmium/
8. Danciger, J., Devadoss, S.L., Mugno, J., Sheehy, D., Ward, R.: Shape deformation in continuous map generalization. GeoInformatica **13**, 203–221 (2009)
9. Deng, M., Liu, Q., Cheng, T., Shi, Y.: An adaptive spatial clustering algorithm based on delaunay triangulation. Comput. Environ. Urban Syst. **35**(4), 320–332 (2011)
10. Dinas, S., Banon, J.M.: A review on delaunay triangulation with application on computer vision. Int. J. Comput. Sci. Eng. **3**, 9–18 (2014)
11. Edelsbrunner, H., Kirkpatrick, D.G., Seidel, R.: On the shape of a set of points in the plane. IEEE Trans. Inf. Theory **29**(4), 551–558 (1983)
12. Funke, S., Mendel, T., Miller, A., Storandt, S., Wiebe, M.: Map simplification with topology constraints: exactly and in practice. In: 2017 Proceedings of the Nineteenth Workshop on Algorithm Engineering and Experiments (ALENEX), pp. 185–196. SIAM (2017)
13. Li, X.Y., Calinescu, G., Wan, P.J., Wang, Y.: Localized delaunay triangulation with application in ad hoc wireless networks. IEEE Trans. Parallel Distrib. Syst. **14**(10), 1035–1047 (2003)
14. Peng, D., Touya, G.: Continuously generalizing buildings to built-up areas by aggregating and growing. In: Proceedings of the 3rd ACM SIGSPATIAL Workshop on Smart Cities and Urban Analytics, pp. 1–8 (2017)
15. Qingsheng, G., Brandenberger, C., Hurni, L.: A progressive line simplification algorithm. Geo-spatial Inf. Sci. **5**(3), 41–45 (2002)
16. The CGAL Project: CGAL User and Reference Manual. CGAL Editorial Board, 5.6 edn. (2023). https://doc.cgal.org/5.6/Manual/packages.html
17. Van Kreveld, M.: Smooth generalization for continuous zooming. In: Proceedings of 20th International Geographic Conference, pp. 2180–2185 (2001)
18. Wei, Z., Liu, Y., Cheng, L., Ding, S.: A progressive and combined building simplification approach with local structure classification and backtracking strategy. ISPRS Int. J. Geo Inf. **10**(5), 302 (2021)
19. Zhai, R., Li, A., Yin, J., Du, J., Qiu, Y.: A progressive simplification method for buildings based on structural subdivision. ISPRS Int. J. Geo Inf. **11**(7), 393 (2022)

In Situ Visualization of 6DoF Georeferenced Historical Photographs in Location-Based Augmented Reality

Julien Mercier[1,2]([✉]) [iD], Erwan Bocher[2] [iD], and Olivier Ertz[1] [iD]

[1] Media Engineering Institute (MEI), School of Engineering and Management Vaud, HES -SO University of Applied Sciences and Arts Western Switzerland, 1400 Yverdon-les-Bains, Switzerland
{julien.mercier,olivier.ertz}@heig-vd.ch

[2] Lab-STICC, UMR 6285, CNRS, Université Bretagne Sud, 56000 Vannes, France
{julien.mercier,erwan.bocher}@univ-ubs.fr

Abstract. Location-based augmented reality (AR) enables in situ visualization of geolocated media in the real world, usually based on latitude and longitude referencing only. By integrating 6DoF georeferenced photographs, they can be positioned along all three rotational axes (pitch, yaw, roll) in addition to the usual perpendicular translation axes (surge, heave, sway), resulting in data registered on all six mechanical degrees of freedom of movement of a rigid body in three-dimensional space. In this paper, we present an integration test of 6DoF georeferenced data from the Smapshot open API to the BiodivAR open authoring tool for location-based AR. While both projects are open source, their data is not interoperable, similarly to most citizen science (CS) projects. After mapping the data and importing it in a new augmented environment, it can be visualized in the mobile AR interface, at the locations specified by the georeferenced images. Visualizing historical photographs in the AR interface from the actual location where they were originally taken allows them to align with their original context, resulting in an eye-catching and impactful visualization. This contextual visualization of historical photographs informs and enriches their meaning, and allows viewers to quickly detect patterns and anomalies at a glance. We perform a basic qualitative evaluation of the visualization made possible by the combination of 6DoF georeferenced data and our authoring system, based on our own observations. We discuss the potential of this proof-of-concept to foster participation and understanding in citizen science and education, especially with regards to biodiversity monitoring and education.

Keywords: 6DoF Georeferenced data · Location-Based Augmented Reality · Data visualization · Citizen Science

1 Introduction

The history of participation by the public in scientific research [35] is as old as science itself [48]. From the 2000 s on however, there has been a rapid growth

M. Lotfian and L. L. L. Starace (Eds.): W2GIS 2024, LNCS 14673, pp. 130–146, 2024.
https://doi.org/10.1007/978-3-031-60796-7_10

in the scope and scale of online citizen science (CS) projects, associated with the widespread use of efficient communication technologies. Mobile technology in particular has extended the data types that could be collected [32]. They are particularly useful for capturing spatial data through geolocation or photogrammetry. Over the recent years, numerous efforts set out to gather open geodata on topics such as environmental studies [1,3,42], cultural heritage sites [17,26,51], or historical photographs [24,43,49]. Noteworthy is the OpenStreetMap (OSM) project, a free and open geographic database built by a large community of volunteers who collect and import data from various open geodata [21]. CS projects are often place-based, built on in-person participation and motivated by local conservation [46]. They are diverse but usually entail two goals:

1. To collect actionable data for further scientific research
2. To raise participants' awareness on a given issue

Regarding the first of these goals, many CS projects fail to generate interoperable geodata, limiting further use. It is thus important to work towards geodata standards [37]. A working group of the Open Geospatial Consortium (OGC) aims to support and promote interoperability in CS [4]. With regard to the second objective of CS-which is to raise public awareness-impactful geodata visualization is one of the key means of achieving it. *Spatial* visualization allows to quickly detect patterns and anomalies at a glance, in a way written words or numerical data doesn't. The visual system shapes a large part of the cognitive human experience, and visualization it is instrumental for comprehension and communication in various contexts [20]. It is therefore likely to play an important role, giving participants a deeper understanding of the data they have helped to collect. CS projects have the potential to transform humans' behaviors and their environment, and the lack of data interoperability as well as impactful data visualization often tend to limit this potential. In this respect, we propose that augmented reality (AR) offers an interesting visualization modality and therefore solution for the spatial visualization of geodata. It can have a positive impact on participants' perceptions, understanding, and awareness. It was found that AR immersive environments enable reliable representation of georeferenced data, whereas 2D imagery is lossy [29]. In AR interfaces, digital objects are overlaid on top of users' field of view in real-time and 3D, through the screen of a mobile device or a head-mounted display. In *location-based* AR, their position (distance and direction relative to the user's location as estimated by the mobile device's GNSS sensor) is computed based on their attributed real-world coordinates. With this technology, augmented environments can be built remotely from any given geodata, as opposed to marker-based AR which requires markers to be physically placed on target locations. By leveraging the appropriate data, it provides an interesting option for contextual and in situ data visualization, and is of particular interest in various fields such as education, urban and infrastructure planning [41], and cultural heritage. When used sensibly in an educational setting, AR may convey the impression of an enriched environment and make educational material more attractive, thus motivating students to learn [6,25]. Location-based AR promotes learning in context [7,19], ecological engagement [10], and causes users to experience a positive interdependence with nature [39], which fosters improved immersion and learning. Last but not least, location-based AR shows positive effects on the physical activity of users across genders, ages, weight status, and prior activity levels [45]. However, location-based AR is relatively immature as a technology, and inaccurate geolocation data causes augmented objects to jitter or drift, which is a factor in downgrading user experience [33]. Such usability issues have been reported by a number of studies [5,19,23,31,47], most of which blame the inaccuracy of mobile devices' embedded GNSS sensors. Some studies considered that these recurring problems made AR distracting and frustrating and eventually favored marker-based AR, which is more advanced and offers better user experience [13,22]. The BiodivAR project initially attempted to investigate these usability issues, so as to use of location-based AR for outdoor education (see below). To this end, a cartographic tool was initially created for the authoring of AR environments [34]. The georeferenced media used in AR are usually registered on two axes only: latitude and longitude. But location-based AR interfaces also provide an optimal framework for anchoring and visualizing more complex spatial data, such as that produced by some of the most recent CS projects. This type of data is an opportunity for singular visualization in AR, which offers more reliable and immersive representations [29] and results in increased awareness. Among the initiatives mentioned above, data from the Smapshot [43] project are of particular interest for in situ visualization with location-based AR: Because it is georeferenced on all 6°C of freedom (6DoF), it can be positioned along three perpendicular translation axes (surge, heave, sway) *and* all three rotational axes (pitch, yaw, roll), as shown in Fig. 1.

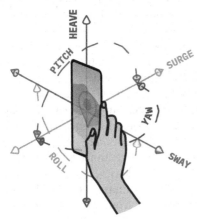

In anticipation of future research investigating the impact of visualizing this type of data in AR, we decided to carry out the present pilot study to assess the initial effort required as well as the achieved outcomes. The questions we aim to address is:

1. Is Smapshot 6DoF data interoperable with BiodivAR?
2. What is its use in an AR context?

In the following sections, we present the steps for the retrieval, mapping, integration, and in situ visualization of 6DoF georeferenced data stemming from the Smapshot API [28] in AR with BiodivAR [34], as schematically illustrated in Fig. 2. We first selected a series of 17 data points from the Smapshot project based on the convenience of their location. We downloaded the images files and their metadata through requests to the open API, and then

Fig. 1. The six mechanical degrees of freedom (6DoF) of a body in 3D space: surge, sway, heave, pitch, yaw, and roll.

mapped that data for its integration into the BiodivAR cartographic authoring tool for location-based AR. We created an augmented environment on the BiodivAR platform and imported the mapped data. We tested AR visualizations of the data on location and reported issues and impressions. We also discuss the benefits of contextual visualization with AR for education, urban planning, and cultural heritage.

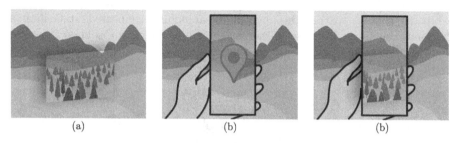

(a)   (b)   (b)

Fig. 2. (a) 6DoF georeferenced photographs placed on top of a digital terrain model for remote contextual visualization, on a desktop screen. (b) Location-based AR typically uses 2D georeferenced objects for contextual visualization. (c) Integrating 6DoF georeferenced photographs in location-based AR enables in situ visualization of historical imagery, blended with its original context.

2 Background

2.1 6DoF Georeferenced Photographs

6DoF georeferenced data is a type of geodata were the full spatial pose of objects' (their position and orientation in 3D space) are represented. It may exploit more fully the potential of location-based AR for in situ and immersive visualization by making the photographs seamlessly integrated within their original surroundings [28]. It may also prove an effective combination to valorize historical photographs [11,14,15]. As reported by Smapshot's authors, historical images enable the analysis of evolving landscape features, such as disappearing glaciers or the impact of urbanization [28]. They also recommend AR as a use case to enable the simultaneous visualization of historical images and their real-world context. 6DoF georeferenced photographs can be positioned in a virtual space so that it aligns perfectly with other geodata, such as a digital terrain model (DTM), as illustrated in Fig. 3. In some cases, DTMs themselves are built from heterogeneous open data scraped from internet in order to produce actionable georeferenced data [49]. 6DoF georeferencing enables the extraction of semantic data from photographs, such as lists of the toponyms that are visible on an image [28]. By retrieving the coordinates where a photograph was taken as well as the direction the camera was pointing, keywords and metadata can be derived [44]. This allows the enriching of the photographs' metadata and improves the structuring of archival databases. When it is coupled with multimodal (metadata and visual) search engines, their access becomes easier [24]. It can be used to promote certain lesser known institutional collections. Visualization of 6DoF georeferenced imagery may also be used for the monitoring of biodiversity: previous states of a plant specimen, an environment or an entire ecosystem can be superposed and compared in context [40]. 6DoF georeferenced historical imagery can be overlaid on top of recent imagery to illustrate the changing landscape and to allow viewers to compare the impacts of urbanization, climate change, etc. In the field of education, contextual visualization refers to visualizing an image in a broader context so that they become meaningfully connected. It facilitates divergent thinking where the learner meaningfully relates an isolated image to the whole image through mental association [52].

Fig. 3. Snapshot interface: a 6DoF georeferenced historical photograph taken in 1999 in Yverdon-les-Bains for landscape documentation before the 2002 national exhibition. It is positioned on a digital terrain model streamed from the Cesium ion service. The off-camera surroundings of the photograph are represented on the 3D model, textured with satellite view. https://smapshot.heig-vd.ch/visit/186653

2.2 Location-Based Augmented Reality

Some researchers consider AR as a concept rather than through the technology it relies upon [53]. AR and its affordances in in situ visualization enhances spatial knowledge representation and experimental learning [30]. However, there are two major types of AR technologies: image-based and location-based. Location-based AR mostly relies on location data, i.e. through the global navigation satellite system (GNSS). Both approaches may result in different affordances [18].

Previous attempts to superpose historical photographs to their original context with AR have been made using a custom image-based method [50]. However, to our knowledge, there is no report on 6DoF georeferenced data integration in location-based AR based on GNSS data only. Image-based AR relies on visual landmarks to register and map a virtual 3D space. Augmented environments can be created using game engines (i.e. Unity, Unreal Engine) or web technologies with 3D computer graphics APIs and libraries (WebXR, three.js, A-Frame.js). With the latter, users may access the application in a web browser, without the need to download and install an application through a store. AR web applications require a browser equipped with the WebXR Device API to run and access the mobile device's necessary hardware (accelerometer, magnetometer). In order to get geolocation data, the web application also needs to access the device's GNSS data through the Geolocation API. The BiodivAR platform is a free and open-source web cartographic authoring tool conceived with user-centered methodologies, aimed at being useful to learners, educators, and citizen scientists [34]. On a desktop environment, the application allows the creation and management of augmented environments while the mobile version is meant for outdoor AR visualization. A comparative user studies were conducted to evaluate the mobile AR tool's usability [33]. Eye tracking measurements were made to evaluate the role of technology during learning activities. An additional ongoing study with pupils aims to evaluate the tool's impact on learning efficiency, nature exploration, and environmental emotions, the results of which are currently being processed. A library [16] for the georeferencing of media entities was created as part of the project, using the A-frame.js framework. In the following chapter, we detail the download of 6DoF data from Smapshot, their adaption to meet BiodivAR's requirements, their importation onto the platform, and their subsequent in situ visualization.

3 Materials and Methods

3.1 Data Collection

Smapshot is an ongoing open-source project for the collaborative georeferencing of historical images [43]. Unlike some CS projects, participants do not collect new data on location but rather enrich existing historical data by retrieving their geolocation. This corresponds to the second level of participation and engagement according to Haklay's categorization, also referred to as 'citizens as interpreters' or 'distributed intelligence' [27]. Through the effort of over 800 participants, the project has georeferenced over 200'000 digitized historical images. On a web platform, users place ground control-points on both an image and a DTM textured with aerial imagery, which enables the computation of the image's full spatial pose as well as the exact position from where it was taken through monoplotting [9,12]. The resulting georeferenced image is stored in a GLTF file, which embeds 6DoF data as a 3D mesh and the original JPG image as a texture. The pose of the mesh is referenced in a local space. The origin is the point of view from which the picture was taken, which is thus the location from which the image must be visualized, with a certain leeway that can be specified by the augmented environment's author. Its attributed world coordinates point to the location where it should be placed, with a circular buffer specified in meters. Among the available data from the Smapshot API, we kept the following attributes (highlighted in red in Fig. 4):

1. The image's id number
2. The title or description of the image
3. The license attributed to the image
4. The date the original photograph was taken
5. The GLTF file, which contains the image and its full 6DoF positional data
6. The world coordinates (location from where the image was originally taken)

The Smapshot open API uses a Representational State Transfer (REST) protocol, which is the most common type. It defines communication routes with a URL which can simply be accessed in a browser, through the HTTP protocol. It is limited to sending text data, and that the image file information are provided as an additional URL pointing to the image file. We downloaded the JSON files containing the attributes of the 17 data points with GET calls to the API. For example, the URL to retrieve the attributes of the image shown on Fig. 3 is https://smapshot.heig-vd.ch/api/v1/images/186653/attributes. The resulting JSON file is represented in Fig. 4. It has to be mapped so that selected attributes can fit BiodivAR's GEOJSON format and be integrated in the AR application.

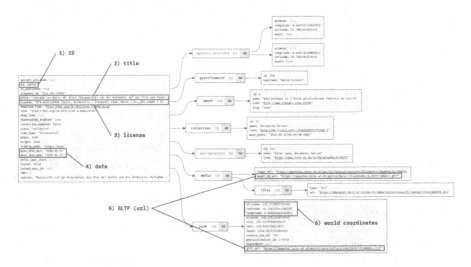

Fig. 4. JSON of a data point from the Smapshot API. The strictly needed attributes for a successful integration into BiodivAR are: a GLTF file and its world coordinates. Additional data are kept for future reference (ID, title, license, and date).

3.2   Data Mapping

The JSON returned from the Smapshot API contains more than enough information to integrate the 6DoF photograph in the BiodivAR authoring tool, but it needs to be mapped to suit the application's expected formatted. First, the Smapshot JSON format is not a GEOJSON, because the world coordinates are stored within a complete 6DoF "pose" object. In a geoJSON file, the coordinates are stored as an array of length three within the "coordinates" object, itself pertaining to the "geometry" object, itself contained in a "feature" object. The photograph's coordinates thus need to be retrieved manually. Secondly, the GLTF file, provided in the form of an url pointing to the hosted file, contains the JPG photograph as an external texture resource, which cannot be linked directly in the new GEOJSON format, or it will result in an empty 3D file. Consequently, the GLTF file needs to be downloaded, as well as the distant JPG texture file within it. To be imported in the BiodivAR authoring tool, the GLTF needs to be self-contained (as opposed to linking to external resources), by embedding the JPG texture as binary data (encoded in base64 for the GLTF file extension or as raw byte arrays in the .glb file extension). Smapshot's GLTF files thus need to be converted, e.g. by opening them in a 3D software (e.g. Blender or Adobe Dimension) and saving them as binary files. All of the other data (world coordinates, title/description, date, image's id, and image's license) are available in their final (string) format in Smapshot's JSON file (see Fig. 4) and may be mapped to a new data format so that they can be integrated as attributes of the point of interest (POI) in the BiodivAR application. The resulting GEOJSON file formatted to BiodivAR's format's expectations is illustrated in Fig. 5.

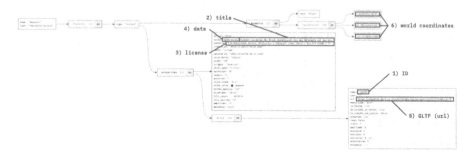

Fig. 5. The attributes from the data point as provided by the Smapshot API (as illustrated in Fig. 4) are mapped into BiodivAR's GEOJSON data format before it can be imported in the AR authoring application.

3.3   Data Integration

While BiodivAR's data does not comply with any particular industry standard for geodata, interoperability has been a key concern throughout the project's conception and its data is compatible with most leading geographic information systems (e.g. QGIS). Recently, a feature for third-party data integration was implemented, opening up the possibility of harnessing virtually any type of geo-data collected by citizen science projects. Provided that the data conforms to the GEOJSON model defined by the application (see Fig. 5), it is now possible to import large thematic datasets and visualize them in context through a mobile, location-based AR interface. As a first test use case, we decided to work with data from the Smapshot API, since its 6DoF georeferencing lends itself particularly well to visualization in context with AR. Once the data from the Smapshot API had been remapped and the GLTF saved as self-containing files, we created a new augmented environment in the BiodivAR application and imported the geodata comprising the 17 data points, as visible in Fig. 6).

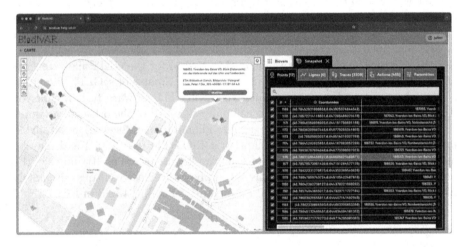

Fig. 6. A view of the BiodivAR map user interface after importing the Smapshot data.

3.4   In Situ Visualization

After populating a new augmented environment with the Smapshot data in the BiodivAR desktop application, we headed out to the area in which the photographs had been taken. We opened the environment in AR mode and walked over to the circles marking the areas in which the georeferenced photographs appear in the interface. At first, the display of the photographs did not align correctly with the landscape: there was a significant offset on the yaw axis, also referred to as azimuth or heading. Indeed, yaw is the angular measurement on the horizontal plane with respect to true north. It is computed based on fused data gathered from the mobile device's inertial measurement unit (IMU) and magnetometer. While IMUs' sensors (gyroscope, accelerometer) provide accurate readings on a rigid body's acceleration and angular velocity, their measures are relative to a local origin and are subject to drifting. Conversely, the magnetometer measures the absolute orientation of a body according to the north magnetic pole. While does not drift from its origin the way IMUs do, magnetic fields are subject to error due to electronic noise potentially stemming from powerlines, other electronic devices, and other components within the mobile device [38]. In addition to noise, wrong calibration can also make the data extremely unreliable [36]. One way to mitigate the imprecision is to calibrate the device by tilting and moving in a figure-eight pattern. However, even after calibration, there can be a significant error. Without accurate determination of users position and orientation, AR suffers from significant registration errors. The limitations of onboard sensors are considered the biggest challenge preventing accurate AR tracking outdoors [8]. Nevertheless, after performing calibration, sometimes repeatedly, the photograph would eventually load with the correct angle and align with its surrounding. The resulting view in the AR interface is pictured in Fig. 7. Although the photograph does not align with reality as perfectly as with the DTM (as visible in Fig. 3), the visual result is eye-catching. The overall impression is particularly effective when, by contrast, environmental and weather conditions are very different from those of the historical image, as was the case on the day of the test. Contemplating the snowy, cold surroundings overlaid with a representation of the same spot on a sunny summer's day provides a brief sensation of time travelling. It offers an immersive moment in which reading the picture and the information it carries is informed and enriched by its context. The differences are immediately noticeable, such as the absence of sailboats, the leaves on the trees, the color of the water and sky, the birds on the lake. We further discuss the potential of in situ visualization of 6DoF georeferenced historical photographs with regards to CS initiatives aim to raise awareness. We also discuss the prospects, limitations and future steps to be implemented to improve the performance of this instrument for this type of purpose.

4   Discussion

One of the aims of this pilot study was to test the obstacles between the availability of a database and its integration into our system, which we are seeking to make easily interoperable. Our use case for the integration of 6DoF georeferenced historical photographs from the Smapshot open API provided a first opportunity to test the geodata import tool recently integrated to the BiodivAR application. It illustrated the common issue of the lack of geodata interoperability within CS, even if it could be tackled with a simple workaround involving data mapping, thus answering our initial question regarding interoperability. Given the important differences between the Smapshot and BiodivAR interfaces, it's possible that no one data format could fit all situations. However, efforts like that of the OGC GeoPose Standard aim at fostering interoperability for geodata through the definition of rules and data structure for the expression of location and orientation of real or virtual geometric objects within reference frames anchored to

Fig. 7. In situ visualization of a 6DoF georeferenced historical photograph from the Smapshot API (as seen in Fig. 3).

the earth's coordinate system [2]. The use case also illustrated that beyond its suitability for 6DoF georeferenced data, location-based AR, if less accurate than its image-based counterpart, can take advantage of many types of geodata, and help valorize it through in situ visualization. As demonstrated with this small-scale use case, augmented environments can be conveniently populated by data stemming from CS projects, which paves the way for the valorization of other geodata through AR visualization. In the future, we would like to experiment with importing larger open CS geodata, such as biodiversity monitoring data from the Global Biodiversity Information Facility (GBIF) [1].

After the data was mapped and imported in the BiodivAR application, we were able to go out on the field and visualize historical photography in situ, although the process was complicated by location-based AR most common pitfall [8]: the inaccuracy of angular data on the yaw axis. Eventually, it was possible to visualize the photographs while they aligned with their original context, which provided a unique type of enriched visualization. On the basis of an instinctive and immediate appreciation, we believe that the combination of historical photographs aligned with their original context is of undeniable interest and potential. Even the initial imprecision in the photographs' alignment presents the viewer with the somewhat playful challenge of trying to realign the augmented object, which could be turned into an advantage. This combination of AR with a novel type of participant-enriched CS geodata [32] for contextual and in situ visualization is likely to foster spatial knowledge representation and experimental learning [30]. This use case allows to experience first-hand the visualization of an image in its broader context, thus creating meaningful connections to the viewer [52]. When appreciated in the context of CS project, which aim to raise participants' awareness on their topical issues, this type of visualization shows an interesting potential. In the continuation of other types of spatial visualization, in situ visualization with AR allows to detect differences and anomalies at once [20]. It could be used to communicate with participants and help them understand the importance and value of the data they collected, possibly fostering future participation. In the context of environmental education, in situ visualization leveraging biodiversity monitoring data (melting of glaciers, deforestation, habitat loss, intensive urban growth) may help the public perceive climate change and biodiversity loss [40]. It would also be interesting to test in situ visualization of videos instead of still images, or even to overlay DTM on top of a real-world context. It would also be interesting to test visualization with AR/MR glasses, which depends only on the availability of GNSS-equipped headsets. Beyond its potential to help raise awareness, AR visualization can also lead to renewed interactions for participatory data collection. For example, participants could comment, annotate, or label the images visualized directly in the AR interface. They could also take and upload new photographs and thus collect new data from the AR interface. It does raise a set of challenges (usability, data accuracy and literacy, impact on participation and learning) that need to be thoroughly investigated and addressed before it can be potentially be beneficial, though. This paper only demonstrates a technical pipeline for 6DoF georeferenced media visualization in AR, and it would also be useful to conduct research on the actual impact of using it within CS or education research projects.

5   Conclusions

In this paper, we presented examples of participant geodata collected as part of CS project and the common interoperability issues preventing that data from being valorized beyond given projects. We discussed the particular interest of 6DoF georeferenced data for location-based AR contextual and in situ visualization. We presented our use case: integrating participant 6DoF georeferenced historical photographs from the Smapshot open API into the BiodivAR cartographic authoring tool, for AR visualization in situ. We described the steps required to map the data to comply with the BiodivAR database and import it in a new augmented environment. Eventually, we went out on the field to make an empiric test visualizing the historical photographs on their original location, overlaid with their real-world surroundings. Based on this simple proof-of-concept, we found that this specific type of contextual and in situ visualization informed and enriched the photographs, and that it holds potential to foster participation and understanding in CS as well as in education. This type of visualization may also have positive effects on learning and raising awareness, especially with regards to environmental topics. However, one remaining question is to methodically evaluate these impacts with dedicated research, especially given that location-based AR suffers from various usability issues that may hinder any benefit. This paper presents a mere technical demonstration of the feasibility and interest of integrating third-party open geodata into the BiodivAR application. On the basis of the groundwork laid in this modest pilot study, we intend to pursue this effort in the coming months by gathering large relevant geodata, especially related to the monitoring of biodiversity. We encourage all initiatives that try to leverage AR affordances for enriched visualization and interaction to positive uses.

References

1. GBIF. https://www.gbif.org/
2. OGC GeoPose 1.0 data exchange standard. https://docs.ogc.org/is/21-056r11/21-056r11.html
3. Pl@ntnet. https://plantnet.org/
4. WebHome < CitizenScienceDWG < ogc public wiki. https://external.ogc.org/twiki_public/CitizenScienceDWG
5. Admiraal, W., Huizenga, J., Akkerman, S., Dam, G.T.: The concept of flow in collaborative game-based learning. Comput. Hum. Behav. **27**(3), 1185–1194 (2011). https://doi.org/10.1016/j.chb.2010.12.013
6. Alnagrat, A., Ismail, R., Syed Idrus, S.Z.: A review of extended reality (XR) technologies in the future of human education: current trend and future opportunity. J. Hum. Reprod. Sci. **1**, 81–96 (2022). https://doi.org/10.11113/humentech.v1n2.27
7. Arvola, M., Fuchs, I.E., Nyman, I., Szczepanski, A.: Mobile augmented reality and outdoor education. Built Environ. **47**(2), 223–242 (2021). https://doi.org/10.2148/benv.47.2.223
8. Azuma, R.T.: The challenge of making augmented reality work outdoors. In: Ohta, Y., Tamura, H. (eds.) Mixed Reality, pp. 379–390. Springer Berlin Heidelberg, Berlin, Heidelberg (1999). https://doi.org/10.1007/978-3-642-87512-0_21
9. Bayr, U.: Quantifying historical landscape change with repeat photography: an accuracy assessment of geospatial data obtained through monoplotting. Int. J. Geogr. Inf. Sci. **35**(10), 2026–2046 (2021). https://doi.org/10.1080/13658816.2021.1871910
10. Bloom, M.A., Holden, M., Sawey, A.T., Weinburgh, M.H.: Promoting the use of outdoor learning spaces by K-12 inservice science teachers through an outdoor professional development experience. In: Bodzin, A.M., Shiner Klein, B., Weaver, S. (eds.) The Inclusion of Environmental Education in Science Teacher Education, pp. 97–110. Springer, Dordrecht (2010). https://doi.org/10.1007/978-90-481-9222-9_7
11. Boboc, R.G., Duguleană, M., Voinea, G.D., Postelnicu, C.C., Popovici, D.M., Carrozzino, M.: Mobile augmented reality for cultural heritage: following the footsteps of ovid among different locations in Europe. Sustainability **11**(4), 1167 (2019). https://doi.org/10.3390/su11041167
12. Bozzini, C., Conedera, M., Krebs, P.: A new monoplotting tool to extract georeferenced vector data and orthorectified raster data from oblique non-metric photographs. Int. J. Heritage Digit. Era **1**, 499–518 (2012). https://doi.org/10.1260/2047-4970.1.3.499
13. Bressler, D.M., Bodzin, A.M.: A mixed methods assessment of students' flow experiences during a mobile augmented reality science game. J. Comput. Assist. Learn. **29**(6), 505–517 (2013). https://doi.org/10.1111/jcal.12008, https://onlinelibrary.wiley.com/doi/abs/10.1111/jcal.12008
14. de Carolis, B., Gena, C., Kuflik, T., Origlia, A., Raptis, G.: AVI-CH 2018: advanced visual interfaces for cultural Heritage, pp. 1–3, May 2018. https://doi.org/10.1145/3206505.3206597

15. Carrozzino, M., Voinea, G.D., Duguleană, M., Boboc, R.G., Bergam-asco, M.: Comparing innovative XR systems in cultural heritage. A case study. Int. Arch. Photogrammetry Remote Sens. Spat. Inf. Sci. **XLII-2-W11**, 373–378 (2019). https://doi.org/10.5194/isprs-archives-XLII-2-W11-373-2019, https://isprs-archives.copernicus.org/articles/XLII-2-W11/373/2019/, conference Name: GEORES 2019
2nd International Conference of Geomatics and Restoration (Volume XLII-2/W11) - 8–10 May 2019, Milan, Italy Publisher: Copernicus GmbH

16. Chabloz, N.: LBAR.js. MIT (2022). https://github.com/MediaComem/LBAR.js

17. Challenor, J., Ma, M.: A review of augmented reality applications for history education and heritage visualisation. Multimodal Technol. Interact. **3**(2), 39 (2019). https://doi.org/10.3390/mti3020039, https://www.mdpi.com/2414-4088/3/2/39, number: 2 Publisher: Multidisciplinary Digital Publishing Institute

18. Cheng, K.H., Tsai, C.C.: Affordances of augmented reality in science learning: suggestions for future research. J. Sci. Educ. Technol. **22**(4), 449–462 (2013). https://doi.org/10.1007/s10956-012-9405-9, http://link.springer.com/10.1007/s10956-012-9405-9

19. Chiang, T.H.C., Yang, S.J.H., Hwang, G.J.: An augmented reality-based mobile learning system to improve students' learning achievements and motivations in natural science inquiry activities. J. Educ. Technol. Soc. **17**(4), 352–365 (2014), http://www.jstor.org/stable/jeductechsoci.17.4.352, publisher: International Forum of Educational Technology & Society

20. Coltekin, A., Griffin, A., Robinson, A.: Visualizations (2021). https://doi.org/10.1093/obo/9780199874002-0224

21. Curran, K., Fisher, G., Crumlish, J.: OpenStreetMap. Int. J. Interact. Commun. Syst. Technol. **2**, 69–78 (2012). https://doi.org/10.4018/ijicst.2012010105

22. Debandi, F., et al.: Enhancing cultural tourism by a mixed reality application for outdoor navigation and information browsing using immersive devices. IOP Conf. Ser. Mater. Sci. Eng. **364**, 012048 (2018). https://doi.org/10.1088/1757-899X/364/1/012048, publisher: IOP Publishing

23. Dunleavy, M., Dede, C., Mitchell, R.: Affordances and limitations of immersive participatory augmented reality simulations for teaching and learning. J. Sci. Educ. Technol. **18**(1), 7–22 (2009). https://doi.org/10.1007/s10956-008-9119-1

24. Geniet, F., Gouet-Brunet, V., Brédif, M.: ALEGORIA: joint multimodal search and spatial navigation into the geographic iconographic heritage. In: Proceedings of the 30th ACM International Conference on Multimedia, MM 2022, pp. 6982–6984. Association for Computing Machinery, New York, NY, USA, October 2022. https://doi.org/10.1145/3503161.3547746

25. Geroimenko, V.: Augmented reality in education: a new technology for teaching and learning. Springer International Publishing (2020)

26. González Vargas, J.C., Fabregat, R., Carrillo-Ramos, A., Jové, T.: Survey: using augmented reality to improve learning motivation in cultural heritage studies. Appl. Sci. **10**(3), 897 (2020). https://doi.org/10.3390/app10030897, https://www.mdpi.com/2076-3417/10/3/897, number: 3 Publisher: Multidisciplinary Digital Publishing Institute

27. Haklay, M.: Citizen science and volunteered geographic information: overview and typology of participation. In: Sui, D., Elwood, S., Goodchild, M. (eds.) Crowdsourcing Geographic Knowledge: Volunteered Geographic Information (VGI) in Theory and Practice, pp. 105–122. Springer, Dordrecht (2013). https://doi.org/10.1007/978-94-007-4587-2_7

28. Ingensand, J., Lecorney, S., Blanc, N., Besse, M., Taylor, J., Rappo, D.: An open API for 3D-georeferenced historical pictures. Int. Arch. Photogrammetry, Remote Sens. Spat. Inf. Sci. **XLVIII-4/W1-2022**, 217–222 (2022). https://doi.org/10.5194/isprs-archives-XLVIII-4-W1-2022-217-2022, https://isprs-archives.copernicus.org/articles/XLVIII-4-W1-2022/217/2022/

29. Kaspar, M., Kieffer, D., Liu, Q.: Holographic mixed reality: an enhanced technology for visualizing and evaluating complex 3D geologic data, October 2023

30. Kye, B., Kim, Y.: Investigation of the relationships between media characteristics, presence, flow, and learning effects in augmented reality based learning. Int. J. Educ. Media Technol. **2**(1) (2008). https://ijemt.org/index.php/journal/article/view/161

31. Lee, G., Duenser, A., Kim, S., Billinghurst, M.: CityViewAR: a mobile outdoor AR application for city visualization, November 2012. https://doi.org/10.1109/ISMAR-AMH.2012.6483989, pages: 64

32. Lotfian, M., Ingensand, J., Brovelli, M.A.: The partnership of citizen science and machine learning: benefits, risks, and future challenges for engagement, data collection, and data quality. Sustainability **13**(14), 8087 (2021). https://doi.org/10.3390/su13148087, https://www.mdpi.com/2071-1050/13/14/8087, number: 14 Publisher: Multidisciplinary Digital Publishing Institute

33. Mercier, J., et al.: Impact of geolocation data on augmented reality usability: a comparative user test. Int. Arch. Photogrammetry Remote Sens. Spatial Inf. Sci. **XLVIII-4/W7-2023**, 133–140 (2023). https://doi.org/10.5194/isprs-archives-XLVIII-4-W7-2023-133-2023, https://isprs-archives.copernicus.org/articles/XLVIII-4-W7-2023/133/2023/

34. Mercier, J., Chabloz, N., Dozot, G., Ertz, O., Bocher, E., Rappo, D.: BiodivAR: a cartographic authoring tool for the visualization of geolocated media in augmented reality. ISPRS Int. J. Geo-Inf. **12**(2), 61 (2023). https://doi.org/10.3390/ijgi12020061, https://www.mdpi.com/2220-9964/12/2/61

35. Miller-Rushing, A., Primack, R., Bonney, R.: The history of public participation in ecological research. Front. Ecol. Environ. **10**(6), 285–290 (2012). https://doi.org/10.1890/110278, https://esajournals.onlinelibrary.wiley.com/doi/10.1890/110278

36. Neumann, R., Peitek, N., Cuadrado-Gallego, J.J.: GeoPointing on indoor maps: enhancing compass sensor accuracy to enable interactive digital object selection in smartphone-based map applications. In: Proceedings of the 10th ACM International Symposium on Mobility Management and Wireless Access, pp. 63–70. ACM, Paphos Cyprus, October 2012. https://doi.org/10.1145/2386995.2387006, https://dl.acm.org/doi/10.1145/2386995.2387006

37. Newman, G., et al.: Leveraging the power of place in citizen science for effective conservation decision making. Biol. Conserv. **208**, 55–64 (2017). https://doi.org/10.1016/j.biocon.2016.07.019, https://www.sciencedirect.com/science/article/pii/S0006320716302841

38. Novakova, L., Pavlis, T.L.: Assessment of the precision of smart phones and tablets for measurement of planar orientations: a case study. J. Struct. Geol. **97**, 93–103 (2017). https://doi.org/10.1016/j.jsg.2017.02.015, https://www.sciencedirect.com/science/article/pii/S0191814117300524

39. O'Shea, P.M., Dede, C., Cherian, M.: Research note: the results of formatively evaluating an augmented reality curriculum based on modified design principles. Int. J. Gaming Comput.-Mediat. Simul. (IJGCMS) **3**(2), 57–66 (2011). https://doi.org/10.4018/jgcms.2011040104, https://www.igi-global.com/gateway/article/www.igi-global.com/gateway/article/54351, publisher: IGI Global

40. Papadopoulou, E.E., et al.: Geovisualization of the excavation process in the Lesvos petrified forest, greece using augmented reality. ISPRS Int. J. Geo-Inf. **9**(6), 374 (2020). https://doi.org/10.3390/ijgi9060374, https://www.mdpi.com/2220-9964/9/6/374, number: 6 Publisher: Multidisciplinary Digital Publishing Institute
41. Peña-Rios, A., Hagras, H., Gardner, M., Owusu, G.: A type-2 fuzzy logic based system for augmented reality visualisation of georeferenced data. In: 2018 IEEE International Conference on Fuzzy Systems (FUZZ-IEEE), pp. 1–8, July 2018. https://doi.org/10.1109/FUZZ-IEEE.2018.8491467, https://ieeexplore.ieee.org/abstract/document/8491467
42. Picaut, J., Fortin, N., Bocher, E., Petit, G., Aumond, P., Guillaume, G.: An open-science crowdsourcing approach for producing community noise maps using smartphones. Build. Environ. **148**, 20–33 (2019). https://doi.org/10.1016/j.buildenv.2018.10.049, https://www.sciencedirect.com/science/article/pii/S0360132318306747
43. Produit, T., Ingensand, J.: 3D georeferencing of historical photos by volunteers. In: Mansourian, A., Pilesjö, P., Harrie, L., Van Lammeren, R. (eds.) Geospatial Technologies for All, pp. 113–128. Springer, Cham (2018). https://doi.org/10.1007/978-3-319-78208-9_6, http://link.springer.com/10.1007/978-3-319-78208-9_6, series Title: Lecture Notes in Geoinformation and Cartography
44. Purves, R.S., Edwardes, A., Fan, X., Hall, M., Tomko, M.: Automatically generating keywords for georeferenced images, April 2010. https://doi.org/10.5167/UZH-40067, https://www.zora.uzh.ch/id/eprint/40067, publisher: [object Object]
45. Rauschnabel, P.A., Rossmann, A., tom Dieck, M.C.: An adoption framework for mobile augmented reality games: The case of Pokémon Go. Comput. Hum. Behav. **76**, 276–286 (2017). https://doi.org/10.1016/j.chb.2017.07.030, https://linkinghub.elsevier.com/retrieve/pii/S0747563217304521
46. Richter, F., Reitmann, S., Jung, B.: Integration of open geodata into virtual worlds. In: Proceedings of the 6th International Conference on Virtual and Augmented Reality Simulations, ICVARS 2022, pp. 9–13. Association for Computing Machinery, New York, NY, USA, August 2022. https://doi.org/10.1145/3546607.3546609, https://dl.acm.org/doi/10.1145/3546607.3546609
47. Ryokai, K., Agogino, A.: Off the paved paths: exploring nature with a mobile augmented reality learning tool. J. Mobile Hum. Comput. Interact. **5**(2), 21–49 (2013). https://doi.org/10.4018/jmhci.2013040102, institution: Agogino, Alice: Department of Mechanical Engineering, School of Information, University of California-Berkley, Berkley, CA, U
48. Strasser, B.J., Baudry, J., Mahr, D., Sanchez, G., Tancoigne, E.: Citizen Science? Rethinking science and public participation. Sci. Technol. Stud. 52–76 (2018). https://doi.org/10.23987/sts.60425, https://sciencetechnologystudies.journal.fi/article/view/60425
49. Themistocleous, K.: The use of open data from social media for the creation of 3D georeferenced modeling. In: Fourth International Conference on Remote Sensing and Geoinformation of the Environment (RSCy2016), vol. 9688, pp. 254–259. SPIE, August 2016. https://doi.org/10.1117/12.2242804, https://www.spiedigitallibrary.org/conference-proceedings-of-spie/9688/96880T/The-use-of-open-data-from-social-media-for-the/10.1117/12.2242804.full

50. Torresani, A., Rigon, S., Farella, E.M., Menna, F., Remondino, F.: Unveiling large-scale historical contents with v-slam and markerless mobile AR solutions. Int. Arch. Photogrammetry, Remote Sens. Spat. Inf. Sci. **XLVI-M-1-2021**, 761–768 (2021). https://doi.org/10.5194/isprs-archives-XLVI-M-1-2021-761-2021, https://isprs-archives.copernicus.org/articles/XLVI-M-1-2021/761/2021/isprs-archives-XLVI-M-1-2021-761-2021.html, conference Name: ICOMOS/ISPRS International Scientific Committee on Heritage Documentation (CIPA)
 28th CIPA Symposium “Great Learning & Digital Emotion& 28 August-1 September 2021, Beijing, China Publisher: Copernicus GmbH

51. Tscheu, F., Buhalis, D.: Augmented reality at cultural heritage sites. In: Inversini, A., Schegg, R. (eds.) Information and Communication Technologies in Tourism 2016, pp. 607–619. Springer, Cham (2016). https://doi.org/10.1007/978-3-319-28231-2_44

52. Ursyn, A., Rodrigues, J. (eds.): Interface Support for Creativity, Productivity, and Expression in Computer Graphics:. Advances in Multimedia and Interactive Technologies, IGI Global (2019). https://doi.org/10.4018/978-1-5225-7371-5, http://services.igi-global.com/resolvedoi/resolve.aspx?doi=10.4018/978-1-5225-7371-5

53. Wu, H., Lattuada, M., Morbidelli, M.: Dependence of fractal dimension of DLCA clusters on size of primary particles. Adv. Colloid Interface Sci. **195-196**, 41–49 (2013). https://doi.org/10.1016/j.cis.2013.04.001, https://linkinghub.elsevier.com/retrieve/pii/S0001868613000353

Can Large Language Models Automatically Generate GIS Reports?

Luigi Libero Lucio Starace$^{(\boxtimes)}$ⓘ and Sergio Di Martinoⓘ

Department of Electrical Engineering and Information Technology,
Università degli Studi di Napoli Federico II, Naples, Italy
{luigiliberolucio.starace,sergio.dimartino}@unina.it

Abstract. Geographical Information Systems (GIS) are essential tools used for storing and performing analyses on spatio-temporal data. GIS reporting plays a crucial role in transforming the result of these analyses into actionable insights, enabling informed decision-making, by uncovering patterns and relationships and presenting them in a human-readable format suitable for the intended target audience. Nonetheless, the traditional process of creating reports involves manual analysis and interpretation of spatio-temporal data, a time-intensive task prone to human error.

This paper aims to investigate the potential of Large Language Models (LLMs), particularly their natural language processing and generation abilities, to streamline the report generation process. To this end, three case studies are conducted, using the GPT-3.5 LLM to analyze real-world GIS data, extract key spatio-temporal insights and generate actionable, human-readable reports. The generated reports are then analyzed, to assess the model's capacity for understanding complex spatio-temporal relationships and patterns and generating coherent reports.

Results show that general-purpose LLMs can be remarkably effective in detecting spatio-temporal patterns and anomalies and in generating concise, effective human-readable reports. Despite this great potential, we also identify several key challenges of LLMs for GIS report generation, including a significant variability among different re-executions, a tendency to report incorrect data in some scenarios, and difficulty in understanding more complex spatial data such as polygons.

Keywords: GIS · Large Language Models · Report Generation

1 Introduction

Geographic Information Systems (GIS) have become integral in unravelling the complexities of spatio-temporal phenomena of interest, providing powerful solutions for analyzing and interpreting geographic and spatio-temporal data [3,12]. In this context, the dissemination of insights derived from GIS analyses and workflows is of paramount importance for effective decision-making, policy formulation, and public understanding. GIS reporting serves as the conduit through

© The Author(s), under exclusive license to Springer Nature Switzerland AG 2024
M. Lotfian and L. L. L. Starace (Eds.): W2GIS 2024, LNCS 14673, pp. 147–161, 2024.
https://doi.org/10.1007/978-3-031-60796-7_11

which the results of intricate GIS analyses, which are typically reported in tabular form and possibly visualized using appropriate plots or maps, can be communicated to decision-makers, stakeholders, and/or the general public, providing actionable insights. More in detail, GIS reporting aims at detecting relevant spatio-temporal patterns, relationships, trends and anomalies emerging from GIS analysis results and presenting them in a format that is understandable to specific target audiences.

The traditional, manual approach to GIS reporting, however, is not without its challenges. Indeed, manual report generation can be time-consuming, prone to human error, and may hinder the scalability of GIS analyses, particularly in the face of growing data volumes and the increasing complexity of spatial analyses [17]. As the demand for timely and accurate spatial information continues to rise, there is a pressing need for innovative solutions that enhance the efficiency and accessibility of GIS reporting.

This paper investigates the feasibility of addressing these challenges by integrating advanced Language Models (LLMs) into GIS workflows, to automatically detect patterns and anomalies in the results of GIS analyses, and generate textual reports. LLMs, with their natural language processing capabilities and promising geospatial reasoning skills [9], may prove useful in automating the generation of GIS reports. To assess the feasibility of the approach, we conducted a case study involving three real-world, diverse GIS reporting scenarios, analyzing the effectiveness and pain points of LLM-based GIS report generation.

The paper is structured as follows. Section 2 provides background notions on LLMs and describes related works investigating their adoption in the GIS context. Subsequently, Sect. 3 describes the approach we employed to automate the generation of GIS reports using LLMs, and Section 4 defines in detail the case study we conducted. In Section 5, we present a detailed qualitative analysis of the LLM-generated reports, while Sect. 6 provides some closing remarks and highlight directions for future research.

2   Background and Related Works

In recent years, the field of natural language processing has witnessed a transformative shift with the emergence of Large Language Models (LLMs) such as ChatGPT [1] or LLaMA [14]. These models leverage the power of massive neural network architectures, comprising billions or even trillions of parameters, to understand, generate, and manipulate natural language.

LLMs are initially pre-trained leveraging extensive and diverse datasets, often extracted from large portions of the internet [14]. During this phase, LLMs learn to predict the next word in a sequence, in a self-supervised fashion, thereby acquiring an implicit understanding of grammar, syntax, and contextual semantics. Following pre-training, LLMs can be fine-tuned on specific tasks, allowing for a high degree of adaptability across various applications. For example, conversational agents such as ChatGPT are often fine-tuned to follow instructions using Reinforcement Learning from Human Feedback [11].

Thanks to their massive scale, LLMs can capture intricate linguistic patterns, nuances, and contextual relationships within vast datasets, and excel in a broad spectrum of applications, ranging from language translation and sentiment analysis [16] to text summarization and question-answering [20]. The sheer size of these models empowers them to generalize across diverse linguistic contexts, thereby enhancing their ability to comprehend and generate natural language text.

Works investigating the feasibility of using LLMs in a GIS context are currently starting to emerge in the literature. In [6], for example, Feng et al. introduce GeoQAMap, a system employing Large Language Models (LLMs) to translate natural language queries into SPARQL queries, retrieve geospatial data from Wikidata, and generate interactive maps as visual answers. The system shows promise for integration with diverse geospatial data sources, facilitating complex geographic question answering with additional spatial operations.

Zhang et al. [19], similarly, propose Map GPT Playground, a system that addresses the challenge of map queries involving multiple locations or locations with additional context. Their work showed the potential of Large Language Models (LLM) to seamlessly answer complex queries by integrating with foundational map services like geocoding and routing.

The work presented in [9] examines the performance of ChatGPT in a real Geographic Information Systems (GIS) exam, aiming to understand the capabilities and limitations of large language models (LLMs) in specialized subject areas. The study evaluates ChatGPT's grasp of geospatial concepts, comparing two models, GPT-3.5 and GPT-4, to explore whether general improvements in LLMs translate to better performance in spatially oriented questions. The findings reveal that both GPT variants can pass a balanced GIS exam and highlight areas where LLMs struggle with spatial concepts.

Liang et al. [8], on the other hand, proposes a framework called LLM-MPE for human mobility prediction during public events, addressing challenges in encoding textual information from online sources into statistical or machine-learning models. LLM-MPE leverages Large Language Models (LLMs) for their ability to process textual data, learn from minimal examples, and generate human-readable explanations. The framework transforms raw event descriptions into a standardized format, segments historical mobility data, and employs a prompting strategy for LLMs to make and rationalize demand predictions based on both historical mobility and event features. A case study at Barclays Center in New York City demonstrates LLM-MPE's superiority over traditional models, particularly on event days, with textual data significantly improving accuracy. The framework also provides interpretable insights into predictions. However, that work also highlights several challenges of LLM usage in that context, including the risk of misinformation and high costs, which hinder the broader adoption of LLMs in large-scale human mobility analysis.

Other works investigated the possibility of leveraging LLMs to automate the setup and execution of GIS workflows. Zhang et al. [20], for example, propose a framework called GeoGPT, which leverages the semantic understanding abilities of LLMs for geospatial tasks. The framework aims to empower non-professional users by enabling autonomous geospatial data collection, processing, and analysis through natural language instructions. Similarly, the work presented in [7] proposes the concept of an Autonomous GIS leveraging LLMs. This AI-powered geographic information system aims to address spatial problems through automatic spatial data collection, analysis, and visualization by utilizing the general abilities of LLMs in natural language understanding, reasoning, and coding. The proposed Autonomous GIS is envisioned to achieve the five key goals of being self-generating, self-organizing, self-verifying, self-executing, and self-growing. The authors developed a prototype system called LLM-Geo using the GPT-4 API, preliminarily demonstrating its capabilities through three case studies. While still in its early stages, LLM-Geo shows promise in making spatial analysis more efficient and accessible, motivating further research and development in autonomous GIS within the GIScience community.

While several works have highlighted the capabilities of LLMs in GIS tasks, to the best of our knowledge, no work in the literature has investigated the feasibility of using LLMs to automatically generate GIS reports, focusing on both the spatial and the temporal nature of data handled by GIS systems.

3   Large Language Models for GIS Report Generation

Generating human-readable reports in GIS involves the key preliminary step of detecting relevant spatio-temporal patterns and anomalies from summarized data produced by a GIS workflow, which should be then presented to the intended audience. In addition to the complexity lying in these knowledge discovery operations, the GIS reporting scenario is further complicated by the need for tailored reports to cater to diverse audiences, potentially in different languages [17]. A single GIS analysis may prompt the generation of reports multiple times a day, each targeted towards specific stakeholders with varying levels of expertise and linguistic preferences.

This diversity in reporting requirements and the inherent difficulty of knowledge discovery processes make the traditional process of creating reports with manual analyses a particularly time-intensive and error-prone task, which would greatly benefit from an automated approach to consistently deliver relevant information to the intended recipients.

To address these challenges, we investigate the feasibility of an extended GIS workflow that incorporates an additional step for automatic report generation using LLMs, as shown in Fig. 1. After the GIS pipeline produces its summarized results, typically in a tabular format, the LLM-based report generation step activates, leveraging a specifically engineered prompt and a suitable, text-based representation of the analysis results to extract patterns and anomalies and produce reports in a human-readable format. The automated process we envision would enable the execution of GIS pipelines multiple times a day, ensuring that reports are generated promptly and tailored to the specific needs of diverse audiences. Integrating LLMs into GIS report generation holds thus the potential

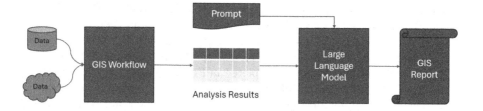

Fig. 1. Overview of the envisioned approach for LLM-based GIS report generation

to streamline the detection of spatio-temporal patterns and anomalies, while simultaneously addressing the complexities associated with generating diverse and tailored reports. In this paper, we focus in particular on the first task (i.e., detecting spatio-temporal patterns and anomalies), leaving the assessment on the LLM capability to tailor generated content to the specific needs, expertise levels, and linguistic preferences of varied audiences across different domains to future works.

4   Case Studies

The aim of this empirical evaluation is to assess the performance of a pre-trained Language Model (LLM) in generating GIS reports from raw data. The evaluation will focus on the correctness (absence of hallucinations) and completeness (detection of all trends and anomalies) of the generated reports.

More in detail, for this study, we leveraged the OpenAI ChatGPT 3.5 service, using the performance-optimized `text-davinci-002-render-sha` model, which is estimated to count 175B parameters [15], and consider three diverse GIS reporting scenarios based on real-world data.

In the remainder of this section, we describe the selected case studies and detail the empirical procedure we employed.

4.1   GIS Reporting Case Studies

Choose three distinct datasets with varied spatial and temporal characteristics. Ensure that the datasets cover different geographical areas and exhibit diverse patterns and anomalies relevant to GIS reporting.

Case Study 1: Earthquake Distribution
As a first case study, we utilized earthquake data collected from the United States Geological Survey (USGS)[1], specifically focusing on seismic events occurring worldwide during the first week of 2024, spanning from January 1, 2024, to January 7, 2024. Moreover, we considered only data about earthquakes with a

---

[1] https://www.usgs.gov/programs/earthquake-hazards.

magnitude above 4.5, which led to a dataset of 130 seismic events. For each event, as reported in Table 1, collected data includes a timestamp, geographic coordinates (Latitude and Longitude), depth of the event, as well as a text description of the area in which the event occurred. The spatial distribution and magnitude of the collected seismic events are depicted in Fig. 2. The selected data captures the spatio-temporal dynamics of earthquakes, offering a comprehensive view of seismic activity in different regions over the specified timeframe. This temporal specificity allows for a detailed exploration of how earthquake occurrences unfold spatially and temporally during this particular week.

Table 1. Sample of earthquake data collected for Case Study 1

Time	Lat.	Long.	Depth	Mag.	Place
01/01/2024 01:37	17.67	145.52	389	4.6	273 km N of Saipan, Northern Mariana Islands
01/01/2024 02:43	−24.41	179.88	509	4.6	south of the Fiji Islands
01/01/2024 04:04	76.09	17.58	10	4.6	243 km S of Longyearbyen, Svalbard and Jan Mayen
01/01/2024 05:49	44.46	149.28	35	4.5	139 km SE of Kuril'sk, Russia
01/01/2024 06:19	−23.34	−179.83	533	4.6	south of the Fiji Islands
⋮	⋮	⋮	⋮	⋮	⋮

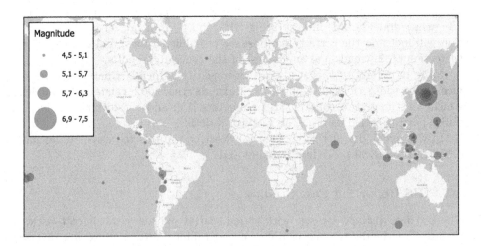

Fig. 2. Visualization of collected earthquake data

Case Study 2: Traffic Accidents

For our second case study, we employed data concerning fatal traffic accidents in the United States, leveraging data published by the National Safety Council (NSC)[2] and based on information provided by the National Highway Traffic

---

[2] https://injuryfacts.nsc.org/motor-vehicle/overview/crashes-by-time-of-day-and-day-of-week/.

Safety Administration (NHTSA). This dataset emphasizes the temporal dimension, providing detailed insights into fatal accidents based on the month, day of the week, and time.

It is worth noting that this dataset lacks geo-referenced information, focusing instead on various time frames within a day, as well as a breakdown across months and days of the week. The temporal granularity of this data enables a nuanced examination of patterns and trends related to fatal traffic accidents throughout different time intervals. A sample of the data is reported in Table 2 and a visualization of the distribution of traffic accidents by month and time of day is depicted in Fig. 3.

Table 2. Sample of traffic accident summary data collected for Case Study 2

Month	Time of day	Day of week							
		Total	Sun	Mon	Tue	Wed	Thu	Fri	Sat
Jan	00:00–03:59 am	402	110	29	25	29	34	86	89
Jan	04:00–07:59 am	322	37	43	39	45	47	70	41
Jan	08:00–11:59 am	335	42	51	46	49	44	58	45
Jan	12:00–03:59 pm	479	66	74	67	59	55	86	72
Jan	04:00–07:59 pm	690	112	75	73	85	99	125	121
Jan	08:00–11:59 pm	583	88	56	50	76	69	131	113
Jan	Unknown	24	5	2	5	2	3	5	2
Jan	Total	2.835	460	330	305	345	351	561	483
Feb	00:00–03:59 am	304	87	48	32	20	22	23	72
Feb	04:00–07:59 am	268	44	46	28	34	41	42	33
Feb	08:00–11:59 am	271	28	35	43	40	51	38	36
⋮	⋮	⋮	⋮	⋮	⋮	⋮	⋮	⋮	⋮

Case Study 3: Spatio-Temporal Road Network Coverage Data

The third case study is based on a Vehicular crowd-sensing (VCS) scenario in which taxis are used to opportunistically collect data in an urban environment [5,12]. More in detail, we consider a GIS report focused on analyzing the spatial coverage achieved by the probe vehicles over the maps, detailing how many times the probe vehicles visited specific areas of interest in the City of Rome.

The report was generated using the Knime Mobility Toolkit presented in [3,4], and leveraging real-world taxi trajectory data collected from approximately 300 taxis in February 2014 [2], restricting the analysis to trajectories from a single day, namely February 1st, 2014. To generate the report, we considered 25 distinct areas over the City of Rome, each representing a cell in an overall larger grid, as depicted in Fig. 4.

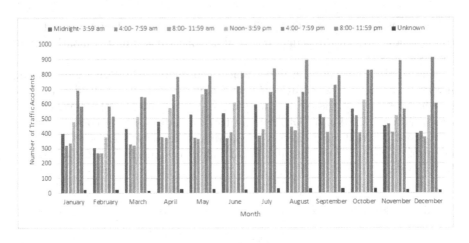

Fig. 3. Distribution of fatal traffic accidents by month and time of day.

The GIS report includes, for each considered area of interest, a numerical identifier, the polygon geometry of the area, defined in Well-Known Text (WKT) format and consisting of a series of longitude and latitude coordinates that outline the boundaries of the area, and the number of visits for that area. A sample of the data is shown in Table 3 and the entire dataset is visualized in Fig. 4. In the figure, the number included between square brackets in each cell represents its numerical ID.

This case study does not include a temporal dimension, but has been included to investigate the extent to which LLMs can handle more complex spatial data such as polygon shapes and infer spatial relations between these more complex objects.

Table 3. Sample of the vehicular crowd-sensing data collected for Case Study 3

Area Id	N. visits	Area Shape
1	540	`POLYGON((12.47 41.89, 12.47 41.90, ...))`
2	217	`POLYGON((12.47 41.90, 12.47 41.91, ...))`
3	94	`POLYGON((12.47 41.91, 12.47 41.91, ...))`
4	54	`POLYGON((12.47 41.91, 12.47 41.92, ...))`
⋮	⋮	⋮

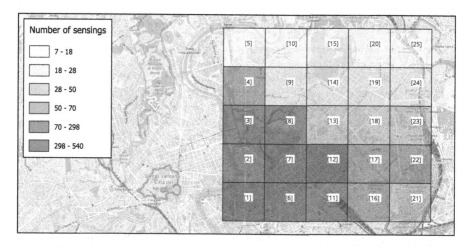

Fig. 4. Visualization of vehicular crowd-sensing coverage over the City of Rome

4.2 Procedure

After collecting the data for our case studies as detailed in Sect. 4.1, we prepared a common data representation in CSV format, which reflects the same structure presented in Tables 1, 2 and 3. Subsequently, we defined, for each case study, a prompt to submit to the LLM. The prompts were defined according to the commonly accepted guidelines defined in [10,18]. More in detail, we start each prompt by providing a general context and description of the input data. Subsequently, we provide step-by-step instructions on how to generate a report (e.g.: start with an overview section, then describe spatio-temporal trends or patterns in data, then highlight any anomaly). For each case study, the prompts we engineered are reported as follows. The CSV-based text representation of the input data was appended at the end of each prompt, symbolized by the ##DATA## placeholder.

Prompt for Case Study 1: Earthquake Distribution Report

Analyze the following data describing earthquakes with their timestamp, magnitude, and geographic position.

Based on the data, you will write a detailed report. The report should start with an overview section, providing general information about the data.

Subsequently, the report should include a section dedicated to describing spatial/temporal trends and patterns in the data, if any.

Last, the report should include a section dedicated to highlighting anomalies in the data, if any. Anomalies can be related to the position of the seismic events, to their temporal frequency, to the depth at which they occur or to their magnitude.

##DATA##

Prompt for Case Study 2: Traffic Accidents Report

Analyze the following data describing fatal traffic accidents in the US in 2021. The data summarizes the number of fatal accidents by month, by time of day, and by day of the week, including some aggregations in the "Total" columns/rows. Based on the data, you will write a detailed report. The report should start with an overview section, providing general information about the data.

Subsequently, the report should include a section dedicated to describing spatial/temporal trends and patterns in the data, if any. Last, the report should include a section dedicated to highlighting anomalies in the data, if any. Anomalies can be related to days of the week, months, or time of day in which traffic accidents are more or less common.

##DATA##

Prompt for Case Study 3: Vehicular Crowd-Sensing Report

Analyze the following data describing how many times each considered area of a city was visited by probe vehicles during a day in a vehicular crowd-sensing setting. Each area is identified by its name and by a polygon representing its shape in WKT format. Each vertex in the polygon is a point with coordinates in the longitude-latitude format. For each area, the data below includes the number of sensings happening in that area.

Based on the data, you will write a detailed report. The report should start with an overview section, providing general information about the data.

Subsequently, the report should include a section dedicated to describing spatial/temporal trends and patterns in the data, if any.

Last, the report should include a section dedicated to highlighting anomalies in the data, if any. Anomalies can be related to areas that receive more or fewer visits w.r.t. neighboring areas, or to the spatial distribution of the areas, or to a combination of both spatial aspects and the recorded number of visits.

##DATA##

Each prompt was executed five times, to account for variability in the LLM text-generation process. For each repetition, the reports generated by the LLM were collected. These reports were subsequently manually analyzed by the authors of this paper. The manual analysis was performed by each of the authors independently. More in detail, each author initially analyzed the input data, to highlight patterns and or anomalies. Then, each author reviewed each generated report, focusing on their *completeness* (i.e., were *all* the patterns and anomalies detected?) and on their *correctness* (i.e., is the reported information *correct*?). Any discrepancies or disagreements among the authors during this analysis were thoroughly discussed, leading to a consensus on the final evaluation of the generated reports.

5   Qualitative Analysis and Discussion

5.1   Case Study 1: Earthquakes

In the first case study, in all considered repetitions of our experiment, LLM-generated reports highlighted the unusual seismic activities linked to the 2024 Noto earthquake that affected Japan on 2024/01/01[3]. This involved both a temporal pattern, with most activities being concentrated in the first two days of the considered time period, and a spatial pattern, with a cluster of seismic events happening in the Noto region, in Japan. In the following snippet, we report a sample from one of the generated reports.

> 🏮: There is a notable concentration of seismic activity in the first two days of January 2024, with several earthquakes occurring within short time intervals, especially around Japan. The most significant event during this period is the earthquake on January 1, 2024, with a magnitude of 7.5 near the Noto Peninsula, Japan.

Moreover, in all the repetitions, LLM-generated reports successfully detected and highlighted as anomalies some earthquakes happening at a notably higher depth w.r.t. other events in the considered dataset. In the following snippet, we report a relevant sample from one of the generated reports.

> 🏮: While most events have shallow depths, there are instances of earthquakes occurring at greater depths, such as the event near the Fiji Islands on January 1, 2024, with a depth of 509.191 km.

While the reported data is correct (i.e., the data includes a seismic event happening on January 1, 2024 near the Fiji Islands at a significant depth of 509.191 km, which is noticeably higher than the average depth in the dataset, which amounts to ≈ 70 km), it is worth noting that a different earthquake with a depth of 611.115 km also happened in the Fiji region, and was not mentioned by the LLM in any of the reports.

5.2   Case Study 2: Traffic Accidents

In the second case study, the LLM performed remarkably worse, possibly also due to the higher complexity of the input data. In this scenario, the LLM-generated reports frequently contained incorrect information, and the reported data often varied among the different repetitions of the experiments.

As an example of such incorrect information and variability among repetitions, in the following snippet, we report two different samples of the reports generated in Repetitions 3 and 1. In the former, the report included correct

---

[3] https://en.wikipedia.org/wiki/2024_Noto_earthquake.

information, while in the latter different months were identified as the months with the most and the fewest accidents.

🎭 **(Rep. 3)**: October recorded the highest total number of fatal accidents (3,799), while February had the lowest (2,340).

🎭 **(Rep. 1)**: The total number of fatal accidents peaked in August (3,715) and reached its lowest in January (2,835).

It is worth noting that the reported figures are always correct (i.e., there were indeed 2,835 accidents in January and 3,715 in August), and the issues always lie in the comparison among the different numbers of accidents to detect the highest/smallest values.

Moreover, the LLM was not fully able to understand the structure of the input data, and the correlation between month and time slot (expressed in rows) and day of the week, encoded in the columns. This is exemplified by the following snippet, extracted from the report obtained in Repetition 3.

🎭 **(Rep. 3)**:
- There is an unexpected peak in fatal accidents during August, particularly in the midnight to 3:59 am time frame, with 179 incidents.
- December shows an anomaly in the 4:00-7:59 pm slot, with 148 accidents, higher than other months in the same period.

In the snippet, the peaks in the number of accidents occurring in August and in December in the indicated time frames are not associated with the entire month, as the report suggests, but rather to specific days of the week (i.e., Sunday and Wednesday, respectively). A different representation of the input data, with the days of the week encoded as rows, might lead to better results in this scenario.

Moreover, in this scenario, LLM-generated reports also consistently failed to reflect a pattern which was detected by both authors during the preliminary analysis of the data. This pattern, which can also be observed in Fig. 3, indicates a higher frequency of accidents during late evening hours (8:00 pm—11:59 pm) in summer and afternoon hours (4:00 pm–7:59 pm) in winter.

5.3   Case Study 3: Vehicular Crowd-Sensing

In this scenario, the limits of the general-purpose LLM in analyzing and understanding more complex spatial data such as Polygons became apparent, and negatively affected the quality of the generated reports. Indeed, in all the considered repetitions, the LLM failed to highlight the key pattern in the input data, i.e., that grid cells in the south-west part of the considered area have a noticeably higher concentration of vehicular sensings than those in the north and north-east areas (see Fig. 4).

Instead, the LLM often incorrectly assumed that the numeric IDs associated with each grid cell were representative of their position w.r.t. the city centre, with lower Area IDs being closer to the centre and higher IDs being increasingly farther away. This led to incorrect results being included in the reports, as in the following snippets.

🏛 **(Rep. 1)**:
- Areas closer to the city center (lower Area IDs) generally exhibit higher visit counts.
- As the Area ID increases, indicating a move towards the city outskirts, the number of visits tends to decrease. - Notably, there's a gradual decline in visit counts from the city center towards the periphery.

🏛 **(Rep. 2)**:
Analyzing the data reveals interesting spatial and temporal trends. For instance, there is a general decrease in the number of visits from the southern to the northern areas of the city. Areas [1] to [5], located in the southern part, have higher visit counts compared to areas [21] to [25] in the northern part, where the visit counts are lower.

Remarkably, in some cases, the LLM hallucinated, confusing spatial data (i.e., the considered areas and their shape) with temporal data, which is not included at all in the input data provided in this case study. This happened, for example, in Repetition 2, in which the LLM produced a report including the following snippet.

🏛 **(Rep. 2)**:
Moreover, there is a noticeable temporal pattern, with a decrease in the number of visits from morning (e.g., Area [1]) to evening (e.g., Area [25]). This temporal trend could be attributed to daily commuting patterns or specific events affecting vehicular movement throughout the day.

5.4   Discussion

Summarizing, the considered LLM proved to be quite effective in consistently detecting spatio-temporal trends and anomalies and in generating accurate reports in the first case study, also due to the simple structure of the input data. When applied in scenarios with more complex input representations (i.e., Case Study 2), the LLM often produced reports containing incorrect or partial information. When faced with a scenario involving more complex spatial data and a more specialized and niche context (i.e., Case Study 3, which involved Vehicular Crowd-Sensing), the LLM was unable to correctly interpret spatial data, and often hallucinated, reporting information unrelated to the provided data.

6 Conclusions

This paper investigated the potential of general-purpose LLMs in detecting spatio-temporal patterns and anomalies in real-world GIS data and in describing them in consistent, human-readable reports. Results show that LLMs are promising tools to support the generation of GIS reports, being able, in some scenarios, to consistently capture some complex spatio-temporal patterns and anomalies in the input data and generate effective reports. However, when faced with more complex input data or with data from more specialized and niche contexts, the LLM performance significantly diminished, leading to reports that contained inaccuracies or partial information and, in some scenarios, also hallucinated details unrelated to the provided data.

Future research directions include further investigation on the impact of prompt engineering and different data representation on the quality of the obtained reports, and exploring ways to enhance the LLM's spatio-temporal reasoning capabilities via fine-tuning on GIS-specific data. Additionally, investigating strategies to mitigate hallucinations and inaccuracies in reports, particularly when dealing with niche contexts, would be a valuable avenue for further research. Last, future works may also analyze the performance of different LLM on GIS report generation tasks, to determine whether open-source models such as LLaMa [14] perform as well as commercial ones such as ChatGPT.

Acknowledgements. This work was partially supported by the PNRR MUR project PE0000013-FAIR.

Data Availability Statement. The data employed in the case studies, as well as the prompts and the generated reports, are available in a dedicated replication package [13].

References

1. Achiam, J., et al.: GPT-4 technical report. arXiv preprint arXiv:2303.08774 (2023)
2. Bracciale, L., Bonola, M., Loreti, P., Bianchi, G., Amici, R., Rabuffi, A.: CRAW-DAD Roma/taxi (2022). https://doi.org/10.15783/C7QC7M
3. Di Martino, S., Landolfi, E., Mazzocca, N., di Torrepadula, F.R., Starace, L.L.L.: A visual-based toolkit to support mobility data analytics. Expert Syst. Appl. **238**, 121949 (2024)
4. Di Martino, S., Mazzocca, N., Di Torrepadula, F.R., Starace, L.L.L.: Mobility data analytics with KNOT: the KNIME mobility toolkit. In: In: Mostafavi, M.A., Del Mondo, G. (eds.) W2GIS 2023. LNCS, vol. 13912, pp. 95–104. Springer, Cham (2023). https://doi.org/10.1007/978-3-031-34612-5_6
5. Di Martino, S., Starace, L.L.L.: Vehicular crowd-sensing on complex urban road networks: a case study in the city of porto. Transp. Res. Procedia **62**, 350–357 (2022)
6. Feng, Y., Ding, L., Xiao, G.: Geoqamap-geographic question answering with maps leveraging LLM and open knowledge base (short paper). In: 12th International Conference on Geographic Information Science (GIScience 2023). Schloss Dagstuhl-Leibniz-Zentrum für Informatik (2023)

7. Li, Z., Ning, H.: Autonomous GIS: the next-generation AI-powered GIS. arXiv preprint arXiv:2305.06453 (2023)
8. Liang, Y., Liu, Y., Wang, X., Zhao, Z.: Exploring large language models for human mobility prediction under public events. arXiv preprint arXiv:2311.17351 (2023)
9. Mooney, P., Cui, W., Guan, B., Juhász, L.: Towards understanding the geospatial skills of ChatGPT: taking a geographic information systems (GIS) exam. In: Proceedings of the 6th ACM SIGSPATIAL International Workshop on AI for Geographic Knowledge Discovery, pp. 85–94 (2023)
10. OpenAI: Prompt engineering guide (2024). https://platform.openai.com/docs/guides/prompt-engineering/strategy-write-clear-instructions
11. Ouyang, L., et al.: Training language models to follow instructions with human feedback. In: Advances in Neural Information Processing Systems, vol. 35, pp. 27730–27744 (2022)
12. Starace, L., Rocco Di Torrepadula, F., Di Martino, S., Mazzocca, N., et al.: Vehicular crowdsensing with high-mileage vehicles: investigating spatiotemporal coverage dynamics in historical cities with complex urban road networks. J. Adv. Transp. **2023** (2023)
13. Starace, L.L.L., Di Martino, S.: Can large language models automatically generate GIS reports? January 2024. https://doi.org/10.5281/zenodo.10535248
14. Touvron, H., et al.: LLaMA: open and efficient foundation language models. arXiv preprint arXiv:2302.13971 (2023)
15. Veres, C., Sampson, J.: Self supervised learning and the poverty of the stimulus. Data Knowl. Eng. **147**, 102208 (2023)
16. Wang, Z., Xie, Q., Ding, Z., Feng, Y., Xia, R.: Is ChatGPT a good sentiment analyzer? A preliminary study. arXiv preprint arXiv:2304.04339 (2023)
17. Yagamurthy, D.N., Azmeera, R., Khanna, R.: Natural language generation (NLG) for automated report generation. J. Technol. Syst. **5**(1), 48–59 (2023)
18. Zamfirescu-Pereira, J., Wong, R.Y., Hartmann, B., Yang, Q.: Why Johnny can't prompt: how non-AI experts try (and fail) to design LLM prompts. In: Proceedings of the 2023 CHI Conference on Human Factors in Computing Systems, pp. 1–21 (2023)
19. Zhang, C., Karatzoglou, A., Craig, H., Yankov, D.: Map GPT playground: smart locations and routes with GPT. In: Proceedings of the 31st ACM International Conference on Advances in Geographic Information Systems, pp. 1–4 (2023)
20. Zhang, Y., Wei, C., Wu, S., He, Z., Yu, W.: GeoGPT: understanding and processing geospatial tasks through an autonomous GPT. arXiv preprint arXiv:2307.07930 (2023)

Transportation Applications

A Digital Twin Architecture for Intelligent Public Transportation Systems: A FIWARE-Based Solution

Alessandra De Benedictis[ID], Franca Rocco di Torrepadula[✉][ID],
and Alessandra Somma[ID]

Department of Electrical Engineering and Information Technology,
University of Naples Federico II, Naples, Italy
{alessandra.debenedictis,franca.roccoditorrepadula,
alessandra.somma}@unina.it

Abstract. Public transportation systems play a vital role for society, but they often fall short in addressing the dynamic needs of commuters. Intelligent Public Transportation Systems (IPTS) hold promise for enhancing efficiency and adapting to these evolving requirements. Digital twins (DT), virtual representations of real-world systems, can be leveraged to create dynamic replicas that guide real-time decision-making and optimization for IPTS. This paper examines the concept of digital twins and their potential for IPTS, highlighting the challenges and opportunities that must be addressed to fully capitalize on this technology. Moreover, a DT-based IPTS architecture is proposed leveraging on FIWARE Smart Data Models for data interoperability. Finally, a small real-world instance of the proposed architecture and data model is illustrated involving a bus-based IPTS where the DT technology is adopted to enable bus passenger demand prediction and bus scheduling update.

Keywords: Intelligent Public Transportation Systems · Digital Twins · FIWARE smart data models · Passenger Demand Prediction

1 Introduction

Public transportation systems are a fundamental aspect of the society, allowing for the movement of people and goods, access to places, and attendance at events [12,22]. However, such systems are not always able to meet the heterogeneous and dynamic needs of citizens with a sufficient quality of service [8,14,20,28], leading to stress, anxiety and loss of productivity for passengers [13,23,25]. For this reason, less sustainable private means of transports are often preferred, with significant environmental effects.

To mitigate these problems, thanks to the increasing availability of mobility data, many research efforts have been focused on improving public transit efficiency, giving rise to the ***Intelligent Public Transportation System*** (IPTS) field. Examples of investigations are on forecasting passenger flow/demand (*e.g.*

M. Lotfian and L. L. L. Starace (Eds.): W2GIS 2024, LNCS 14673, pp. 165–182, 2024.
https://doi.org/10.1007/978-3-031-60796-7_12

[1, 11, 29]), or metro/bus arrival times (*e.g.*, [3, 24, 27]). Based on such predictions, transport companies can proactively adapt their services by applying new policies, in order to meet new needs. Still, evaluating the impact of new scheduling/planning solutions, and assessing their sustainability at a city-wide scale, is another crucial aspect of urban planning and policy-making.

As a result of the growing of processing capabilities and computational power, the microscopic movement of individuals and vehicles in a urban scenario and the interactions between neighbouring vehicles or between vehicles and pedestrians can be realistically modeled and simulated. Simulation is a fundamental tool for understanding and predicting a system behavior, but it can be taken a step further by establishing a dynamic bidirectional link between the virtual representation and the physical system, in order to enable real-time interaction and feedback loops that can allow for proactive intervention and optimization. This is what a ***Digital Twin*** (DT) does, as it creates a living digital replica of the real-world entity, capturing its current state and continuously updating it as the physical system evolves.

Consider a transportation network with multiple traffic signals, roads, and vehicles. A simulation model of this network could be used to predict traffic congestion under various scenarios, such as changing traffic patterns or introducing new traffic signals. However, a Digital Twin of the transportation network would go a step further, continuously monitoring real-time traffic data and adjusting traffic signals accordingly to optimize traffic flow. A few examples of DT initiatives in the transportation domain exist, such as those carried out by the Hamad International Airport[1] and the Port of Rotterdam[2], which are using digital twins to improve their operations. The first provides a real-time view of airport operations, optimizes resources, and minimizes asset downtime, while the latter helps to schedule ships and cranes more efficiently, reduce waiting times, and improve cargo handling.

While the concept of DT has been around for a while and is gaining traction in academia and industry, it needs to be carefully adapted to meet the specific requirements of mobility, which differ from those of manufacturing and industry in terms of the geographic areas involved and, above all, of the complexity of human factors involved. Technical interoperability, clear communication between stakeholders, and reliable data to test different scenarios (including disaster and social challenges), are just a few of the other very important facets that it highlights for consideration. In addition, there are governmental, regulatory and legal challenges that may need to be addressed including data ownership, confidentiality and liability issues.

In this paper, we propose a DT-based conceptual architecture for IPTS meant to support transport companies in optimizing the provided services, as well as citizens in satisfying their mobility needs. To cope with interoperability issues

---

[1] https://www.sita.aero/pressroom/blog/digital-border-and-airport-technologies-smoothing-the-way-for-visitors-to-the-world-cup/.

[2] https://ditto-oceandecade.org/use-cases/a-digital-twin-for-the-port-of-rotterdam-by-esri/.

and provide a common language to share data and collaborate among the different entities of an IPTS, we investigate the integration of the FIWARE Smart Data Models[3], which are currently being adopted by a number of organizations (including the European Commission) to develop and deploy their applications. Finally, to provide a practical example of how the proposed architecture and data model can be instantiated, we present a case study on a bus-based IPTS where the Digital Twin technology can help to predict passenger demand based on real-time data collected from buses and possibly to update bus schedule accordingly.

The remainder of the paper is organized as follows. Section 2 discusses some related work on the integration of the DT technology in the transportation domain. Section 3 presents an architecture proposal for a DT-based IPTS. Section 4 introduces the mapping of the proposed architecture onto FIWARE components, while Sect. 5 describes a bus transport case study, illustrating the adopted FIWARE Smart Data Models (SDMs) and technological components. Finally, Sect. 6 draws our conclusion.

2   Related Work

Transportation digital twins offer immense potential to revolutionize the way we manage and optimize transportation systems. They can be utilized to improve the efficiency and effectiveness not only of traffic planning and management, but also of traffic forecasting, energy management and energy consumption forecasting (for electric vehicles for instance), parking lot management, driver behavior analysis, pedestrian behavior investigation, and so on [10,26]. Unfortunately, despite some solutions exist that claim to represent a DT example in the transportation domain, most of them do actually miss the main peculiar feature of DTs, namely them being continuously updated by real-time data coming from the physical system. For example, in [7], a proof-of-concept application of DT for Adaptive Traffic Signal Control (ATSC) was presented. Despite being called a "digital twin approach", the application leveraged on simulation data that was not based on real-world traffic conditions, but generated by the simulation model itself. In many other cases, the DT concept is used as a buzz word without any concrete reference, such as in [19].

In [15], the authors proposed a run-time synchronized DT of the Geneva motorway leveraging the SUMO simulator and the real-time motorway traffic data (in minute resolution) from the Open Data Platform Mobility Switzerland (ODPMS). In this solution, the number of passing vehicles, their speeds and vehicle category are continuously fed into the running simulation through the SUMO's Traffic Control Interface (TraCI) so that the simulation-based motorway DT is updated (in a spatio-temporal manner) as the physical motorway traffic changes. This work is particularly significant in the context of DT-based IPTS, as it represents an actual example of run-time calibrated digital simulation model of a transportation system, continuously updated with actual

---

[3] https://www.fiware.org/smart-data-models/.

high-resolution traffic data. Nevertheless, the focus of the work is on the system implementation, which leverages on the integration of an existing simulator, *i.e.*, SUMO, with suitable data sources for its dynamic calibration. Our goal is wider, as we aim to propose a general architecture for DT-based IPTSs that may use different system modeling and simulation capabilities and where the core functionalities that are common to any IPTS and DT are outlined. Moreover, in [15] the data interoperability problem is not addressed, as there is only one data source, while in several scenarios the data is generated and shared by multiple sources in different formats and under different policies.

The architectural aspect has been addressed in [2], where an architecture for DTs applied to transportation systems is introduced. The architecture devises three layers: the data access layer realizes real-time data perception by modeling both the static traffic environment (roads, facilities, driving behaviors, etc.) and the dynamic traffic elements (data from roadside and vehicle sensors, pedestrian crossing, etc.); the computational simulation layer collects the traffic data and builds the traffic model by discovering the existing hierarchical relationships, interactions, and evolutionary processes among traffic elements. Finally, the application management layer suitably combines simulation calculation results and decision optimization models to build practical applications. While the proposed architecture captures some fundamental features of DTs in a traffic management scenario, it does not provide any concrete implementation of such architecture, nor it addresses data interoperability issues.

3   An Architecture Proposal for DT-Based IPTS

In this section, we describe the architecture we envision for a DT-based IPTS, organized into nine layers, as shown in Fig. 1. Public transports are complex systems involving several entities, including but not limited to buses, metros, passengers, road networks and infrastructures. All these *Real-World (Physical) Entities* can be monitored through apposite devices in order to obtain mobility-related data, on top of which it is possible to realize several services.

In our conceptual architecture, the **Physical Twin Layer** is the interface with the physical world, for both sensing and control/actuation. On one hand, it is responsible for acquiring data related to the physical entities under control. To this purpose, different kind of sensors are used. For instance, GPS/GNSS devices are typically exploited to acquire data related to the trajectories of vehicles/passengers, while Automatic Passenger Counting (APC) systems are used for understanding how many people are in a vehicle or are waiting at a stop/station. On the other hand, based on the outcomes of DT-based services, this layer allows to control and perform some actions on the physical entities, by means of specific controllers and/or actuators.

Since different entities are monitored, and several sensors are employed, the resulting data are highly heterogeneous. For this reason, the **Data Ingestion Layer** is meant to homogenize the data collected through the Physical Layer in a standard format, before being stored, analyzed and/or processed. The **Storage**

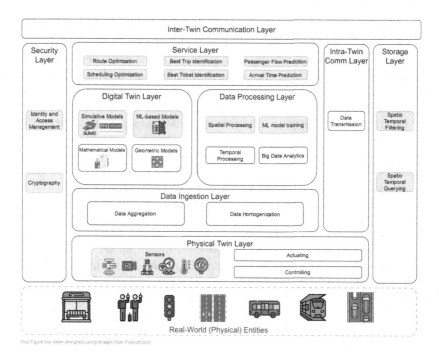

Fig. 1. Architecture for a DT-based Intelligent Public Transport System. Components whose design and implementation is specific to mobility systems are highlighted in green. (Color figure online)

Layer is responsible for the persistence of data generated by all the other layers. Hence, in our vision, this layer stands as orthogonal to the others. However, it is worth noticing that, within the realm of public transport systems, data exhibit a distinct spatio-temporal nature. Therefore, this layer should be designed in order to explicitly incorporate support for spatio-temporal data filtering and querying. Similarly, in the implementation phase, technologies with this kind of support should be employed. Within the *Data Processing Layer* data are elaborated for diverse purposes, including conducting data analytics, training machine learning models, and their integration into simulation environments.

The core of the architecture lies in the *Digital Twin Layer*, which represents the modeling capability of the system. Here, digital replicas of monitored entities take form through mathematical models, simulations, machine learning algorithms, and so on. For instance, in the context of public transport, predictive models based on machine learning techniques (such as Recurrent or Convolutional Neural Networks) can be deployed to predict the system's future state. Moreover, urban mobility simulators (such as Eclipse SUMO[4] or PTV Vissim[5])

---

[4] https://eclipse.dev/sumo/.

[5] https://www.ptvgroup.com/en/products/ptv-vissim.

can be exploited to simulate and analyze both the current and the future behavior of the system.

On top of these models and the processed data, the **Service Layer** provide different services, with the common goal of enhancing and optimizing public mobility. For example, based on the historical data, bus/metro arrival time or passenger demand prediction can be performed. Such predictions allow passengers to plan their trip also based on this information, as well as transport operators to better manage their own resources. Moreover, the resulting information can be combined for realizing more sophisticated services, ranging from public transport routing and scheduling optimization, tailored for public transport operators, to trip and ticket calculation services, designed to benefit passengers.

The communication among various components within the DT-based architecture is managed by the **Intra-Twin Communication Layer**. The latter acts as a publish-subscriber broker, meant to maintain loose coupling among components. Moreover, given the complex nature of smart cities, which are composed of different subsystems, each potentially incorporating its own Digital Twin, we envision an additional layer, *i.e.*, the **Inter-Twin Communication Layer**. This layer is meant to allow the exchange of data and services among different DTs within the smart city framework. Its objective is to ease a unified and cooperative environment, enabling DTs to exchange information and insights. This contributes to the comprehensive functionality and efficiency of the broader smart city infrastructure. Finally, the **Security Layer** includes the main capabilities needed for accessing and using data in a compliant way w.r.t the considered local privacy/data regulations.

Data interoperability is one of the biggest challenges that an IPTS has to face, as the ability to seamlessly share and exchange data between different systems and devices is fundamental in their context. Key data interoperability problems are related to the co-existence of different data formats and data models (*i.e.*, the way that data is structured and organized), and to the prevalence of poor data quality (missing, corrupted or inconsistent data) in many real cases. Moreover, the availability of different security capabilities at the different sub-systems of an IPTS often represents a further barrier to interoperability, as data cannot be shared securely by involved entities as requested by existing policies and regulations. Adopting common data formats and models and improving overall data security and quality are key concerns that must be taken into account when instantiating the above illustrated architecture.

4   An Open Standards-Based IPTS Implementation: FIWARE and Smart Data Models

The DT-based IPTS architecture presented in the previous section is platform-independent. A few solutions currently exist to implement digital twins, including open source frameworks like Eclipse Ditto[6] or FIWARE[7], and commercial solutions like Azure Digital Twins[8] and Siemens Insights Hub[9].

In this work, we leverage on the **FIWARE** technology, an open-source, open standards-based initiative that facilitates the development and deployment of smart solutions across various domains. FIWARE's open-source nature, multi-domain applicability, cloud-agnosticism, data-driven approach, and community support make it a compelling choice for organizations seeking a versatile and scalable digital twin platform. Its ability to integrate with existing IoT systems and leverage open standards further enhances its appeal for a wide range of use cases.

FIWARE provides a set of building blocks for the creation of smart applications known as *Generic Enablers* (GEs) [4,16]. They are grouped in five main categories[10] [5,6]: i) *Core Context Management* includes software components based on publish-subscribe pattern in charge of context data storage and manipulation; ii) *interfacing with the IoT, robots and third-party systems* to capture changes in context information and translate necessary actions; iii) *processing, analysis and visualization* of context data; iv) *Open Data and API* management components and *Identity and Access Control Management*; v) *deployment tools*. Furthermore, FIWARE is supported by the European Commission and the main and only mandatory component of any "powered by FIWARE" project is the **Context Broker** (CB) belonging to GEs first category and to the Connecting Europe Facility (CEF) building blocks[11].

As shown in Fig. 2 (a), a FIWARE-based solution has an *event-driven architecture* [16], where events refer to something that happened in the system, *e.g.*, changes in contextual information such as updated of already existing entities and/or the creation of new ones. In fact, context information are captured from the real world and managed in the CB layer for further processing, analysis and monitoring. Results from these activities are used to actuate actions in the real world.

FIWARE GEs communicate with one another through the **Next Generation Service Interfaces** (**NGSI**) protocol [21], standardized by European Telecommunications Standards Institute (ETSI). NGSI exists in two versions, NGSI-v2 and its evolution NGSI-LD where LD stands for *Linked Data*, developed to increase interoperability. The main constructs of NGSI-LD are Entity, Property and Relationship, represented in Fig. 2 (b) as a navigable knowledge graph. Every *NGSI-LD Entity* must have a *unique ID* that is a Uniform Resource Identifier (URI), usually a Uniform Resource Name (URN); the URI should correspond to a well-defined data model which can be found on the Web. Moreover,

---

[6] https://projects.eclipse.org/projects/iot.ditto.

[7] https://www.fiware.org/.

[8] https://learn.microsoft.com/en-us/azure/digital-twins/overview.

[9] https://blogs.sw.siemens.com/insights-hub/.

[10] https://github.com/fiware/catalogue.

[11] https://www.fiware.org/2018/08/08/fiware-context-broker-launches-as-a-cef-building-block/.

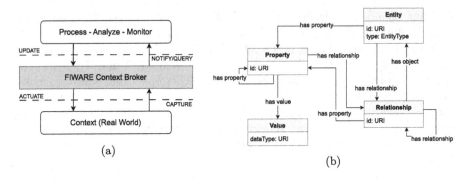

Fig. 2. (a) FIWARE event-driven architecture; (b) NGSI-LD Context Information Model.

entities have a *type* used to define the structure of stored data and that must be a URI. An entity can have properties and relationships: a *NGSI-LD Property* has a *value* that reflects the state of that property and may have further properties (properties-of-properties); a *NGSI-LD Relationship* connects the entity with another data object through its URI/URN. NGSI-LD entities are represented using *JSON-LD*, a JSON-based serialization format for linked data to avoid ambiguity when expressing linked data in JSON. In fact, introducing the concept of *@context* elements[12], JSON-LD provides additional information to structure data in a format parsable by machines and to easily compare data attributes when coming from a multitude of separate data sources.

The FIWARE **Smart Data Models** initiative aims at integrating reference data model with NGSI API, that is *domain-agnostic* and thus provides mechanisms to access context information without defining how the context data are modeled. Promoted by FIWARE in collaboration with TM Forum[13], India Urban Data Exchange (IUDX)[14] and Open & Agile Smart Cities (OASC)[15], SDMs are compliant with both NGSI-v2 and NGSI-LD with the objective of being portable for different solutions [5,18]. Currently, there are 13 domains related to smart cities, smart environment, smart sensors, smart agrifood and so on[16].

SDMs define how data should be represented, exchanged, and consumed in the context of smart solutions. They provide a standardized way of describing data entities, relationships, and attributes, enabling interoperability and data exchange across different systems and platforms. Among the 13 different

---

[12] Please note that JSON-LD @context is different from the concept of context-aware data system. Context can be defined as "any information that can be used to characterize the situation of an entity" [18], *i.e.*, the state in which an entity is at a given time. Instead, the @context is used to define short-hand names that are part of JSON-LD payloads.

[13] https://www.tmforum.org/.

[14] https://iudx.org.in/.

[15] https://oascities.org/.

[16] https://github.com/smart-data-models/data-models.

data models dealing with the `Smart Cities` domain, two of them are particularly interesting for us: i) `Urban Mobility`[17] maps GTFS[18] fields with NGSI attributes. ii) `Transportation`[19] provides a description of the primary entities involved in smart solutions that address transportation issues. In order to create an actual DT for a specific transportation scenario, such reference data models have to be extended with suitable attributes. An example will be provided by our case study described in the next section.

Before diving into specific aspects of our practical example, in Fig. 3 we illustrate the mapping between the functionalities discussed with respect to the proposed DT-based IPTS architecture and a possible set of technical components (both belonging to FIWARE and external) that can be used to implement those functionalities. The *Physical Twin Layer* is characterized by generic data sources and/or IoT networks incorporating sensing, actuating and controlling capabilities. To interface with sensors and actuators, several platforms and components may be used in the *Data Ingestion Layer*. Existing IoT Platforms may be adopted, as long as they use the FIWARE CB to manage context information. Alternatively, the IoT Agents provided as part of the FIWARE *Interface to Internet of Things (IDAS) Framework* may be used. FIWARE **IoT Agents** are software components that act as intermediaries between IoT devices and FIWARE platforms, by providing a translation layer between the different protocols used by IoT devices and the FIWARE Context Broker. In case of systems that do not natively comply with the NGSI-LD standard, suitable *System Adapters* may be developed based on the IDAS IoT Agent library. Finally, as in the transportation domain media processing systems are typically available (*e.g.*, for the elaboration of video streaming data from the cameras), in Fig. 3 we also included a *Media Stream Processing* component. To this aim, the FIWARE *Kurento* component[20] can be used for the analysis and enhancement of data coming from cameras via WebRTC. These data are used for two purposes: i) describe the *static JSON-LD context*, *i.e.*, the characterization of the physical system based on baseline SDMs; ii) feed the data models in (near) real-time to obtain the living replica.

As we already said, the main component is the **Context Broker** populating the *Intra-Twin communication Layer*, in charge of managing the entire life cycle of context information, for instance updates, queries, registration and subscriptions. There exist four different CBs, *i.e.*, *Orion*[21], ***Orion-LD***[22], *Scorpio*[23]

---

[17] Available at https://github.com/smart-data-models/dataModel.UrbanMobility, the data model has been adopted in the SynchroniCity European project https://cordis.europa.eu/project/id/732240.

[18] General Transit Feed Specification is an open standard used by public transport agencies to publish their transit data in a format that can be consumed by a wide variety of software applications.

[19] https://github.com/smart-data-models/dataModel.Transportation.

[20] https://kurento.readthedocs.io/en/stable/.

[21] https://fiware-orion.readthedocs.io/.

[22] https://github.com/FIWARE/context.Orion-LD.

[23] https://scorpio.readthedocs.io/en/latest/.

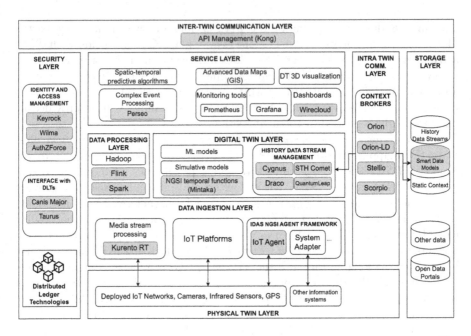

Fig. 3. A FIWARE-enabled instance of the proposed DT-based IPTS architecture. The instance leverages on FIWARE GEs (marked in blue) and other external tools that can easily interact with FIWARE components. (Color figure online)

and *Stellio*[24] differing for NGSI REST API version implemented. Conventionally, CBs deal only with current context; this means that they have *no memory*. However, to offer historical context data in a variety of JSON based formats and thus build a proper DT, either *temporal functions* or *subscriptions* can be adopted. The former represent an additional interface for NGSI-LD CBs, which can rely upon any persistence mechanism once it has been activated; when the subscription mechanism is used instead, the CB subscribes to an individual context entities and context data are stored into a time-series database. In both cases, additional components must be included to manage context information, which logically belong to the Digital Twin layer. An implementation of the NGSI-LD temporal retrieval interface is **Mintaka**[25] that will be used in our case study described in Sect. 5. The subscription mechanism is instead enabled by additional components, such as **QuantumLeap**[26], *Cygnus*, *Draco* and *STH Comet*, usually set-up with other storage solutions. Please note that the advantage of using a subscription is that only subscribed entities are persisted, saving memory space, while the temporal interface benefit is directly provided by the CB, thus no subscriptions are needed and network traffic is reduced. As shown by the arrows, through the CB the history data stream managers retrieve changes

---

[24] https://stellio.readthedocs.io/en/latest/.
[25] https://github.com/FIWARE/mintaka.
[26] https://quantumleap.readthedocs.io/.

in the context saving it in a storage (*e.g.*, QuantumLeap has support for both Timescale-DB and CrateDB). In the *Digital Twin Layer*, there are also ML models and simulative models that can possibly interact with data models.

External tools can be connected to the architecture and thus to FIWARE components. For example, the *Data Processing Layer* can easily leverage on Apache Flink, the stream processing framework, through the *Cosmos Flink*[27] connector, or on Apache Spark, open-source distributed general-purpose cluster-computing framework, through the *Cosmos Spark*[28] connector. Finally, there is the *Service Layer* in which there are the components needed to implement the desired services. Apart from generic tools such as spatio-temporal predictive algorithms particularly useful in mobility domain, there is the FIWARE *Perseo*[29] GE, an Esper-based Complex Event Processing (CEP) software designed to be fully NGSI-v2-compliant. Moreover, for monitoring and visualization purposes, *WireCloud*[30] offers a platform to allow end users without programming skills to easily create web applications and dashboards.

For *Inter-Twin Communication*, there is FIWARE *Kong*[31] that can implement API management and extend the API Gateway with further functionalities required for FIWARE-based environments and thus helping into realizing the communication among different Digital Twins. Regarding the security aspects, there are: *Keyrock*[32] component responsible for Identity Management; *Wilma*[33] that is a Policy Enforcement Point (PEP); *AuthZForce*[34] that is the authorization Policy Decision Point (PDP). Moreover, *CanisMajor*[35] is a blockchain adapter that supports persistence and verification of NGSI-LD Entity-Transactions (*e.g.*, create/delete/update-operations) in various blockchains; while *Taurus*[36] is still an under-development Distributed Ledger Technology (DLT) component responsible for listening to events and storing data in FIWARE ecosystem.

5 Case Study

In this section, we illustrate a simple case study involving a urban bus-based transportation system composed of a set of bus lines managed by a public transportation company, normally operated via a fixed bus schedule. The DT concept can be used in this scenario to introduce a dynamic bus scheduling based on real-time passenger information acquired via suitable sensors installed both on the vehicles and at the bus stops.

---

[27] https://fiware-cosmos-flink.readthedocs.io/.
[28] https://fiware-cosmos-spark.readthedocs.io/.
[29] https://fiware-perseo-fe.readthedocs.io/.
[30] https://wirecloud.readthedocs.io/.
[31] https://github.com/FIWARE/kong-plugins-fiware.
[32] https://fiware-idm.readthedocs.io/.
[33] https://fiware-pep-proxy.readthedocs.io/.
[34] https://authzforce-ce-fiware.readthedocs.io/.
[35] https://github.com/FIWARE/CanisMajor.
[36] https://github.com/FIWARE-Blockchain/Taurus.

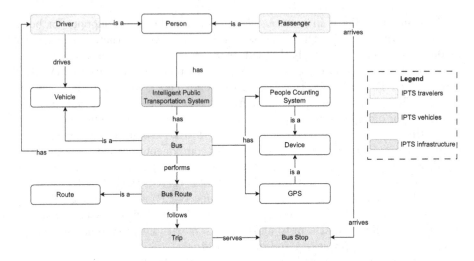

Fig. 4. Intelligent Public Transportation System ontology model. The IPTS components, *i.e.*, infrastructure, travelers and public transportation vehicle, are colored differently, with green, yellow, and blue respectively.

In Fig. 4, there is the ontology model describing an IPTS at high-level, specifically a bus-based public transport system. A typical IPTS system includes the following components [9, 17]:

- **infrastructure** that includes routes, trips, stops and stations. The *route* (also referred to as a line) is the itinerary of a public transport networks and is made of *trips* that are displayed to riders as a single service according to a timetable[37]. *Stops* are physical locations where vehicles stop to pick up or drop off passengers. A *station* is a collection of close stops.
- **traveler** who is usually the passenger that catches public transportation vehicles to move between stops. Sometimes, even public vehicle drivers are considered travelers.
- **public transportation vehicle** which is the vehicle meant for transporting passengers, performing defined routes that follow one or more trips. The public transport network combines different transport modes, *i.e.*, guided mode (*e.g.*, bus), free mode (*e.g.*, cars) and non-motorized mode. In our case study, we consider only the guided mode and in particular buses as transport vehicles.

To collect real-time data from the bus service system, two types of devices are installed on each bus, namely a *people counting system* (APC device) and a GPS sensor. At each bus stop, the APC device determines the number of passengers who are dropped off and/or picked up, while the *GPS sensor* is responsible for determining the public vehicle's location. APC and GPS devices implement the

---

[37] https://developers.google.com/transit/gtfs.

sensing capability of the *Physical Twin Layer*, while *Real-World Physical Entities* are buses, infrastructure and travelers (passengers and driver).

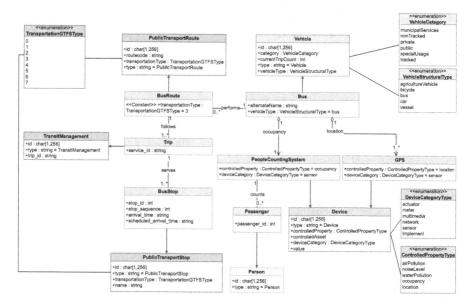

Fig. 5. Class diagram of IPTS Digital Twin model based on FIWARE Smart Data Models. Violet, blue, orange and yellow classes belong to `Urban Mobility`, `Transportation`, `Device` and `Organization` data models respectively. Green classes are peculiar of the considered domain. (Color figure online)

In order to create proper digital twins specific to the scenario under investigation, we modified baseline SDMs adding properties and relationships. For example, we extended the *PublicTransportStop* data model by adding some important attributes for our case, such as the bus `stop_sequence` and `scheduled_arrival_time`. In this way, the CB is able to hold the bus stop context. Furthermore, in our case study, there are involved entities not strictly related with the transportation domain, *e.g.*, the APC is an hardware device with a running software in charge of counting people entering and/or leaving the bus. In Smart Sensing domain, there is the *Device* data model that can be used to model data of the aforementioned system. Passengers can be described through the *Person* data model of *Organization* domain.

For this reason, in Fig. 5 we described the DT model through a class diagram in which we distinguished the entities of our urban bus-based scenario, depicted in green, and FIWARE data models on which we leveraged to define the DT itself. More in detail, in *Urban Mobility* the data models that we extended are *PublicTransportRoute*, *PublicTransportStop* and *TransitManagement*, marked in violet. Each SDM requires mandatory attributes/properties that are listed in the respective classes; this means that our scenario's entities inherit properties

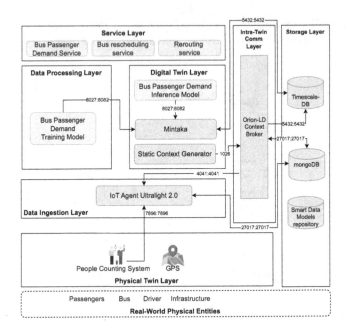

Fig. 6. Digital Twin-based IPTS architecture in an urban bus scenario leveraging on FIWARE GEs marked in blue. Components related to the implemented service are colored in yellow. (Color figure online)

from data models and can define specific attributes if needed. As we said before, BusStop entity will be extended with scheduled_arrival_time, stop_sequence, stop_id and arrival_time. Regarding the *Transportation* data model, we used the *Vehicle* model, coloured in blue, to describe the Bus entity. Finally, *Device* data model has been used for GPS and PeopleCountingSystem entities and *Person* for Passenger.

As shown in Fig. 6, occupancy and locations measurements coming from the *Physical Twin Layer* are collected in the *Data Ingestion Layer* by the IoT Agent Ultralight 2.0, a bridge between HTTP/MQTT messaging (with an Ultra-Light 2.0 payload) and NGSI-LD. For this case study, we used real-world data acquired on two bus routes of a major Italian city. Through HTTP protocol, these data are sent to the agent that will be listening for the so-called *northbound traffic* on port 7896. The IoT Agent sends this information to the Orion-LD Context Broker that exposes localhost port number 1026 for updating the entities' state by keeping track of the last context in MongoDB, accessible on port number 27017. *Southbound traffic* is composed by HTTP requests generated by the CB consisting of commands made to actuator devices which alter the state of the real world by their actions. The port used for configuring the IoT Agent and receiving context updates from the CB is 4041: please note that MongoDB database is used by Orion-LD to hold context data information (*e.g.*, data entities, subscriptions and registrations), but also by the IoT Agent for storing device information such as device URLs and Keys. Finally, even though we do not have access to real actuators in the Italian city, the actuation that can be provided by our DT-based prediction is the *dynamic bus re-scheduling*.

In the *Digital Twin Layer*, there is the `static context generator`, a Python script for our scenario's entities description. We used ***ngsildclient***[38], a Python NGSI-LD client implementation, that helps to cope with tediousness of writing large NGSI-LD compliant entities using JSON-LD, risking error-prone and significant amount of code. The library ngsildclient wraps the NGSI-LD API providing primitives to build and manipulate NGSI-LD entities without effort and with respect to the ETSI specification. An example of the description and the creation of a bus entity is presented in Fig. 7.

```
from ngsildclient import Entity, CORE_CONTEXT, Rel
#bus entity definition sample
bus = Entity("Vehicle", bus_progressive_id, ctx=transportation_ctx)
bus.prop("category", "public").prop("vehicleType", "bus").prop("currentTripCount", 0).prop("alternateName", "0E314")
bus.rel("performs", busroute.id)
bus.prop("occupancy", 0).rel(Rel.OBSERVED_BY, pcs_device.id, nested=True)
bus.gprop("location", coord).rel(Rel.OBSERVED_BY, gps_device.id, nested=True)

#entities creation sample
cb= Client("localhost", port=1026, port_temporal=8027,tenant="openiot", overwrite=True)
mobility_entities = [bus, trip, busroute, busstop, gps_device, pcs_device]
cb.create(mobility_entities)
```

Fig. 7. Sample code of entities definition and creation in the CB.

As said in Sect. 4, to cope with memory-less context brokers, we activated the NGSI-LD temporal operations by adding `Mintaka` which services the temporal interface exposing port number 8027 and is also responsible for persisting historic context in a `Timescale` timeseries database available on port number 5342. In fact, `Client` function in Fig. 7 is invoked with `port_temporal=8027` parameter; in this way, historical context can be retrieved through Mintaka by using `temporal.query()` function available in ngsildclient. To ensure that everything works properly, ***Temporal Representation of Entities*** *(TRoE)* has to be implemented in Orion-LD, meaning that in `docker-compose.yml` file the following variables have to be set: i) `ORIONLD_TROE=TRUE`; ii) `ORIONLD_TROE_USER=set_user`; `ORIONLD_TROE_PWD=set_password`.

Our objective is to use a DT-based IPTS to provide a `passenger demand prediction service` that aims at forecasting how many people will use a specific public service since this prediction has been proved to be significantly useful both for passengers and transport operators. To this purpose, we defined and trained a machine learning predictive model with pre-processed data collected from `Mintaka`: we applied a Long Short Term Memory (LSTM) Network because of its intrinsic capabilities in dealing with time series data. The `trained model`

---

[38] https://ngsildclient.readthedocs.io.

is in the *Data Processing Layer*, while the `inference model` is in the *Digital Twin Layer* accessing, through Mintaka, to data not used in the training phase. The outputs of the LSTM-based model are used in the *Service Layer* firstly to offer a basic prediction service; moreover, a major advantage of having a Digital Twin is that the prediction results are further processed to simulate alternative scenarios for `bus rescheduling` and/or `bus rerouting` in different real situations (*e.g.*, strikes) and choose the best option to be actuated.

Finally, it is worth nothing that our case study is currently compliant with 2 over 10 OASC MIMs, the ***Minimal Interoperability Mechanisms***[39], vendor-neutral and technology-agnostic tools for achieving interoperability of data, systems, and services between cities. More specifically, for *MIM1 - the Context Information Management* we used Orion-LD Context Broker and as regards for *MIM2 - Data Models* we leveraged on FIWARE Smart Data Models.

6   Conclusions

In this paper, we have investigated the usage of Digital Twin technology for Intelligent Public Transportation Systems to enhance the quality of services and consequently decreasing the use of private transportation. Indeed, thanks to the growing availability of mobility-related data and leveraging on the bidirectional communication between physical and virtual worlds of DTs, smart services such as passenger flow/demand prediction can be further improved. However, despite the increasing interest of both academia and industry in IPTS and DT topics, the application of DT in transportation domain requires attention to deal with mobility peculiarities, notably interoperability, complexity of involved human factors, data reliability and so on.

For this reason, in our work, we present a general DT architecture for IPTS identifying the main functionalities to be implemented. To provide minimum common data models enabling interoperability for applications and among different digital twins, we mapped our architectural proposal onto FIWARE Generic Enablers, *i.e.*, technological components based on NGSI v2/LD standard. Finally, to prove the effectiveness of our solution, we instantiated the architecture in real bus-based mobility scenario modeling real world entities through FIWARE Smart Data Models and integrating ML models to offer passenger demand prediction service.

Acknowledgments. This work has been partially supported by the Spoke 9 "Digital Society & Smart Cities" of ICSC - Centro Nazionale di Ricerca in High Performance-Computing, Big Data and Quantum Computing, funded by the European Union - NextGenerationEU (PNRR-HPC, CUP: E63C22000980007).

---

[39] https://mims.oascities.org/basics/oasc-mims-introduction.

References

1. Amato, F., Di Martino, S., Mazzocca, N., Nardone, D., Rocco di Torrepadula, F., Sannino, P.: Bus passenger load prediction: challenges from an industrial experience. In: Karimipour, F., Storandt, S. (eds.) W2GIS 2022. LNCS, vol. 13238, pp. 93–107. Springer, Cham (2022). https://doi.org/10.1007/978-3-031-06245-2_9
2. Bao, L., Wang, Q., Jiang, Y.: Review of digital twin for intelligent transportation system. In: 2021 International Conference on Information Control, Electrical Engineering and Rail Transit (ICEERT), pp. 309–315 (2021). https://doi.org/10.1109/ICEERT53919.2021.00064
3. Bin, Y., Zhongzhen, Y., Baozhen, Y.: Bus arrival time prediction using support vector machines. J. Intell. Transp. Syst. **10**(4), 151–158 (2006)
4. Cirillo, F., Solmaz, G., Berz, E.L., Bauer, M., Cheng, B., Kovacs, E.: A standard-based open source IoT platform: FIWARE. IEEE Internet Things Mag. **2**(3), 12–18 (2019). https://doi.org/10.1109/IOTM.0001.1800022
5. Conde, J., Munoz, J., Alonso, A., Lòpez-Pernas, S., Salvachua, J.: Modeling digital twin data and architecture: a building guide with FIWARE as enabling technology. IEEE Internet Comput. **26**, 7–14 (2021). https://doi.org/10.1109/MIC.2021.3056923
6. Conde, J., Munoz-Arcentales, A., Alonso, A., Huecas, G., Salvachùa, J.: Collaboration of digital twins through linked open data: architecture with FIWARE as enabling technology. IT Prof. **24**(6), 41–46 (2022). https://doi.org/10.1109/MITP.2022.3224826
7. Dasgupta, S., Rahman, M., Lidbe, A.D., Lu, W., Jones, S.L.: A transportation digital-twin approach for adaptive traffic control systems. CoRR abs/2109.10863 (2021). https://arxiv.org/abs/2109.10863
8. Gavalas, D., et al.: Smart cities: recent trends, methodologies, and applications (2017)
9. Ghariani, N., Elkosantini, S., Darmoul, S., Ben Said, L.: A survey of simulation platforms for the assessment of public transport control systems. In: 2014 International Conference on Advanced Logistics and Transport (ICALT), pp. 85–90 (2014). https://doi.org/10.1109/ICAdLT.2014.6864088
10. Jafari, M., Kavousi-Fard, A., Chen, T., Karimi, M.: A review on digital twin technology in smart grid, transportation system and smart city: challenges and future. IEEE Access **11**, 17471–17484 (2023). https://doi.org/10.1109/ACCESS.2023.3241588
11. Jenelius, E.: Data-driven bus crowding prediction based on real-time passenger counts and vehicle locations. In: 6th International Conference on Models and Technologies for Intelligent Transportation Systems (MTITS2019) (2019)
12. Kale, A.: Collaboration of automotive, connected solutions and energy technologies for sustainable public transportation for Indian cities. In: 2019 IEEE Transportation Electrification Conference (ITEC-India), pp. 1–6. IEEE (2019)
13. Kim, K.M., Hong, S.P., Ko, S.J., Kim, D.: Does crowding affect the path choice of metro passengers? Transp. Res. Part A Policy Pract. **77**, 292–304 (2015)
14. Kirimtat, A., Krejcar, O., Kertesz, A., Tasgetiren, M.F.: Future trends and current state of smart city concepts: a survey. IEEE Access **8**, 86448–86467 (2020)
15. Kui, K., Schumann, R., Ivanjko, E.: A digital twin in transportation: real-time synergy of traffic data streams and simulation for virtualizing motorway dynamics. Adv. Eng. Inform. **55**, 101858 (2023). https://doi.org/10.1016/j.aei.2022.101858. https://www.sciencedirect.com/science/article/pii/S1474034622003160

16. Martínez, R., Pastor, J.A., Àlvarez, B., Iborra, A.: A testbed to evaluate the FIWARE-based IoT platform in the domain of precision agriculture. Sensors **16**(11) (2016). https://www.mdpi.com/1424-8220/16/11/1979

17. Megalingam, R.K., Raj, N., Soman, A.L., Prakash, L., Satheesh, N., Vijay, D.: Smart, public buses information system. In: 2014 International Conference on Communication and Signal Processing, pp. 1343–1347 (2014). https://doi.org/10.1109/ICCSP.2014.6950068

18. Munoz-Arcentales, A., López-Pernas, S., Conde, J., Alonso, l., Salvachúa, J., Hierro, J.J.: Enabling context-aware data analytics in smart environments: an open source reference implementation. Sensors **21**(21) (2021). https://doi.org/10.3390/s21217095. https://www.mdpi.com/1424-8220/21/21/7095

19. Nie, L., Wang, X., Zhao, Q., Shang, Z., Feng, L., Li, G.: Digital twin for transportation big data: a reinforcement learning-based network traffic prediction approach. IEEE Trans. Intell. Transp. Syst., 1–11 (2023). https://doi.org/10.1109/TITS.2022.3232518

20. Paiva, S., Ahad, M.A., Tripathi, G., Feroz, N., Casalino, G.: Enabling technologies for urban smart mobility: recent trends, opportunities and challenges. Sensors **21**(6), 2143 (2021)

21. Privat, G.: Guidelines for modelling with NGSI-LD (ETSI white paper) (2021)

22. Ramstedt, L., Krasemann, J.T., Davidsson, P.: Movement of people and goods. In: Edmonds, B., Meyer, R. (eds.) Simulating Social Complexity, pp. 651–665. Springer, Heidelberg (2013). https://doi.org/10.1007/978-3-540-93813-2_24

23. Tirachini, A., Hensher, D.A., Rose, J.M.: Crowding in public transport systems: effects on users, operation and implications for the estimation of demand. Transp. Res. Part A Policy Pract. **53**, 36–52 (2013)

24. Tsai, T.H.: Self-evolutionary sibling models to forecast railway arrivals using reservation data. Eng. Appl. Artif. Intell. **96**, 103960 (2020)

25. Wang, P., Chen, X., Chen, J., Hua, M., Pu, Z.: A two-stage method for bus passenger load prediction using automatic passenger counting data. IET Intel. Transp. Syst. **15**(2), 248–260 (2021)

26. Wang, W., et al.: Introduction to digital twin technologies in transportation infrastructure management (TIM). In: Edmonds, B., Meyer, R. (eds.) Simulating Social Complexity. Understanding Complex Systems, pp. 1–25. Springer, Heidelberg (2024). https://doi.org/10.1007/978-981-99-5804-7_1

27. Yu, B., Lam, W.H., Tam, M.L.: Bus arrival time prediction at bus stop with multiple routes. Transp. Res. Part C Emerg. Technol. **19**(6), 1157–1170 (2011)

28. Zear, A., Singh, P.K., Singh, Y.: Intelligent transport system: a progressive review (2016)

29. Zhang, J., et al.: A real-time passenger flow estimation and prediction method for urban bus transit systems. IEEE Trans. Intell. Transp. Syst. **18**(11), 3168–3178 (2017)

An Analysis of Container Transportation Multiplex Networks from the Perspective of Shipping Company

Yang Xu[1,2], Peng Peng[1(✉)], Christophe Claramunt[1,3], and Feng Lu[1,2]

[1] State Key Laboratory of Resources and Environmental Information System, Institute of Geographic Sciences and Natural Resources Research, Chinese Academy of Sciences, Beijing 100864, China
pengp@lreis.ac.cn
[2] College of Resources and Environment, University of Chinese Academy of Sciences, Beijing 100864, China
[3] Naval Academy Research Institute, 29240 Lanvéoc, France

Abstract. Shipping companies play a crucial role in coordinating container transportation, as their decisions about shipping routes and ports have a direct impact on the development of the container network. Hence, understanding the similarities and distinctions across ship companies is crucial for gaining insight into the container shipping market. This study uses a multiplex network method to provide insight into identifying various transportation patterns and significant ports. The model is enhanced with a set of structural indices, together with a novel overlap measure that assesses the distinct function of a particular port across several layers of ship companies. The entire methodology is applied and tested using AIS data from the top 10 shipping companies, which facilitates the creation of a multiplex network and the calculation of structural metrics. The experiments conducted on the global maritime transportation network aim to identify crucial ports and emphasize notable variations at both the regional and trade flow levels. This study enhances the existing knowledge in the field of transport geography and uncovers the route organization strategies employed by shipping companies. These findings can offer valuable insights for port managers when making decisions.

Keywords: Global Container Shipping Network · Complex Networks · Vessel Trajectory Data

1 Introduction

Multiplex networks serve as valuable models of complex systems, wherein a common set of nodes can be linked by varying sorts of relationships [1]. Systems that can be represented as multiplex networks encompass social networks, transportation systems with several modes of transportation, and biological systems that incorporate various forms of interactions [1, 2]. Maritime transportation is the fundamental support of global trade, and the Global Container Shipping Network (GCSN) is essential for the progress and

© The Author(s), under exclusive license to Springer Nature Switzerland AG 2024
M. Lotfian and L. L. Starace (Eds.): W2GIS 2024, LNCS 14673, pp. 183–191, 2024.
https://doi.org/10.1007/978-3-031-60796-7_13

durability of the global economy [3, 4]. Several vital ports serve significant roles within distinct shipping company subnetworks, thereby strengthening the overall container shipping network. Therefore, the entire maritime transportation network can be characterized as a complex network consisting of interconnected single-layer subnetworks that complement each other [5]. Consequently, it is imperative to comprehend the similarities and distinctions among the subnetworks of different shipping companies.

Previous studies [6, 7] on container transportation commonly employ AIS data from various ship companies which is then consolidated into an aggregated network. Therefore, the use of the new multiplex network framework in analyzing the container transportation system could provide a more comprehensive understanding of intricate matters such as appropriately assessing the global container transportation scenario and the significance of key ports. In a container multiplex network, ports are represented as nodes and organized into layers based on ship companies. The trade relationships between ports are represented as edges, which indicate the intra-connections within each layer [8]. This study employs vessel trajectory data from 2015 to construct a directed weighted complex network. We perform a case study on 10 shipping companies that have the highest 10 throughput rankings globally.

The remainder of this paper is structured as follows. In Sect. 2, we provide a concise summary of our approach, methodology, and experimental data. Section 3 outlines the main analysis, which employs the multiplex model to examine the structure of 10 container shipping networks. It also includes a comparison between single-layer, aggregated, and multiplex approaches. The findings and discussions are finally consolidated in Sect. 4.

2   Materials and Methodology

2.1   Data Collection

To support the multiplex network modelling and analytic work, this study utilized global container AIS data, worldwide port and vessel attribute data from 1 January to 31 December 2015. The maritime dataset is provided by Elane (a database in the container shipping industry, https://www.elane.com/). The dataset contains 396,650 voyage records covering 1,474 ports, data fields include ship MMSI number, ship company, departure port, departure time, arrival port, arrival time, and port position (longitude and latitude). This paper splits the dataset by different ship company and select top 10 company data as multiplex GCSN database, and we employed a data preprocessing method for AIS data which contains noise elimination, data screening, and data calibration. Table 1 depicts the example of final data format.

Table 1. The fields of GCSN database of top 10 ship company

Company	Departure	Position	Arrival	Position	Frequency
Maersk	Zhoushan	122.1,30	Tanjung Pelepas	103.5,1.35	13
MSC	Shanghai	121.5,31.22	Pusan	129,35.1	3
CMA CGM	Los Angeles	-118.25,33.75	Oakland	-122.33,37.82	42
…	…	…	…	…	…
Wan Hai	Hong Kong	114.2,22.27	Kao-Hsiung	120.25,22.62	136

2.2 Methodology

Firstly, the directed weighted GCSN in three styles is derived from the maritime routes of different ship companies. Then we introduce the structural characteristic analysis indexes of the GCSN based on the established directed weighted networks mentioned above. The structural characteristic analysis indexes of single-layer network including average shortest path length and clustering coefficient, indexes of all three network styles including node degree and node betweenness. Finally, we also complemented an additional index named overlap ratio to highlight the degree to which the multiplex network exhibits structural properties that confirm or diverge from specific single-layer networks.

Network Construction. Figure 1 shows the global container transportation system modelled as a directed weighted network in three styles. Figure 1a depicts a single-layer directed weighted network where $G = (N, E, W)$ represents the GCSN. N denotes the ports of the GCSN, while E denotes the routes, that is, the directed edges among ports. $E_{ij}=1$ if there is a direct route between port i and port j; otherwise, $E_{ij}=0$. The weight W of a given edge E is valued by the number of ship routes among the two ports i and j of that edge. Then an aggregated network is constructed as shown in Fig. 1b. The aggregated network denotes a single layer aggregated from all connections represented as different single layers, the edge's weight is equal to the sum of the edge weights of all single layers. Finally, a multiplex maritime network is depicted in Fig. 1c. A regular assumption is that different layers contain the same ports, and there is no difference between taking intra-layer steps in different layers, but not all ports need to be involved in all types of links.

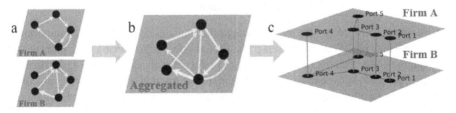

Fig. 1. Construction process of directed weighted global container shipping network in 3 formats.

Average Shortest Path Length. The average shortest path length L of the single-layer directed network is given by the average topological distance between any two single ports which formulated as Formula (1). Where N denotes the number of nodes in the network and d_{ij} is the topologically shortest path distance between ports i and j.

$$L = \frac{1}{N(N-1)} \sum_{i \in N} \sum_{j \in N, j \neq i} d_{ij} \tag{1}$$

Average Clustering Coefficient. The clustering coefficient C of the single-layer directed network can reflect the tightness of the port connections in a given maritime network. Where N is the number of nodes in the network, k_i is the number of all connected nodes with node i, E_i denotes the numbers of node pairs between all neighbors of node i. Therefore, $k_i(k_i - 1)$ is the possible maximum number of node pairs between all neighbors of node i and formulated as Formula (2). A higher C denotes a relatively clustered neighborhood, this, for example, showing that a cargo can be transported rapidly within the local trade area.

$$C = \frac{1}{N} \sum_{i \in [1,N]} \frac{E_i}{k_i(k_i - 1)} \tag{2}$$

Node Degree. Node degree is one of the most basic measures of complex network. Referring to a single-layer network, a node's degree is the number of nodes that are adjacent to it. One can generalize the notion of degree for directed network that the node degree shows the sum of in-degree and out-degree, which reflect the importance of the node in a network. The larger the node degree is, the more important it is in the network. In a multiplex network, the same node exists in different layers at the same time. Therefore, the node degree (in-degree, out-degree, degree) of multiplex directed network can be calculated by Formula (3), (4), (5), respectively. Where $D_{i^a}^{[a]}$ denotes the degree of node i^a of the a layer network. Apparently, the total node degree of node a of the whole network is $D_i = \sum_{a=1}^{M} D_{i^a}^{[a]}$. Noticing that relationships between inter-layer is virtual connection

$$inD_{i^a}^{[a]} = \sum_{j^a=1, j^a \neq i^a}^{N^a} E_{j^a i^a}^a \tag{3}$$

$$outD_{i^a}^{[a]} = \sum_{j^a=1, j^a \neq i^a}^{N^a} E_{i^a j^a}^a \tag{4}$$

$$D_{i^a}^{[a]} = inD_{i^a}^{[a]} + outD_{i^a}^{[a]} = \sum_{j^a=1, j^a \neq i^a}^{N^a} (E_{j^a i^a}^a + E_{i^a j^a}^a) \tag{5}$$

Betweenness Centrality. Betweenness centrality indicator can measure the importance of a node which based on the shortest path, if the shortest path of many node pairs passes through the node, then the node is important in the network. For a single-layer directed network, the node betweenness shows the sum of the fraction of the shortest paths of all pairs passing through the node in the network which can be formulated as Formula (6). Where $BCs_{i^a}^{[a]}$ denotes the betweenness centrality of node i^a of the a layer network. d_{uv} Shows the number of shortest paths between node u and v, $d_{uv}^{[a]}(i^a)$ shows the number of shortest paths between node u and v that passing through the node i^a. In a multiplex network, the same node exists in different layers at the same time. Therefore, the node betweenness of multiplex directed network should be $BCm_{i^a} = \sum_{a=1}^{M} BCs_{i^a}^{[a]}$.

$$BCs_{i^a}^{[a]} = \sum_{u,v \in N_a, u \neq v} d_{uv}^{[a]}(i^a)/d_{uv} \qquad (6)$$

Overlap Ratio. The overlap ratio between ports and routes of any two single-layer networks is formulated as Formula (7) which can evaluate the respective multiple functions of a given port. Where $overlap_i^{[\alpha\beta]}$ denotes the number of routes for node i which appear in layer α and layer β at the same time, while $aggRoute_i^{[\alpha\beta]}$ denotes the number of union routes for node i appear in layer α and layer β.

$$overlapRatio_i^{[\alpha\beta]} = \frac{overlap_i^{[\alpha\beta]}}{aggRoute_i^{[\alpha\beta]}} \times 100\% \qquad (7)$$

3   Experimental Results

3.1   Structural Characteristic Analysis

Table 2 shows the main characteristics of the global container shipping network (GCSN) for the top 10 ship companies worldwide. It is obvious that there are some variances in the GCSN, and by examining their structural qualities, we may gain insights into the differences among these companies. To demonstrate these differences, we calculate several network indices for both individual and combined network formats, as presented in Table 2. As an example, MSC GCSN has the highest number of shipping routes, with a total of 4018. This is due to their fleet of 288 ships that operate in 594 ports. In contrast, WAN HAI GCSN has a smaller fleet of 70 ships that operate in 132 ports, resulting in 735 shipping routes. The average degree (AD) of each GCSN indicates the normal level of connectivity and volume of commerce inside the network. The AD values of business MSC and MAERSK are 10.63 and 10.44 respectively, indicating their significant presence in container trade link. On the other hand, firm RICKMERS and CSCL have lower densities with values of 7.51 and 7.56 respectively. The average clustering coefficient quantifies the degree of interconnectedness across all ports in the GCSN. WAN HAI exhibits the highest value (0.65), indicating a greater level of tightness. Conversely, MSC and Hapag-Lloyd display the lowest values (0.46), suggesting a lower level of tightness. Simultaneously, WAN HAI exhibits the lowest average shortest path length of 2.71, whilst MSC has the highest value of 3.26. It is possible to deduce that the values of these two indexes (ACC and ASPL) may be influenced by the extent of services provided by the shipping businesses.

We enhance our study by incorporating one of the fundamental metrics of graph theory, known as the degree. Based on the degree calculation results, we observed that certain ports exhibit comparable degree values throughout all three networks (single-layer, aggregated, and multiplex) simultaneously. What is particularly intriguing is the fact that these ports frequently possess three distinct characteristics: 1) These ports specialize in serving a single shipping industry. 2) The ports on the shipping route either

Table 2. Main characteristics of maritime networks under study, ordered by decreasing ship amount

Ship company	Ship amount	Ports	Routes	AD	ACC	ASPL
MSC	288	594	4018	10.63	0.46	3.26
MAERSK	263	375	2491	10.44	0.57	2.87
CMA	130	286	1635	9.13	0.51	3.14
COSCO	117	196	1102	8.82	0.56	2.96
PIL	113	208	1152	8.65	0.58	3.02
EVERGREEN	112	235	1260	8.42	0.52	3.01
RICKMERS	78	351	1593	7.51	0.45	3.55
Hapag-Lloyd	76	217	1189	8.84	0.46	3.08
CSCL	75	188	906	7.56	0.54	3.00
WAN HAI	70	132	735	8.53	0.65	2.71
Aggregated	1319	830	9537	17.34	0.54	2.93

belong to the same country or are located in close proximity to each other. 3) The frequency of container shipping excursions via these ports is consistently low. As an illustration, the Antofagasta port exclusively serves the CSCL company out of a total of 10 ship companies. The port on the shipping route that passes through Antofagasta is San Antonio, and both ports are located in Chile. The frequency of voyages between both ports is limited to only 1, maybe due to the availability of land transport options over a short distance. Additionally, there are other ports facing comparable circumstances, such as Benoa in Indonesia and Albany in Australia, which respectively engage in operations with MSC and COSCO. However, despite the significant differences amongst ship companies, there is a common occurrence of substantial variation in the degree values of most ports throughout the three networks (single-layer, aggregated, and multiplex).

Furthermore, some ports with a low degree of connectivity are crucial for the functioning of the Global Connectivity and Shipping Network (GCSN). If the majority of shipping routes rely on these ports for transfers within the GCSN, it indicates that the significance of these ports is directly linked to the construction and operation of the network. Thus, this research utilizes betweenness centrality to depict the significance of these ports. Firstly, the rank of the port's betweenness centrality has seen significant changes in comparison to the rank of its degree centrality. To show the varied features, we will use the top 10 ports with the highest betweenness centrality in the aggregated network, due to space constraints. Three ports have notably ascended into the top 10 rankings: Valencia, which rose from 11th to 3rd place, Mina Jabal Ali, which rose from 13th to 4th place, and Marsaxlokk, which rose from 29th to 10th place. Furthermore, let us examine Valencia and Mina Jabal Ali port as prime examples of significant transshipment hubs and ports in the Mediterranean and Middle East regions. While both of these ports have achieved a position in the top 10 in terms of betweenness centrality in the aggregated network, their rankings differ significantly when considering the multiplex perspective, with one port ranked at 20 and the other at 5. Valencia had minimal involvement with firm PIL and WAN HAI, whereas Mina Jabal Ali port, as the primary port for global operations, had extensive dealings with all of the top 10 shipping corporations. Therefore, we may better comprehend the necessity of ports and dig more into the distinct serving scopes of each port.

3.2 Analytics of Inter-layer Relationships

The previous section provided a concise overview of the structural attributes of several formats of the GCSN. By integrating the aforementioned study and referring to Table 2, it becomes evident that the aggregated network consists of 830 ports and 9537 shipping routes. However, out of the total 10 ship firms, only 2782 ports are utilized over 16081 shipping routes. This indicates that many ports and shipping routes are concurrently operated by various shipping companies. Thus, while the combined network may identify important ports in the GCSN, it unavoidably disregards the significance and diversity among individual network layers. In this section, we will examine several interactions and assess whether the combined network is sufficient for comprehending the GCSN.

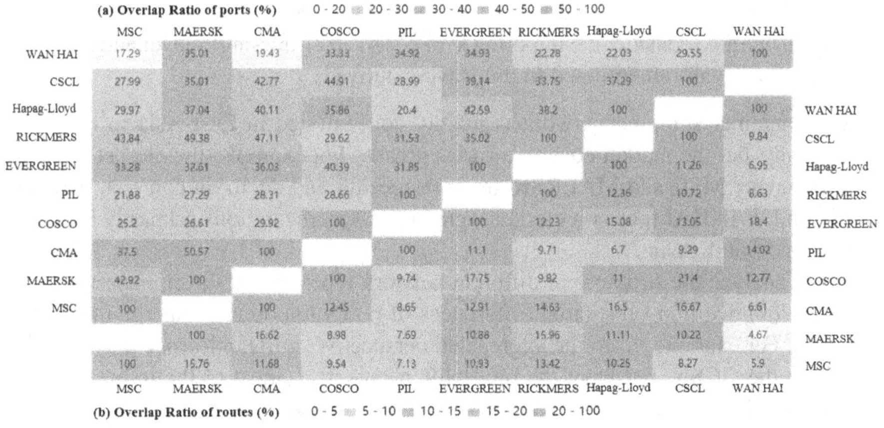

(a) Overlap Ratio of ports (%) 0 - 20 ▪ 20 - 30 ▪ 30 - 40 ▪ 40 - 50 ▪ 50 - 100

	MSC	MAERSK	CMA	COSCO	PIL	EVERGREEN	RICKMERS	Hapag-Lloyd	CSCL	WAN HAI	
WAN HAI	17.29	35.01	19.43	33.33	34.92	34.93	22.28	22.03	29.55	100	
CSCL	27.99	35.01	42.77	44.91	28.99	39.14	33.75	37.29	100		
Hapag-Lloyd	29.97	37.04	40.11	35.86	20.4	42.59	38.2	100		100	WAN HAI
RICKMERS	43.84	49.38	47.11	29.62	31.53	35.02	100		100	9.84	CSCL
EVERGREEN	33.28	32.61	36.03	40.39	31.85	100		100	11.26	6.95	Hapag-Lloyd
PIL	21.88	27.29	28.31	28.66	100		100	12.36	10.72	6.63	RICKMERS
COSCO	25.2	26.61	29.92	100		100	12.23	15.08	13.05	18.4	EVERGREEN
CMA	37.5	50.57	100		100	11.1	9.71	6.7	9.29	14.02	PIL
MAERSK	42.92	100		100	9.74	17.75	9.82	11	21.4	12.77	COSCO
MSC	100		100	12.45	8.65	12.91	14.63	16.5	16.67	6.61	CMA
		100	16.62	8.98	7.69	10.88	15.96	11.11	10.22	4.67	MAERSK
	100	15.76	11.68	9.54	7.13	10.93	13.42	10.25	8.27	5.9	MSC
	MSC	MAERSK	CMA	COSCO	PIL	EVERGREEN	RICKMERS	Hapag-Lloyd	CSCL	WAN HAI	

(b) Overlap Ratio of routes (%) 0 - 5 ▪ 5 - 10 ▪ 10 - 15 ▪ 15 - 20 ▪ 20 - 100

Fig. 2. Overlap Ratio between any two ship companies

Figure 2 illustrates the degree of overlap between the GCSNs (Global Container Shipping Networks) of any two ship companies. It is evident that the port overlap ratio (Fig. 2.a) is significantly larger than the route overlap ratio (Fig. 2.b). One observation reveals that the companies MAERSK and CMA have the highest overlap ratio of ports, reaching 50.57% and overlapping a total of 222 ports. The overlap ratio between company MSC and WAN HAI is just 17.29%, and the number of overlapping ports is 107. Upon closer examination of the multi-functionality of ports, it becomes evident that 299 ports (36.02%) are exclusively used by a single ship company, while only 39 ports (4.7%) are utilized by all ship companies. This stark contrast highlights the significant heterogeneity present within the single-layer network. Moreover, 531 ports (63.98%) are utilized by two or more ship companies, suggesting that the majority of ports provide several functions for different shipping companies. The higher the overlap ratio, the more significant these ports are. In contrast, the route overlap ratio is significantly smaller when compared to the port overlap ratio. The GCSN (Global Container Shipping Network) of companies MSC and MAERSK have the first and second biggest numbers of shipping routes. However, the firm COSCO and CSCL have the highest overlap ratio in terms of routes, which accounts for 21.4%. MAERSK and WAN HAI have the lowest route overlap ratio, amounting to a mere 4.67%. A higher route overlap ratio indicates a greater number of duplicated container trade connections across different GCSN layers. Conversely, a lower ratio suggests a GCSN with varying transportation efficiency, potentially influenced by the competitiveness and cooperation among ship firms. Hence, the intricate nature of the worldwide container shipping network cannot be accurately represented solely through the aggregated network modelling.

4   Conclusion

Ship companies are the organizers of container transportation and their choice of shipping routes and ports directly affects the construction of container network. This study utilizes vessel trajectory data of top 10 ship companies in 2015 to study the intra and inter connected structure, mine the differences among ship companies and global shipping routes, and we also consider the importance of ports across the single-layer and multiplex perspective. The aforementioned findings were derived.

1. The container shipping network is mainly concentrated in East Asia in most ship company, but the market coverage varies greatly. For example, the market coverage of company MSC and MAERSK are both breadth and depth, in contrast, company PIL and WANHAI focus on market segments in specific regions primarily located in East and South Asia.
2. When analyze the structure of different network types (single-layer, aggregated and multiplex), we find substantial differences of port's importance emerge in different layers. For example, from the aggregated perspective, ports in Europe play a critical role in the GCSN, but from the multiplex perspective, most of the important ports distributed in East Asia.

As an on-going work, there are still many limitations like the analysis of relationships between ship companies, community detection of ports from the multiplex perspective, etc. However, this research also opens many opportunities for further work. We will implement our work to address such analysis and questions in the future, conduct some necessary geo-visualization to help us understand the advantages of multiplex network modelling. We also believe that this will offer valuable opportunities for assisting scholars and policymakers in planning maritime transportation operations and regulation.

References

1. Kivelä, M., Arenas, A., Barthelemy, M., Gleeson, J.P., Moreno, Y., Porter, M.A.: Multilayer networks. J. Compl. Netw. **2**, 203–271 (2014). https://doi.org/10.1093/comnet/cnu016

2. Aleta, A., Meloni, S., Moreno, Y.: A multilayer perspective for the analysis of urban transportation systems. Sci. Rep. **7**, 44359 (2017). https://doi.org/10.1038/srep44359

3. Xu, M., Pan, Q., Muscoloni, A., Xia, H., Cannistraci, C.V.: Modular gateway-ness connectivity and structural core organization in maritime network science. Nat. Commun. **11**(1), 1–15 (2020). https://doi.org/10.1038/s41467-019-13993-7

4. Li, K.X., Li, M., Zhu, Y., Yuen, K.F., Tong, H., Zhou, H.: Smart port: a bibliometric review and future research directions. Transp. Res. Part E Logist. Transp. Rev. **174**, 103098 (2023). https://doi.org/10.1016/j.tre.2023.103098

5. Ducruet, C.: Multilayer dynamics of complex spatial networks: the case of global maritime flows (1977–2008). J. Transp. Geogr. **60**, 47–58 (2017). https://doi.org/10.1016/j.jtrangeo.2017.02.007

6. Jiang, J., Lee, L.H., Chew, E.P., Gan, C.C.: Port connectivity study: an analysis framework from a global container liner shipping network perspective. Transp. Res. Part E Logist. Transp. Rev. **73**, 47–64 (2015). https://doi.org/10.1016/j.tre.2014.10.012

7. Huang, L., Tan, Y., Guan, X.: Hub-and-spoke network design for container shipping considering disruption and congestion in the post COVID-19 era. Ocean Coast. Manag. **225**, 106230 (2022). https://doi.org/10.1016/j.ocecoaman.2022.106230

8. Peng, P., Lu, F., Cheng, S., Yang, Y.: Mapping the global liquefied natural gas trade network: a perspective of maritime transportation. J. Clean. Prod. **283**, 124640 (2021). https://doi.org/10.1016/j.jclepro.2020.124640

Doctoral Symposium

A Spatial Interaction Model for the Identification of Urban Functional Regions

Marjan Ghanbari[1,2(✉)] ⓘ, Mohammad Karimi[1] ⓘ, Christophe Claramunt[3] ⓘ,
and Claire Lagesse[2] ⓘ

[1] Faculty of Geodesy and Geomatics Engineering, K. N. Toosi University of Technology,
Tehran, Iran
marjan.ghanbari@email.kntu.ac.ir, mkarimi@kntu.ac.ir
[2] Franche-Comté University, CNRS, ThéMA, 25000 Besançon, France
{marjan.ghanbari,claire.lagesse}@univ-fcomte.fr
[3] Naval Academy Research Institute, Lanvéoc, Poulmic, France
claramunt@ecole-navale.fr

Abstract. Urban Functional regions represent dynamic formations molded by spatial interactions, illustrating the intricate connections between different geographic areas. Identifying functional regions is essential for supporting urban planning efforts and promoting sustainable development. This study presents a comprehensive framework to characterize critical road network locations, integrating structural, functional, and geographical dimensions of the built environment. Addressing limitations in one-dimensional networks and multivariate issues, the study utilizes spatial density-based hotspot detection approaches and develops a method to identify critical locations as multivariate hotspots. Emphasizing critical locations as foundational units for functional regions, it then addresses spatial interaction data limitations through flexible modeling approaches, enhancing local modeling with Artificial Neural Networks (ANNs) within Geographically Weighted Regression (GWR) models. Lastly, dynamic spatial interactions are considered using overlapping community detection methods, offering a structured framework for identifying overlapping functional regions in urban landscapes. This study enhances the identification and analysis of urban functional regions, providing deeper insights into spatial complexities and facilitating more effective decision-making for sustainability.

Keywords: Urban functional regions · Road network critical locations · Spatial interaction modeling

1 Introduction

In geography, defining regions is crucial for understanding spatial characteristics and human interactions [1, 2]. These regions, whether formal or functional, highlight shared physical or cultural traits [3]. Functional regions, shaped by spatial interactions, reveal

M. Lotfian and L. L. L. Starace (Eds.): W2GIS 2024, LNCS 14673, pp. 195–204, 2024.
https://doi.org/10.1007/978-3-031-60796-7_14

the complexity of connectivity across geographical areas [4]. They encompass agglomeration, intra-regional activity, and resource movements [5], playing a vital role in urban understanding, planning, and sustainable development [6], particularly in recent focused territorial development initiatives [7]. In urban geography, functional regions are shaped by three key elements: the origin and destination of spatial interactions, the interactions themselves, and the method of identification. These regions arise from basic spatial units acting as origins and destinations, engaging in dynamic interactions with varying intensities. The resulting network, characterized by spatial configuration and interaction patterns, delineates the intricate nature of functional regions. Identification relies on established methods analyzing the interplay among these basic units, with each element's precise understanding crucial for effective identification and comprehension of their dynamics.

As urban space delineation evolves, there's a shift away from conventional methods using grid cells or administrative zones for functional region detection. Recent evaluations highlight the underestimated role of transportation network layout in shaping urban spatial structures. Emphasizing functional urban road network elements, particularly critical locations, is crucial for identifying functional regions, given their significant influence on spatial interactions within urban environments [8]. Previous studies highlight the importance of road network elements' structural and functional attributes in identifying critical locations [9, 10]. However, they often overlook the broader urban context, especially the significant role of geographical characteristics in shaping urban landscapes and influencing transportation demand. Therefore, there is a need for a new approach that integrates various multivariate characteristics to address this complexity [11]. This includes extending hotspot detection methods [12–17] beyond one-dimensional road networks to capture multivariate hotspots effectively.

Functional region detection traditionally relies on spatial interaction data, like travel patterns, but limitations such as temporal constraints and incomplete datasets call for paradigm shifts towards spatial interaction modeling based on diverse factors like socioeconomic variables and infrastructure. This offers increased flexibility, adaptability, and predictive capability. While traditional spatial interaction models struggle with capturing spatial variations, recent advancements advocate for local modeling, with the Geographically Weighted Regression (GWR) model enabling variable relationships across space [18–21]. However, challenges persist with spatial similarity metrics and kernel functions, impacting accuracy in capturing spatial heterogeneity and transportation network complexities.

Multiple methodologies are used to identify functional regions, including rule-based, numerical, and graph-oriented approaches. Among these, graph theory-based community detection methods have gained prominence [4]. In this method, each vertex in the graph represents a region of interest, connected by edges indicating the strength of spatial interaction [22]. Grouping vertices based on dense within-group and sparse between-group connections [23] offers a promising approach to adapting non-geographical methods for functional region identification [22]. Researchers recognize the dynamic nature of functional regions, influenced by temporal and spatial modifications, urban planning, and shifting population lifestyles [24, 25]. This dynamicity introduces spatial uncertainty [4], posing challenges for precise boundary delineation due to their interconnected nature.

Studies have addressed this uncertainty using a probabilistic perspective, with fuzzy set theory facilitating the identification of overlapping functional regions [26–29]. However, comprehensive methods for systematically identifying and analyzing overlapping regions are still lacking, despite their significance in understanding dynamic variations within functional regions.

This study aims to address these limitations through specific objectives, each associated with corresponding research questions and hypotheses, as outlined in Table 1.

Table 1. Research objectives, questions, and hypotheses.

Research Objectives	Research Questions	Research Hypothesizes
1. Identification of critical urban road network locations	**1.** How can critical road network locations be effectively characterized?	**1.** A comprehensive point of view by integrating **multivariate attributes** related to the structural, functional, and geographical characteristics of the urban built environment will effectively characterize critical locations
	2. How can a multivariate hotspot detection approach be developed for one-dimensional networks?	**2.** Incorporating **multivariate densities** into **density-based spatial hotspot detection methods** in **one-dimensional networks** captures local and semantic intricacies
2. Spatial interaction modeling for urban transportation flows	**3.** How are the limitations caused by relying on spatial interaction data-driven approaches in urban functional region detection addressed?	**3.** The **spatial interaction modeling** is hypothesized to offer enhanced flexibility, predictive capability, and the ability to capture the dynamic nature of urban systems, providing a forward-looking perspective on functional region detection
	4. How can improvements be made to the Geographically Weighted Regression (GWR) model to effectively capture complex spatial heterogeneity in transportation flow modeling?	**4.** The capacity of **Artificial Neural Networks (ANNs)** to learn intricate and non-linear patterns and **integrating them with the GWR model** enhances its capability to capture complex, non-stationary spatial relationships within transportation flows
3. Identification of urban functional regions	**5.** What structured framework can effectively be utilized for systematically identifying and analyzing functional regions concerning their dynamic and interconnected nature within urban landscapes?	**5. Overlapping community detection methods** will enhance the identification and analysis of functional regions by providing a systematic approach to recognizing the coexistence of spatial units in multiple regional classes

2 Preliminary Work and Initial Results

2.1 Case Study and Data Resources

Chicago, as a major urban center with diverse socio-economic characteristics and a complex urban fabric, stands out as an exemplary case study for identifying functional regions. With open and ample data and resources, comprehensive research on functional regions is feasible in Chicago. Insights from studying Chicago can provide valuable recommendations for policymakers and urban planners worldwide facing similar challenges.

This study utilizes a diverse range of data sources within the urban area, including:

- GIS Data Layers: Geographic Information System (GIS) data layers provide essential information on various spatial features of the urban environment. These layers encompass data on land use, transportation networks, zoning, and other pertinent spatial characteristics (See Figs. 1, 2, and 3).
- Demographic Data: Demographic data plays a crucial role in understanding the composition of urban populations. This study utilizes population counts at multiple geographic levels, such as census tracts and blocks.
- Transportation Data: Transportation data is instrumental in analyzing urban mobility patterns. Data on road networks, traffic volumes, and commuting patterns between different locations.

All necessary data, comprising land use layers, transportation networks layers, population counts, and taxi trip records (as transportation data, See Table 2) spanning from 2012 to 2018, are gathered. This data is sourced from the Chicago Data Portal[1], with the selection of years based on availability. Ensuring the availability and documentation of these datasets is essential for enhancing the replicability and validity of the study in other urban areas.

Table 2. Chicago taxi trips details sample.

ID Trip	Trip Start Timestamp	Trip End Timestamp	Pick-up Latitude	Pick-up Longitude	Drop-off Latitude	Drop-off Longitude
f24e*	12:00 am	12:15 am	41.9386662	-87.71121059	41.92726096	-87.76550161
8e40*	5:00 pm	5:30 pm	41.88099447	-87.63274649	41.91461629	-87.63171737

---

[1] https://data.cityofchicago.org.

Fig. 1. GIS data layers comprise Chicago's road network, city boundaries, and community areas.

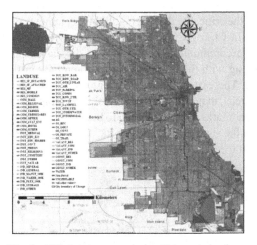

Fig. 2. GIS data layer comprise Chicago's land use.

2.2   Results and Discussion

A multivariate framework is established to achieve the first objective. Structural attributes measure network element significance using centrality metrics, while functional attributes evaluate performance based on quantified vehicle movement. Geographical attributes estimate local spatial urban density and land use diversity. To identify critical locations, a method based on network kernel density estimation integrates multivariate characteristics. This approach combines spatial and multivariate density, aiming to precisely identify hotspots within the urban road network.

Fig. 3. GIS data layer comprise Chicago's Census Tracts.

Figure 4 presents the criticality degree, highlighting elements positioned at the center of community areas in Chicago. The visualization provides an early insight into the criticality observed in community areas located in the eastern and central regions of the case study, aligning with the actual scenario (potentially critical areas highlighted with a black border). The eastern and central regions of Chicago are characterized by high-density urban areas, major transportation hubs, bustling commercial districts, and prominent cultural landmarks, all contributing to their critical role in urban functionality. The findings confirm the significance of these locations in the urban landscape.

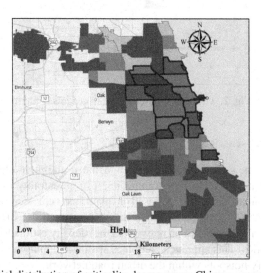

Fig. 4. Spatial distribution of criticality degree across Chicago community areas.

The pursuit of the second objective involves integrating Artificial Neural Networks (ANNs) with the Geographically Weighted Regression (GWR) model. This integration seeks to capture spatial heterogeneity and improve precision in modeling interactions within transportation networks. As part of this ongoing process, Fig. 5 provides a preliminary comparison between the predictions of the developing model and observed transportation flows from community areas 1 and 32 to all others. This visualization aims to offer an early indication of the alignment between predicted and actual flow volumes, demonstrating the potential accuracy of our ANNs and GWR-based spatial interaction model in capturing spatial dynamics.

Finally, the third objective of this study involves utilizing the critical urban road network locations and the spatial interactions between them, with a specific focus on identifying densely interacted communities. It constitutes a cohesive strategy. A method will be selected to identify communities with overlapping characteristics. This approach allows for the identification of urban functional regions with dynamic overlaps over time, providing valuable insights into their evolving nature. Through this integrated methodology, a comprehensive understanding of the functional characteristics of urban regions is attained.

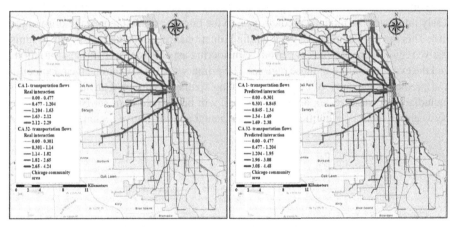

Fig. 5. The ANNs and GWR-based spatial interaction model predicated transportation flows from areas 1 and 32, aligning with actual patterns.

3 Evaluation

In this section, the results are evaluated to determine the effectiveness and efficiency of the methodology in fulfilling the study's objectives. This assessment aims to ascertain how well the research questions are addressed and the hypotheses are validated by the methodology.

In evaluating the first objective, emphasis is placed on a holistic approach contributing to a comprehensive understanding of specific potential critical points. To assess, conventional accuracy-based metrics are adapted, relying on ground truth and contextualizing evaluations within the broader urban landscape. The alignment between identified and potential critical locations is scrutinized on a case-by-case basis, ensuring a detailed and context-sensitive evaluation. Figure 4 demonstrates the primary method's accuracy (above 85%) and adaptability in utilizing the urban road network of Chicago, validating its performance and indicating its potential.

Turning to the second objective, the evaluation strategy emphasizes precise prediction of spatial interactions. To assess predictive capacity over time, a comparative analysis is conducted against traditional Geographically Weighted Regression (GWR)-based models and recent advancements. This perspective enables a comprehensive evaluation of our model's efficacy in capturing dynamic urban mobility. Figure 6 depicts model performance across different time slots, evaluating R-squared, Root Mean Squared Error (RMSE), and Mean Absolute Error (MAE) metrics. The high R-squared values indicate a strong correlation between predicted and observed values, while the low RMSE and MAE values suggest minimal prediction errors. Overall, these findings highlight the robustness and accuracy of our model for capturing spatial interaction patterns.

Through the utilization of a spatial interaction model, the evaluation approach seamlessly integrates the model's predictions into the ongoing assessment of the third objective. This involves comparing the identified functional regions with real-world administrative regions across different periods, considering aspects such as overlaps, variations, and the evolving nature of these regions. The primary goal is to examine the adaptability and predictive capacity of capturing evolving spatial dynamics. Quantitative metrics, including precision, recall, and the F1 score, will be utilized to quantify the alignment between the model's identifications and the actual administrative regions.

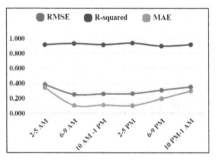

Fig. 6. The proposed spatial interaction model performance in urban transportation flow prediction.

In conclusion, the evaluation of the methodology reveals promising outcomes concerning the achievement of the study's objectives. Through analyses, it has exhibited effectiveness in identifying critical locations and predicting spatial interactions, indicating potential for further exploration.

4   Conclusion

This study presents an innovative methodology for identifying and analyzing urban functional regions and addressing challenges in urban geography. A comprehensive approach integrating multivariate structural, functional, and geographical attributes effectively characterizes critical urban road network locations, as exemplified by the case study in Chicago. It proposes an advanced framework combining Artificial Neural Networks (ANNS) with the Geographically Weighted Regression (GWR) model to capture complex spatial heterogeneity in transportation flow modeling. Additionally, the study utilizes overlapping community detection methods to identify dynamic urban functional regions systematically.

The evaluation plan includes 1) conventional accuracy-based metrics for critical location identification, relying on ground truth and contextual evaluations; 2) comparative analyses against traditional GWR models to assess predictive capacity in transportation flow modeling; and 3) quantitative measures such as precision, recall, and the F1 score to validate the identification of functional regions and their evolution over time.

Preliminary results demonstrate the feasibility and potential of the proposed approaches, offering deeper insights into urban spatial complexities and facilitating more effective decision-making in urban planning and sustainability efforts.

Acknowledgements. This research is supported by the Tehran Research and Planning Center [137.1204088].

Disclosure of Interests. The authors have no competing interests to declare that are relevant to the content of this article.

References

1. Haining, R.P.: Spatial Data Analysis: Theory And Practice. Cambridge University Press (2003)
2. Halás, M., et al.: A definition of relevant functional regions for international comparisons: the case of Central Europe. Area **51**(3), 489–499 (2019)
3. Minshull, R.: Regional Geography: Theory and Practice. Routledge (2017)
4. Klapka, P., Halás, M.: Conceptualising patterns of spatial flows: five decades of advances in the definition and use of functional regions. Moravian Geograph. Rep. **24**(2), 2–11 (2016)
5. Halás, M., Klapka, P., Tonev, P.: The use of migration data to define functional regions: the case of the Czech Republic. Appl. Geogr. **76**, 98–105 (2016)
6. Halás, M., et al.: An alternative definition and use for the constraint function for rule-based methods of functional regionalisation. Environ. Plan A **47**(5), 1175–1191 (2015)
7. Rodríguez, M., Molina, J., Camacho, J.: Mapping functional areas in Spain using mobile positioning data. Eur. Urban Region. Stud. **29**(2), 145–151 (2022)
8. Zhou, Y., Thill, J.-C.: Urban nodal regions through communities of functionally critical locations in the transportation network. In: Development Studies in Regional Science: Essays in Honor of Kingsley E. Haynes, pp. 293–311 (2020)
9. Demšar, U., Špatenková, O., Virrantaus, K.: Identifying critical locations in a spatial network with graph theory. Trans. GIS **12**(1), 61–82 (2008)

10. Zhou, Y., et al.: Functionally critical locations in an urban transportation network: identification and space–time analysis using taxi trajectories. Comput. Environ. Urban Syst. **52**, 34–47 (2015)
11. Litman, T., Steele, R.: Land Use Impacts on Transport. Victoria Transport Policy Institute Canada (2017)
12. Cheng, Z., Zu, Z., Lu, J.: Traffic crash evolution characteristic analysis and spatiotemporal hotspot identification of urban road intersections. Sustainability **11**(1), 160 (2018)
13. Getis, A., Ord, J.K.: The analysis of spatial association by use of distance statistics. Geogr. Anal. **24**(3), 189–206 (1992)
14. Ma, Q., Huang, G., Tang, X.: GIS-based analysis of spatial-temporal correlations of urban traffic accidents. Eur. Transp. Res. Rev. **13**(1), 1–11 (2021)
15. Xie, Z., Yan, J.: Kernel density estimation of traffic accidents in a network space. Comput. Environ. Urban Syst. **32**(5), 396–406 (2008)
16. Okabe, A., Satoh, T., Sugihara, K.: A kernel density estimation method for networks, its computational method and a GIS-based tool. Int. J. Geogr. Inf. Sci. **23**(1), 7–32 (2009)
17. McSwiggan, G., Baddeley, A., Nair, G.: Kernel density estimation on a linear network. Scand. J. Stat. **44**(2), 324–345 (2017)
18. Simini, F., et al.: A universal model for mobility and migration patterns. Nature **484**(7392), 96–100 (2012)
19. Noulas, A., et al.: A tale of many cities: universal patterns in human urban mobility. PLoS ONE **7**(5), e37027 (2012)
20. Kordi, M., Fotheringham, A.S.: Spatially weighted interaction models (SWIM). Ann. Am. Assoc. Geogr. **106**(5), 990–1012 (2016)
21. Zhang, L., Cheng, J., Jin, C.: Spatial interaction modeling of OD flow data: comparing geographically weighted negative binomial regression (GWNBR) and OLS (GWOLSR). ISPRS Int. J. Geo Inf. **8**(5), 220 (2019)
22. Farmer, C.J., Fotheringham, A.S.: Network-based functional regions. Environ. Plan. A **43**(11), 2723–2741 (2011)
23. Newman, M.E., Girvan, M.: Finding and evaluating community structure in networks. Phys. Rev. E **69**(2), 026113 (2004)
24. Zhao, Y., et al.: Dynamic community detection considering daily rhythms of human mobility. Travel Behav. Soc. **31**, 209–222 (2023)
25. Liu, X., et al.: Spatial-interaction network analysis of built environmental influence on daily public transport demand. J. Transp. Geogr. **92**, 102991 (2021)
26. Coombes, M.: Defining locality boundaries with synthetic data. Environ. Plan. A **32**(8), 1499–1518 (2000)
27. Feng, Z.: Fuzziness of travel-to-work areas. Reg. Stud. **43**(5), 707–720 (2009)
28. Watts, M.: Rules versus hierarchy: an application of fuzzy set theory to the assessment of spatial grouping techniques. In: Adaptive and Natural Computing Algorithms: 9th International Conference (ICANNGA 2009), Kuopio, 23–25 April 2009, Revised Selected Papers 9. Springer (2009)
29. Watts, M.: Assessing different spatial grouping algorithms: an application to the design of Australia's new statistical geography. Spat. Econ. Anal. **8**(1), 92–112 (2013)

Enhancing Efficiency and Privacy of Intelligent Public Transportation Systems Through Federated Learning and EdgeAI

Franca Rocco di Torrepadula$^{(\boxtimes)}$ 🄳

Department of Electrical Engineering and Information Technology,
University of Naples, Federico II, Naples, Italy
`franca.roccoditorrepadula@unina.it`

Abstract. In the realm of intelligent public transportation systems, deep learning (DL) techniques are widely used to extract valuable insights from mobility-related data, on top of which it is possible to realized several use-cases. However, since DL models are expensive in terms of resource and energy consumptions, they are typically deployed on third-party clouds, posing challenges such as latency, privacy, and scalability. To address these issues, Federated Learning (FL) and EdgeAI have emerged as promising solutions. Despite their potential, several open challenges persist. The application of FL in public transport systems lacks exploration, while the theoretical understanding of KD's effectiveness remains incomplete. This research aims at addressing these challenges by leveraging FL to prevent data exchange among transport entities, and systematically employing KD for model compression. The ultimate goal is to facilitate the efficient integration of federated learning and EdgeAI to mitigate privacy and efficiency issues in distributed Intelligent Public Transportation Systems.

Keywords: Intelligent Public Transportation Systems · EdgeAI · Federated Learning

1 Problem Description

In the realm of intelligent public transportation systems, the Internet of Things (IoT) and the Internet of Vehicles (IoV) [7] allow the collection of a multitude of different data, ranging from real-time vehicle location to passenger demand or traffic condition. To obtain valuable insights from these data, deep learning (DL) techniques have been widely employed, being the state-of-the-art solutions on many different tasks. On top of the extracted knowledge, it is possible to develop several use cases, with the general goal of exploiting the available public transport resources in a smarter, more effective, and even proactive way [5,13].

Due to the significant amount of parameters and computations involved, such models tend to be very expensive in terms of storage and computational costs.

© The Author(s), under exclusive license to Springer Nature Switzerland AG 2024
M. Lotfian and L. L. Starace (Eds.): W2GIS 2024, LNCS 14673, pp. 205–210, 2024.
https://doi.org/10.1007/978-3-031-60796-7_15

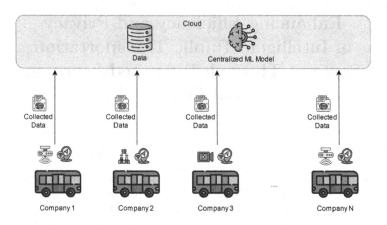

Fig. 1. An example of IPTS with centralized learning.

Hence, traditionally, they are placed on a centralized remote back-end, or on a third-party cloud. As a result, data must be continuously moved from data source locations to the centralized cloud (Fig. 1), introducing several challenges including [2]:

- *low-latency*, since sending data to the server through the network may cause further propagation and queuing delays,
- *privacy*, as data may be exposed to malicious attacks during such transmission.

It is worth noticing that data related to public transportation systems contain sensitive information regarding the habits of individual citizens. Hence, privacy concerns are central in the scenario under investigation.

Federated Learning (FL) and EdgeAI have come to the forefront as potential solutions to these issues [2,10]. From a technical standpoint, FL is a distributed and collaborative training approach that allow multiple devices (*i.e.* clients) to coordinate with a central server, without sharing their private data [9]. In a nutshell, the clients share their local model, while the central server combine them into a new improved global model. In this way, training quality can be enhanced, while privacy leakage is minimized [10]. This paradigm is particularly useful in scenarios characterized by sensitive data, belonging to different entities. This is typical in urban transport, where different companies may manage different kind of transportation systems, or different areas of the city.

On the other hand, the EdgeAI research field aims at distributing training and/or inference of deep models nearest to the data sources, on edge devices, avoiding the movement of data toward the centralized server. However, these devices are typically characterized by limited storage and computational capabilities, challenging the deployment of deep models. Hence, several *model compression* techniques have been proposed to reduce network structure and complexity, without significantly sacrificing its accuracy [4]. Among them, Knowledge Distillation (KD) consists of training a small model (*i.e.* the *student*), designed ad hoc

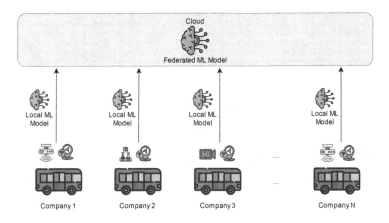

Fig. 2. An example of IPTS with FL.

for the deployment at the edge, by exploiting the knowledge acquired through a more complex model (called the *teacher*)[8]. This results in higher accuracy compared to training the same student from scratch, namely without KD.

Despite the promising potential of FL and KD, there are still several open challenges that are not completely investigated in the scientific literature. As for FL, its employment on public transport systems is barely studied, probably also due to the lack of urban scale dataset. Hence, how to realize an effective FL framework for these scenario is still an open issue. Regarding KD, in spite of its proven effectiveness, there is still a lack of a comprehensive and theoretical explanation of why and how it actually works [3,6,11]. As a consequence, realizing an effective distillation is often an expensive process.

2 Goal Statement

The goal of my research is addressing privacy and latency issues in distributed IPTS, through the application of FL and/or KD. To this purpose, my current investigation mostly focused on how to shift from centralized to federated learning, and how to compress the trained networks for their deployment at the edge.

More in detail, the introduction of FL is meant to prevent the exchange of sensitive data among different companies involved in public transport systems. To this purpose, I am currently investigating how FL can be effectively applied to public transport systems (Fig. 2), exploring also potential personalization mechanisms to accommodate the heterogeneity inherent in urban public transport networks. The output of this activity will be a FL framework, customizable for different urban scenarios.

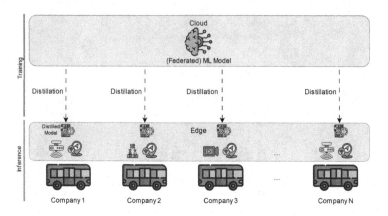

Fig. 3. Integrating EdgeAI into IPTS.

On the other hand, KD allows to deploy the trained models (potentially through the federated approach) within resource-constrained environments. This include scenarios where edge-devices are installed directly on buses or at stops/stations (Fig. 3). In this context, I am focusing on systematically and automatically apply KD as a model compression technique, concentrating especially on how to correctly and efficiently configuring the temperature hyper-parameter. The result of this investigation will be a systematic methodology for temperature configuration, implemented as a tool for KD optimization.

3   Method

To realized and evaluate the proposal, several experiments and studies need to be conducted, as described in the following.

3.1   Federated Learning

As for FL, the first study involves investigating the effectiveness of such an approach for urban public transport networks. To this purpose, an extensive experimental campaign is needed, and the passenger demand prediction problem is considered as reference task [1]. This problem consists of predicting how many people will use a specific public transport service, based on historical data.

Considering a urban scenario, the city can be conceptually divided in different areas, each one served by several public transport services, potentially managed by different companies. It is reasonable that services within a particular area exhibit comparable behaviors and trends. Consequently, implementing a centralized machine learning/deep learning model for each area could be advantageous. However, for this endeavor, the participating companies would need to disclose their sensitive data to a centralized server.

To avoid this issue, for each area, the federated learning approach can be applied, and the performance of the federated model can be compared with the performance of the centralized model. Although the accuracy of the model may degrade slightly, the resulting advantage in terms of privacy as well as network overhead is significant. The illustrated framework can be tailored to meet more specific needs. For instance, to cope with the heterogeneity of the services within a specific area, a personalization mechanism can be integrated during the update of the local models. Knowledge distillation (KD) can be employed for this purpose.

3.2 Knowledge Distillation

Regarding KD, the aim of my investigation is systematically assessing the impact of the temperature on the effectiveness of the distillation. This entails testing various types of networks (such as ResNet, DenseNet, MobileNet, and YOLO) on diverse benchmark datasets (like CIFAR10, CIFAR100, and COCO), while varying temperature values. The result should be deeply analyzed in order to discover any systematical effect that can be extracted for the construction of the methodology.

To evaluate the effectiveness of the KD, the performance of the distilled models (namely the students) can be compared with the performance of the teacher, as well as with the performance of the same models trained without distillation (*i.e.* from scratch). This comparison encompasses not only accuracy but also factors such as energy consumption, storage requirements, and computational costs. Consequently, the distilled networks are deployed on edge devices to collect these measurements.

4 Preliminary Work

The experimental campaign detailed in the previous section is currently underway. As for FL, in order to assess its viability for public transportation, a dataset at an urban scale was necessary. To achieve this, a synthetic dataset was developed using the Eclipse SUMO simulator. Leveraging some real-world origin-destination matrices and the GTFS files, this simulator was utilized to simulate both private and public transport scenarios within a prominent Italian city [12]. The city was then segmented into distinct areas based on geographical characteristics. On this basis, both centralized and federated learning approaches are now being tested in each of these areas.

In parallel, the experimental campaign on KD is being conducted considering ResNet and DenseNet as reference deep learning models. At the moment, these experiments have shown that the temperature hyperparameter cause some systematical effects on the distillation process. Essentially, the most effective temperature depends on the complexity of the problem, and on the gap between the teacher and the student, in terms of network structure. Moreover, the performance of the obtained students have been tested on Xilinx Zynq Ultrascale+

ZCU102 and STM32F4, confirming a significant improvement in terms of energy and resource consumptions.

References

1. Amato, F., Di Martino, S., Mazzocca, N., Nardone, D., di Torrepadula, F.R., Sannino, P.: Bus passenger load prediction: challenges from an industrial experience. In: Karimipour, F., Storandt, S. (eds.) International Symposium on Web and Wireless Geographical Information Systems, pp. 93–107. Springer, Cham (2022). https://doi.org/10.1007/978-3-031-06245-2_9
2. Chen, J., Ran, X.: Deep learning with edge computing: a review. Proc. IEEE **107**(8), 1655–1674 (2019). https://doi.org/10.1109/JPROC.2019.2921977
3. Cheng, X., Rao, Z., Chen, Y., Zhang, Q.: Explaining knowledge distillation by quantifying the knowledge. In: Proceedings of the IEEE/CVF Conference on Computer Vision and Pattern Recognition, pp. 12925–12935 (2020)
4. Deng, L., Li, G., Han, S., Shi, L., Xie, Y.: Model compression and hardware acceleration for neural networks: a comprehensive survey. Proc. IEEE **108**(4), 485–532 (2020)
5. Elkosantini, S., Darmoul, S.: Intelligent public transportation systems: a review of architectures and enabling technologies. In: 2013 International Conference on Advanced Logistics and Transport, pp. 233–238. IEEE (2013)
6. Gou, J., Yu, B., Maybank, S.J., Tao, D.: Knowledge distillation: a survey. Int. J. Comput. Vision **129**, 1789–1819 (2021)
7. Guo, L., et al.: A secure mechanism for big data collection in large scale internet of vehicle. IEEE Internet Things J. **4**(2), 601–610 (2017)
8. Hinton, G., Vinyals, O., Dean, J.: Distilling the knowledge in a neural network. arXiv preprint arXiv:1503.02531 (2015)
9. McMahan, B., Moore, E., Ramage, D., Hampson, S., y Arcas, B.A.: Communication-efficient learning of deep networks from decentralized data. In: Artificial Intelligence and Statistics, pp. 1273–1282. PMLR (2017)
10. Nguyen, D.C., Ding, M., Pathirana, P.N., Seneviratne, A., Li, J., Poor, H.V.: Federated learning for internet of things: a comprehensive survey. IEEE Commun. Surv. Tutor. **23**(3), 1622–1658 (2021)
11. Phuong, M., Lampert, C.: Towards understanding knowledge distillation. In: International Conference on Machine Learning, pp. 5142–5151. PMLR (2019)
12. Rocco Di Torrepadula, F., Russo, D., Di Martino, S., Mazzocca, N., Sannino, P.: Using sumo towards proactive public mobility: Some lessons learned. In: Proceedings of the 1st ACM SIGSPATIAL International Workshop on Sustainable Mobility, pp. 51–58 (2023)
13. Zhu, L., Yu, F.R., Wang, Y., Ning, B., Tang, T.: Big data analytics in intelligent transportation systems: a survey. IEEE Trans. Intell. Transp. Syst. **20**(1), 383–398 (2018)

Towards a Framework for Personalising Leisure Walking Route Recommendations

James Williams(✉)📵

Nottingham Geospatial Institute, University of Nottingham, Nottingham, UK
James.Williams@Nottingham.ac.uk

Abstract. This research investigates how a greater understanding of leisure walking can be used to support the personalisation and curation of new leisure walking experiences. Existing solutions are often limited in the range of routing properties a user has access to. The purpose of this research is to explore a richer understanding of how, what, why, and where leisure walkers engage with walks. Through a grounded theory approach combining a walking behaviour survey, a think-aloud study, and an expert interview study, a framework for personalising leisure walking route recommendations has been designed. The remaining work includes finalising the development of a web-based GIS demonstrator system for curating personalised routes and conducting an evaluation of this approach.

Keywords: Leisure Walking · Route Recommendation · Mobile Geospatial Computing · Place-Based Information

1 Problem Description

Leisure walking is a broad term and activity that can relate to a variety of rationales and purposes including health, well-being, or connecting with nature (e.g., [5,11]). Despite this, providing route recommendations to leisure walkers often focuses on routes with specific supporting qualities or characteristics, for example, recommending routes with considerations of safety, amenities, and walking ability [14]; or investigating the use of landmarks as points along a route [12]. Existing research rarely explores the more experiential, subjective, and personal factors that are more commonly associated with leisure walking, such as local connections to place [6]. Some research presents approaches to combining multiple subjective characteristics, such as visual and facility-based diversity, to present different walking routes in cities [18], but it is only explored in the context of urban settings. Few route recommendation systems have attempted to represent multiple types of route quality, as identified in a survey on pedestrian quality-aware route navigation [15]. The survey also reviews existing literature and classifies the work into the safety, well-being, effort, exploration, and pleasure taxonomy of pedestrian navigation route qualities [15].

M. Lotfian and L. L. L. Starace (Eds.): W2GIS 2024, LNCS 14673, pp. 211–217, 2024.
https://doi.org/10.1007/978-3-031-60796-7_16

The work presented in this article attempts to bridge this gap in research by expanding existing work in the area of route quality and classification to better integrate multiple leisure walking characteristics. A review of the state-of-the-art in social local search [7] identifies that relevant supporting data such as the environment or social web are ignored in favour of popular points of interest. Some literature has explored the use of user-generated content, such as mobile application routes classified by land use [1]. Previous research has also explored the assessment of difficult routes [3] and dynamic routing areas [8]. However, more work is needed to understand the personalisation of these properties, which provides the impetus of exploring how leisure walking experiences can be curated by users.

The remainder of this article is organised as follows: Sect. 2 presents the goal statement of the research project, highlighting the goals and problems addressed during the project. Section 3 presents the overall methodology, the studies conducted, and the artifacts developed during the research project. Section 4 discusses the emerging results of the work. Finally, Sect. 5 provides preliminary conclusions formed during the work and presents potential avenues for future research.

2   Goal Statement

The limitations of the existing literature, such as the focus on single-route quality types [15] as opposed to the multifaceted motivations of users, highlight the need to improve the recommendations of leisure walking routes personalised to user preferences. Therefore, the purpose of this research project is to provide a deeper understanding of how and why users take certain routes to support the personalisation of new route recommendations. The aims of the project are defined as follows:

1. **To Understand the User**: This aim will explore what walkers consider to be a leisure walk, what engagements occur and why during leisure walks, and how these engagements are captured using existing tools and techniques from an expert perspective.
2. **To Understand the Data**: Attempts to understand the data generated through the initial aim and design a framework for personalising leisure walking experiences. Exploring if and how existing geospatial datasets can be extrapolated to fit the identified route characteristics.
3. **Design and Test**: Explores the development of a prototype web-based Geographic Information System (GIS) and routing demonstrator based on the proposed framework and investigates the evaluation of the framework and approach.

The research aims of this project attempt to address the problems with existing approaches and solutions, using the methods presented in Sect. 3. The problem of limited grounded research on what users engage with while walking is addressed by (1) exploring a deeper understanding of the user requirements and engagements that occur during a walk. The problem of representing the characteristics of experiential walking routes in computational form is addressed by (2) investigating the data generated during the first aim of the project and designing a framework to integrate these, enabling the exploration of existing geospatial datasets. Finally, the issue of conducting an evaluation of the theoretical and more experiential aspects of leisure walking is explored by (3) presenting the approach with a demonstrator system and evaluating this with potential users.

3   Methods

The research follows the design science research methodology [2], implementing a combination of theoretical and practice-based research. Theoretical concepts are explored through a grounded theory approach, where qualitative studies are conducted and emerging themes are identified. The practice-based aspects of the work includes the development of a route recommendation demonstration system, which is used as prototype solution to be evaluated.

3.1   Grounded Theory Approach

A grounded theory approach was taken and initial data was collected in which emerging themes and concepts were coded to categories themes and properties [10]. The use of the grounded theory approach enabled a more exploratory understanding of leisure walking, where data could be captured for an emerging framework and categories determined over the course of the study.

Leisure Walking Behaviour Survey. For a preliminary understanding of what leisure walking is, how often participants would walk for leisure, and how leisure walkers captured their own data, a leisure walking behaviour survey was conducted. The leisure walking behaviour survey was designed using a combination of behavioural questions [13] that questioned frequency for the purpose of self-evaluation (e.g., How often have you...) and open-ended qualitative questions to capture new knowledge of the rationale and purpose of leisure walking.

Think-Aloud Study. Based on the results of the leisure walking behaviour survey, a think-aloud walking study was conducted. During the study, participants received a chest-mounted video recorder, a GPS tracker, and a prompt sheet. Participants were asked to take a self-selected leisure walk for a duration of 30 min to 1 h and to think aloud [4]. The think-aloud study allowed a rich understanding of how, why, when, and where participants would engage with the experiential aspects of leisure walks, while also providing details of why certain engagements would occur.

During this stage of the project, a custom qualitative geographic information system (QGIS) was developed [17], allowing the analysis of multiple modalities of data while also providing a fuzzy extraction method through a web-based QGIS.

The tool enabled multimodal data sources (transcriptions, audio, and video) to be combined with a platial analysis approach, implementing a fuzzy spraycan tool to capture the uncertain and fuzzy aspects of place [9].

Expert Interviews. An understanding of the user was gathered during the leisure walking behaviour survey and think-aloud study, however, these study captured limited perspectives from a route management or mobile application development perspective. Therefore, it was necessary to conduct a small array of semi-structured expert interviews, these interviews lasted between 30 min and 1 h and focused on the experts role related to leisure walking.

3.2 Framework Design

Based upon the grounded theory approach taken a framework was designed to integrate the results from the leisure walking behaviour survey, the think-aloud study, and the expert interviews. The framework was designed based on a combination of results and themes identified from each of the studies, grouped into: 'Tasks', 'Activities', 'Influences', and 'Properties', each property having related evidence.

3.3 Demonstrator System and Evaluation Plan

To integrate the framework and provide a usable example, a demonstrator system will be developed. This prototype research artifact will be produced as a tool to support the experiences of people leisure walking. The web-based GIS will allow existing data sources to be used as a dynamic selection of route characteristics for the generation of new routes.

The final study will evaluate how the proposed framework (presented through the demonstrator system) supports the user in curating personalised leisure walking experiences. The preliminary proposed approach of this study is to provide the system to end users and capture think-aloud utterances in addition to semi-structured questions on the quality of the recommended routes and any surprising occurrences or results.

4 Discussion of Emerging Work

The initial results are mostly focused on the completion of the grounded theory studies, the emerging framework design, and work towards the development of the final system. Therefore, these preliminary results are expected to support the continued development and integration of the findings into the final framework. These preliminary results are still emerging, and the final evaluation study has not yet been conducted.

4.1   Grounded Theory Results

Leisure Walking Behaviour Survey. The leisure walking behaviour survey provided an early understanding of what leisure was for the participants, their usual leisure walking behaviours, and their rationale for walking for leisure. The online survey was completed by a total of 329 participants, with rationales for leisure walking including health and exercise, social activities, and walking the dog. The study also identified several design considerations for future leisure walking technologies, highlighting the importance of using local knowledge, enabling the escape of technology, and providing users with the opportunity for self-analysis.

Think-Aloud Study. The design of the think-aloud study was based on the results of the survey on leisure walking behaviours. A total of 14 studies were conducted, with nine walks by individuals and five walks by groups of two. Results related to rich engagements while leisure walking and methodological findings on the think-aloud approach were captured during the study. The emerging themes of the think-aloud study were reported as preliminary themes identifying the platial and subjective elements of the walk [16].

Expert Interviews. Expert interviews were conducted based on a lack of understanding of the technical requirements of leisure walking data and technology. A total of nine expert interviews were conducted, with experts identifying key themes that included the importance of user-generated content, such as reviews to capture new information on how users interact with digital technologies and the challenges of providing functionality in locations with poor signal.

4.2   Framework

The framework was produced through a combination of the grounded theory studies. Based on a iterative and thematic analysis approach, an analysis was conducted and produced three main tasks: planning a leisure walk, doing a leisure walk, and reflecting on a leisure walk. These tasks were segmented into activities, influences, and properties with corresponding evidence from the study. The process has now continued to explore the related datasets for each of these properties and the practicalities of implementation.

These results also aligned with the general themes captured from each study, where the survey on leisure walking behaviours were often relating to the planning of a leisure walk, the think-aloud results often relating to the doing of a leisure, and the expert interview often presenting a reflective view of the properties of leisure walking.

4.3   Demonstrator System and Evaluation

The final and remaining aspect of the study is the development of a demonstrator system, and conducting an evaluation. The demonstrator system is based on the results captured, where the properties from the framework will be explored for use in the system through linked datasets. The web-based demonstrator system will present a GIS capable of enabling dynamic weightings of route properties, enabling dynamic route selections, hierarchical management of the datasets in a grid, and the ability for the data to be pre-processed.

The final study will be an evaluation of how the system can support users in curating personalised leisure walks through user-selected properties. This study will explore what properties participants select and how these impact the curation of new and dynamic routes. This will include semi-structured interview questions and think-aloud statements from participants. The evaluation study has not yet been completed, but should enable the identification of new insights based on the planning stage of walking.

5   Conclusions and Future Work

The research presented in this article has highlighted the methods used and preliminary results of a research project exploring how digital technologies can support route recommendations for the leisure walking experience. Early results have indicated the importance of the experiential aspects of leisure walking, which are often subjective and personal to a user and the importance of representing these in a framework. The current focus is to complete this implementation stage, enabling a user study to evaluate if and how the framework and demonstration tool support the personalisation of leisure walking routes.

Acknowledgement. This work was supported by the Engineering and Physical Sciences Research Council [grant number EP/S023305/1] and by Ordnance Survey. Supervision and advice was provided by James Pinchin, Adrian Hazzard, Gary Priestnall, and Sarah Sharples at the University of Nottingham. Additional guidance was provided by Lee Newton and Stefano Cavazzi at Ordnance Survey and Andrea Ballatore at Kings College London. No new study data was created for this article.

References

1. Ballatore, A., Cavazzi, S., Morley, J.: The context of outdoor walking: a classification of user-generated routes. Geogr. J. **189**(3), 485–500 (2023). https://doi.org/10.1111/geoj.12511
2. vom Brocke, J., Hevner, A., Maedche, A.: Introduction to Design Science Research, pp. 1–13. Springer, Cham (2020). https://doi.org/10.1007/978-3-030-46781-4_1
3. Calbimonte, J.P., Martin, S., Calvaresi, D., Cotting, A.: A platform for difficulty assessment and recommendation of hiking trails. In: Wörndl, W., Koo, C., Stienmetz, J.L. (eds.) Information and Communication Technologies in Tourism 2021, pp. 109–122. Springer, Cham (2021). https://doi.org/10.1007/978-3-030-65785-7_9
4. Ericsson, K.A., Simon, H.A.: Verbal reports as data. Psychol. Rev. **87**(3), 215–251 (1980). https://doi.org/10.1037/0033-295x.87.3.215
5. Ettema, D., Smajic, I.: Walking, places and wellbeing. Geogr. J. **181**(2), 102–109 (2015). https://doi.org/10.1111/geoj.12065

6. Evans, J., Jones, P.: The walking interview: methodology, mobility and place. Appl. Geogr. **31**(2), 849–858 (2011). https://doi.org/10.1016/j.apgeog.2010.09.005

7. Gasparetti, F.: Personalization and context-awareness in social local search: state-of-the-art and future research challenges. Pervasive Mob. Comput. **38**, 446–473 (2017). https://doi.org/10.1016/j.pmcj.2016.04.004

8. Huang, H., Mathis, T., Weibel, R.: Choose your own route - supporting pedestrian navigation without restricting the user to a predefined route. Cartogr. Geogr. Inf. Sci. **49**(2), 95–114 (2022). https://doi.org/10.1080/15230406.2021.1983731

9. Huck, J., Whyatt, J., Coulton, P.: Spraycan: a PPGIS for capturing imprecise notions of place. Appl. Geogr. **55**, 229–237 (2014). https://doi.org/10.1016/j.apgeog.2014.09.007

10. Knigge, L.G.: Grounded Theory, pp. 1–5. Wiley (2017). https://doi.org/10.1002/9781118786352.wbieg0339

11. Lumber, R., Richardson, M., Sheffield, D.: Beyond knowing nature: contact, emotion, compassion, meaning, and beauty are pathways to nature connection. PLoS One **12**(5), 1–24 (2017). https://doi.org/10.1371/journal.pone.0177186

12. Nuhn, E., Timpf, S.: Do people prefer a landmark route over a shortest route? Cartogr. Geogr. Inf. Sci. **49**(5), 407–425 (2022). https://doi.org/10.1080/15230406.2022.2075469

13. Rips, L.J.: Behavioral Question, p. 52. Sage, Thousand Oaks, CA (2008). https://doi.org/10.4135/9781412963947.n35

14. Sasaki, W., Takama, Y.: Walking route recommender system considering saw criteria. In: 2013 Conference on Technologies and Applications of Artificial Intelligence, pp. 246–251 (2013). https://doi.org/10.1109/TAAI.2013.56

15. Siriaraya, P., et al.: Beyond the shortest route: a survey on quality-aware route navigation for pedestrians. IEEE Access **8**, 135569–135590 (2020). https://doi.org/10.1109/ACCESS.2020.3011924

16. Williams, J., Pinchin, J., Hazzard, A., Priestnall, G., Cavazzi, S., Ballatore, A.: Emerging platial narratives and themes from a leisure walking study. In: Fourth International Symposium on Platial Information Science (PLATIAL 2023), pp. 23–28. Dortmund, Germany (2023). https://doi.org/10.5281/zenodo.8286259

17. Williams, J., Pinchin, J., Hazzard, A., Priestnall, G., Cavazzi, S., Ballatore, A.: WalkGIS: exploring platial analysis of leisure walks via linked video narratives. In: 31st Annual Geographical Information Science Research UK Conference (GISRUK), pp. 1–6. Glasgow, Scotland (2023). https://doi.org/10.5281/zenodo.7825302

18. Zhang, Y., Siriaraya, P., Wang, Y., Wakamiya, S., Kawai, Y., Jatowt, A.: Walking down a different path: route recommendation based on visual and facility based diversity. In: Companion Proceedings of the The Web Conference 2018, pp. 171–174. WWW 2018, International World Wide Web Conferences Steering Committee, Republic and Canton of Geneva, CHE (2018). https://doi.org/10.1145/3184558.3186971

Author Index

M. Lotfian and L. L. L. Starace (Eds.): W2GIS 2024, LNCS 14673, p. 219, 2024.
https://doi.org/10.1007/978-3-031-60796-7

Printed in the United States
by Baker & Taylor Publisher Services